Children's Work, Schooling, and Welfare in Latin America

Children's Work, Schooling, and Welfare in Latin America

David Post
Education Policy Studies and
Population Research Institute
The Pennsylvania State University

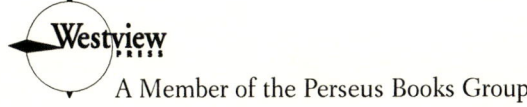

All rights reserved. Printed in the United States of America. No part of this publication may be reproduced or transmitted in any form or by any means, electronic or mechanical, including photocopy, recording, or any information storage and retrieval system, without permission in writing from the publisher.

Copyright © 2001 by Westview Press, A Member of the Perseus Books Group

Westview Press books are available at special discounts for bulk purchases in the United States by corporations, institutions, and other organizations. For more information, please contact the Special Markets Department at The Perseus Books Group, 11 Cambridge Center, Cambridge MA 02142, or call (617) 252-5298.

Published in 2002 in the United States of America by Westview Press, 5500 Central Avenue, Boulder, Colorado 80301-2877, and in the United Kingdom by Westview Press, 12 Hid's Copse Road, Cumnor Hill, Oxford OX2 9JJ

Find us on the World Wide Web at www.westviewpress.com

Library of Congress Cataloging-in-Publication Data

Post David
  Children's work, schooling, and welfare in Latin America / by David Post
    p. cm
  Includes bibliographical references (p.) and index.
  ISBN 0-8133-3915-4 (pbk.)
  1. Child labor—Latin America. 2. Education—Latin America 3. Child welfare—Latin America. I. Title

HD6250.L292 P67 2002
331.3'1'098—dc21
                                                        2001045000

The paper used in this publication meets the requirements of the American National Standard for Permanence of Paper for Printed Library Materials Z39.48–1984.

10 9 8 7 6 5 4

Contents

List of Illustrations   vii
Preface   xi

1. Policies And Realities For Working Children In Latin America   1

2. The Nature And Politics Of Child Labor   44

3. The Norms And Institutions Of Education   94

4. A Multivariate Model Of Child Labor and School Attendance   139

5. Region And Gender Differences In Children's Work And Schooling   174

6. Conclusion: Social Mobilization, NGOs, and Policy Change   215

Appendix   237
List of Formal Interviews   251
References   253
Index   271

LIST OF ILLUSTRATIONS

Tables

4.1 Multinomial Logistic Regression Model Estimates and Relative Risk Ratio, Rural Mexico, 1992
4.2 Multinomial Logistic Regression Model Estimates and Relative Risk Ratio, Urban Mexico, 1992
4.3 Multinomial Logistic Regression Model Estimates and Relative Risk Ratio, Rural Mexico, 1996
4.4 Multinomial Logistic Regression Model Estimates and Relative Risk Ratio, Urban Mexico, 1996
4.5 Multinomial Logistic Regression Model Estimates and Relative Risk Ratio, Rural Peru, 1985
4.6 Multinomial Logistic Regression Model Estimates and Relative Risk Ratio, Urban Peru, 1985
4.7 Multinomial Logistic Regression Model Estimates and Relative Risk Ratio, Rural Peru, 1997
4.8 Multinomial Logistic Regression Model Estimates and Relative Risk Ratio, Urban Peru, 1997
4.9 Multinomial Logistic Regression Model Estimates and Relative Risk Ratio, Rural Chile, 1990
4.10 Multinomial Logistic Regression Model Estimates and Relative Risk Ratio, Urban Chile, 1990
4.11 Multinomial Logistic Regression Model Estimates and Relative Risk Ratio, Rural Chile, 1996
4.12 Multinomial Logistic Regression Model Estimates and Relative Risk Ratio, Urban Chile, 1996

5.1 Determinants of School Years Attained by Age 17 in Chile, Peru, and Mexico: Direct and Time-Period Interaction Effects of Income Quintile and Rural Residence
5.2 Determinants of Full-time Schooling for Mexicans, Ages 12-17: Individual, Family, and State-level Contextual Effects Over 1992-1996 Period
5.3 Determinants of Full-time Schooling for Chileans, Ages 12-17: Individual, Family, and Provincial-level Contextual Effects Over 1990-1996 Period

Figures

1.1 International Relationship Between Rates of Adolescent Student-Employment and Average Math Achievement
1.2 Demographic Trends in Chile, Peru, and Mexico
1.3 Economic Indicators for Chile, Peru, and Mexico
1.4 Percentages of Chilean, Peruvian, and Mexican Children, Ages 12-17
1.5 Trends in Activities of Girls and Boys, Ages 12-17
1.6 Full Range of Activities of Mexicans, Ages 12-19, in 1995

2.1 Conceptual Framework on Children, Rationale for Regulating Their Activities, and Situations of International Advocates

3.1 Age Sequences and Levels of Compulsory and Non-Compulsory Education in Chile, Peru, and Mexico
3.2 Chile's Per-Pupil Government Spending in 1997 Pesos and US$
3.3 Chile's Constant Public Spending and Enrollments in Educacion Media
3.4 Constant Recurrent Spending and Total Enrollments in Peru (all levels)
3.5 Enrollment Trends in Mexican Secundaria and Media Superior
3.6 Constant Spending and Total Public Enrollments in Mexico's Educacion Media Superior
3.7 Expenditures on Public Education in Chile, Peru, and Mexico

5.1 Trends in the Effects of Income and Rural Residence on Educational Attainment at Age 17

List of Illustrations ix

5.2 Peruvian Trends in School Attendance and Economic Activity, 1985-1997, by Region
5.3 Regional Inequality in Economic and School Activities for Mexican Children (12-17), 1992 and 1996
5.4 Percent of Chilean Children in School, by Child's Rural/Urban Residence and Provincial Concentration of Rural Children in Population
5.5 Trends in Regional Education Inequality in Chile: Relations of Provincial Rates of Attendance and Mean Education of Household Heads
5.6 Trends in Regional Educational Inequality in Mexico: Relations of State Rates of Full-time Enrollment and State Mean Parents' Education
5.7a Percent of Primary Students Continuing to Secondary, 1985
5.7b Percent of Primary Students Continuing to Secondary, 1995
5.8 Trends in Regional Educational Inequality in Mexico: Relation of State Rates of Transition from Primary to Secondary Level and State Levels of Adult Education
5.9 Predicted Probabilities of Work and Schooling in Mexico (Children 12-17) by Quintiles of Family Income and State Child Poverty Rate, 1992 and 1996
5.10 Trends in Peruvian Girls' Relative School Participation
5.11 Provincial Relation of Adult Education and Female Underrepresentation in Chilean Media-Level Schools, 199
5.12 Percentage of Students Beginning Secondary School Who Are Female, 1995
5.13 State and Municipio Relation of Adult Education and Female Underrepresentation in Mexican Secondary Schools, 1995
5.14 Predicted Probability of Weekly Activity by Mexican Children (12-17), by Gender and Poverty Status

6.1 Material and Symbolic Impact of State Action on Household Decisions and Children's Activities
6.2 Transnational Advocacy and the Socialization of Human Rights Norms

Preface

Questions about the future of child labor and basic education are supposed to be settled matters, at least in most countries of Latin America. Not, of course, because all Latin American children succeed in school or because the region has no underage workers. Rather, these matters are supposedly "settled" because of the inexorable movement toward those ultimate resolutions. In one familiar version, ever-more-democratic societies embrace global human rights to create a childhood free of exploitation, as farm families and street vendors, industrialists, and the police all accept this universal norm. In another version, world trade will create incentives for nations and families to invest in the stock of their human capital: Early labor becomes bad business for all. A sociological variant sees isomorphic institutions that inevitably standardize the regulation of youth through similar types of school systems and welfare safety nets. More children are officially students whose parents have registered them in schools. Proportionally fewer, it is then supposed, must be working. The forces of economic growth and the spirit of progress lift entire societies, as the experiences of childhood everywhere come naturally to resemble those enjoyed by children in what were once called "first world" countries.

Several glitches now appear in this rosy scenario. At the end of the twentieth century, the World Trade Organization failed to compromise between *competing* "universal norms" of neoliberal, opened markets for nations and core labor standards to protect all workers. The International Labour Organization (ILO) estimated that there remained 250 million working children in the world (albeit many of them attending school). Not in dispute was the disturbing truth that few of the world's poorer countries ever came close to meeting the ambitious goals set by the International Labour Organization's 1973 Convention on the minimum age for work (age fourteen). Few developing countries even had formally ratified it. And the ideals embodied in the 1989 United Nations Convention on the Rights of the Child remain just that: important ideals, yet to be legislated into national laws in much of the world. With the unequal economic growth characteristic of the 1990s, many nations, including parts of Latin America, became home to millions of children who resembled "grit in the prosperity machine" (Loker 1999). By 1995, the World Bank's annual report had concluded, "There is no worldwide trend toward convergence between rich and poor workers. Indeed, there are risks that workers in poorer countries will fall further behind, as lower investment and educational attainment widen disparities." And J. Brian Atwood, former head of the U.S. Agency for International Development, had these dark words upon stepping down: "It is time to end the hypocrisy. Globalization is thus far leaving out about two-thirds of the world... If economic growth is limited to an already educated elite, then it has limited development benefit and it is a poor indicator of sustainability" (cited in M. Levinson 1999, p. 21).

We might blame an uneven demographic transition for the sorry state of childhood in Latin America, at least in part. Although birth rates have declined in the region as a whole, the decline was much slower among the poor. One result is that increasing proportions of children live in poverty, even when poverty rates do not increase. At the same time, each nation's population includes proportionally fewer children. Children are thus receiving lower priority as social policy concerns–they become easier to ignore politically–at the very moment when poverty is becoming more concentrated among them (McNicoll 1997, p.48). In fact, the problem is even worse because, as we will see, the adjustment shocks during the 1980s exacerbated poverty among the families who already were poor prior to the ascendency of neoliberalism.

Preface   xiii

Against this backdrop, the welfare of children–those who can least advocate for themselves–becomes a humanitarian as well as a political preoccupation. The full development of our potential requires a time period–childhood–that is protected from abuse, hardship, or exploitation. Although poverty among children may be impossible to eradicate, the searching question for social scientists is just how inexorable is the supposed tide uplifting childhood everywhere. In starkest terms, is there any need for nations to *do* anything? Is there, a case for leadership or intervention by governments, non-governmental organizations, lending agencies, or multinational institutions such as the ILO and the U.N.? Finally, if there is a need for leaders, what should be their priorities for children and for which populations: the minority who are not in school, or the majority who are full-time students?

The broad view by respected economists like Gary Becker (1997) is that a common history is shared by today's wealthy countries–where child labor became irrelevant as incomes rose–and nations of the South–where the slow retreat of child labor may similarly occur as economies become more productive and as individual incomes grow. During the industrial revolution, argues one prominent historical account, "children worked ... because their families were poor; as family income increased, child labor decreased" (Nardinelli, 1990, p.112). In nineteenth century Europe, there was little apparent effect of law, public policies, or even school availability on children's work. Smelser (1991) argues that, in an important sense, Britain's compulsory school legislation *followed* changes in the family economy that freed children for education.

Will the exploitation of Latin American children stop of its own accord when it stops making sense to desperate families? Perhaps, but that too-facile question requires a complex response. A recent World Bank summary of child labor reduction agreed that, although "poverty reduction is the most powerful long-term approach ... this a lengthy process that, even when successful, will in practice tend to raise the incomes of the poor unevenly, thus leaving room for a substantial incidence of child labor for some time to come (Fallon and Tzannatos 1998, p. 10). In the meantime, can children be expected to forgo labor or to attend school full time while poverty persists? AFL-CIO President John Sweeney, testifying before the U.S. Senate's foreign relations committee, argued against waiting for global prosperity: (October 21, 1999) "There are those who assert that child labor must be tolerated, that it can only be overcome when poverty is vanquished, that poor children have no alternatives to exploitation and abuse 'necessary' to a nation's economic strength. We reject these arguments. We believe that economic development is based in education; that school is the best place for all children, regardless of their personal social standing or their nation's economic vitality."

School is the best place, and education leaders would like to make it even better. But can these improvements reach children most in need of them? In the world movement for education reform, many non-governmental organizations and ministries have narrowed their agenda to the critical deficiencies in the quality of instruction. Real learning, not mere attendance, is the ultimate goal of the "Education For All" movement. Today the top priority for most agencies is to increase achievement (usually measured by standardized test results) among individuals whose major activity *already* is the business of schooling. An implicit assumption behind this reorientation is that children who labor will be likely to stop working of their own accord once schools are improved. After schools are improved and education makes better sense, working children would be expected to join the majority of children who–in many countries, though not in Peru, as we will see–already complete compulsory schooling before concentrating on economic production.

Regarding this assumption and the focus on education quality, two comments are necessary. First, the emergence of full-time schooling for all will be a long time in coming, if it comes at all. If the United States is any example, then new opportunities for employment and new adolescent consumer "needs" are likely to emerge in Latin America, even if poverty does diminish. By the most conservative estimates, more than one out of ten fifteen-year-old American students works for pay after school (U.S. Department of Labor, 2000). And there are indications from my own research that Mexico is following the U.S. example, although not in the way John Sweeney had hoped: During the 1990s, *more* Mexican students also became part-time workers. A second comment is that I am sympathetic with a focus on education quality and will have more to say on improved quality as a means to increase parents' preferences for schooling over labor. However, "quality" is notoriously difficult to measure, or even to agree upon. In the 1990s, separate attempts were made by UNESCO and by the International Association for the Evaluation of Achievement (IEA) to assess language and mathematics achievement in Latin America. Even when ministries were convinced to participate, the results of these assessments have been kept secret in several countries (including Peru and Mexico). National pride and concern about saving face will always politicize the measurement of quality.

Rather than *directly* investigating the progress of Latin America's younger generation, in this book I take an indirect and inferential approach by investigating children's activities. Indicators of school or labor force participation are analogous to indicators of infant mortality in the field of public health or murder rates in criminology. Such indicators do not measure all of the important characteristics of an education system or of a labor force. But, like infant mortality, children's participation rates are hard to disguise and, thus, they are less prone to equivocation than other important indicators of children's educational well-being. Since all nations today are at least minimally committed to insuring school attendance and reducing child labor whenever possible, a focus on the time that children allocate to work and education is the best place to begin.

An integral approach to work and education sharpens a focus on child labor that began a generation ago. The world's most optimistic and ambitious attempt to regulate children's activities dates to 1973, and to the International Labour Organization's convention on minimum age, No. 138. This convention committed members of the ILO to the eradication of forms of employment by young people which, among other undesirable characteristics, conflicted with compulsory schooling during the age ranges in which schooling had been legislated in each member country. Countries that had established age ranges for compulsory schooling were expected, once they formally ratified the convention, to legislate protections and restrictions on children's employment so that their work would not interfere with compulsory education. In any case, children under fourteen were prohibited from most employment. As already mentioned, the problem was that few countries with high rates of child labor ever ratified the convention or took steps to modify their own labor laws so as to accommodate its directive. Rather than reworking their national labor legislation to fit a mold set by Convention 138, many countries either implicitly or explicitly have attempted to accommodate schooling with work. As will be discussed in Chapter 3, Peru openly moved in this direction in a 1992 presidential decree, one making school and work more legally compatible. Can this benefit Peru's children? What lessons are there for other nations?

In addition to the ILO's Convention 138, during the 1990s all nations of the world (except for Somalia and the United States) formally ratified the 1989 United Nations Convention on the Rights of the Child. This treaty, the most widely adopted of any in legal history, gives a child's development priority over most competing interests and makes explicit the responsibility of national governments to protect children from the exploitation associated with working at the expense of their education. As we will see, a discourse on children's rights has succeeded, where earlier protection doctrines have failed, by energizing civil society to become advocates for children.

While we should take these developments as on balance positive for the welfare of children in Latin America, important issues remain unsettled. The integrative approaches to child welfare and labor policy–seen most clearly in ILO Convention 138 and the U.N. CRC–join together compulsory school policies with an international commitment to the rights of the child. The question of whether or not child labor inherently or *necessarily* conflicts with schooling is avoided both by Convention 138 and the U.N. Convention on the Rights of the Child. As I will discuss in much

Preface

greater detail, it also is avoided by the national labor codes of Chile, Peru, and Mexico. But this question now occupies the center of international debate, after the ILO's adoption of a *new* convention focusing on only the "worst forms" of abusive child labor. That instrument (Convention No. 182, already accepted by the United States, Mexico, and Chile) downplays the importance of schooling and, instead, calls only for the immediate elimination of the most blatantly "intolerable" forms of child labor. By omitting education participation as a criterion for defining "tolerable" child labor, Convention 182 makes no assumption that working necessarily conflicts with schooling. Employment by children of school age is not viewed, in and of itself, as inherently exploitative nor in conflict with children's individual rights. Is "tolerable" child labor consistent with the human-resource training needs of ILO member nations?

The shift to a new international criterion may be a good strategy, given that so few countries in the South ever succeeded in ratifying Convention 138. Indeed, there are excellent strategic arguments not to include those types of work that conflict with schooling as inherently among the "worst forms" of child labor. Eradicating "exploitation," too broadly construed, becomes an unenforceable goal if it requires such far-reaching redistribution of opportunity that it conflicts with other vested interests within many societies. Creating new stakeholders who are committed to eliminating work by children may be a wiser course. As one longtime ILO researcher has argued, "No real solutions will be realized without the full participation of working children and their families" (Myers 1999, p. 23). The new ILO approach is conciliatory rather than confrontational.

But, apart from the understandable *strategic* reasons to narrow the focus of the international campaign against child labor to the worst forms of exploitations, and to treat families as allies rather than adversaries, are there also substantive reasons to support the reordering of priorities that are evident in the new ILO convention? What has social science research to say on this subject? What does the preponderance of the evidence show about the compatibility of work and schooling? Does a labor market for the time and energy of children and adolescents prevent them from investing in their future skills via education?

It is surprising that few integrative assessments of children's activities in school and work have been conducted anywhere in the world. In the context of the international policy debate over what to do about children's labor and schooling, this book offers a comprehensive view of children's labor, schooling, and family welfare in three countries of Latin America. An integrated appraisal of the determinants of children's activity is important for promoting coherent policies that can sustain social development in the region. But labor, schooling, and welfare are too seldom considered jointly in the research literature, mirroring their infrequent articulation in national governance and policy debate. As a UNICEF official, Marta Maurás, commented, "Until relatively recently it was common to encounter studies on child labor that barely mentioned education. Most educational research in developing countries, moreover, has grossly neglected the obvious link between not being in school, or performing poorly, and being a working child" (Salazar and Alarcón 1996).

This book thus argues for an integral assessment of children, incorporating findings from both education policy and child labor research. The book presents original analysis of household survey and school enrollment data to show trends in children's unpaid domestic work, paid employment, and schooling. In Mexico, Chile, and Peru, the purpose is to show how household and community characteristics shaped families' allocations of children's time to school, domestic work, and paid employment. The larger goal of the book is to interpret these trends since the mid-1980s, within and between countries. To do this, I use a comparative case study approach. For Chile, Peru, and Mexico I discuss the interest groups, global economic forces, and public policies that affected education, child labor, and family welfare.

This book culminates five years of effort, for which multiple thanks are due. First, I am deeply indebted to my collaborators, students, and research assistants over the years, some of whom were the co-authors of Chapter 4. These include: Leif Jensen, David Abler, Hector Robles, Jose Rodriguez, Patricia Muñoz, Silvana Vargas, Rosario Garcia, Rocio Flores, Martin Benavides, Claudia Galindo, Riho Sakurai, and Marleni Ramirez. The work of the Penn State students is further indebted to generous support from the Ford Foundation, and the research project received other key support from the Spencer Foundation. I am grateful to the early guidance of their program officers, Cynthia Sanborn (Ford) and Rukmini Banerji (Spencer), as well as to inspiration from Rosa María Rubalcava and Fernado Cortés, and for key logistic support from Penn State's Population Research Institute. A Fulbright-Hayes grant from the U.S. Department of Education allowed me to spend concentrated time in the countries under study, based at Peru's GRADE. A sabbatical leave from Penn State gave me time to continue working on the project in the supportive environment of Stanford's Center for Latin American Studies and School of Education, to which sincere thanks are due.

—David Post

1
Policies and Realities for Working Children in Latin America

A grim joke circulated among Latin American researchers and advocates during the early 1980s, a time of threatened development loan defaults by several countries (including Peru, where that threat became a reality in 1986 under President Alan Garcia). "If you owe the bank a hundred dollars," went the joke, "then you have a problem. But if you owe the bank a hundred million dollars, then the bank has a problem." Policy discussions about working children and early school dropout share the same bitter insight. In a nation where few parents are forced to rely on child labor or allow their children to leave school prematurely, these aberrant parents can be seen as a "problem" for their children. But in a nation, or in a world, where substantial numbers of children are employed, either at the expense of their schooling or as an added burden to it, then the problem is not only with the family. The International Labour Organization estimates that there are 250 million working children in the world. When a nation adopts but cannot implement compulsory schooling, it is not out-of-school children or underage workers who are individually to blame for the nation's failure to attain development targets. As stated succinctly by the Peruvian labor economist Francisco

1

Verdera, "That a family opts to send their children to work rather than sending them to school is a reflection of a nation's quality of life." This same view is taken by UNICEF: "Like poverty itself, the prohibitive cost of education that keeps children out of school and increases the likelihood of their remaining in hazardous work, must also be seen not as natural or even unavoidable, but as a consequence of faulty policies and priorities" (UNICEF 1997).

This is a book about the social realities and policy analysis of children's work and schooling. The comparative case studies are of three Latin American countries, but the welfare issues it discusses are equally relevant to Pakistan, The Philippines, Ghana, Thailand, and many other societies. In this first chapter, I present an overview of the historical context of children's labor. I then outline the moral foundations of the terms of debate over children as they are reflected in international law and echoed by children's advocates around the world. Next, I pose the major welfare considerations before policymakers: When does work help children? When does it pose a threat to their intellectual growth? I review the evidence about these questions that has been uncovered by labor economics and school psychology. Next, I describe the recent political economy of each of the country cases of our comparative study, emphasizing the critical events since the 1980s that have raised concern among children's advocates and lawmakers in Chile, Peru, and Mexico. Finally, I describe the main sources of this book's empirical contributions to the analysis of children's activities. I explain the national survey sources used by my collaborators and me, highlighting their strengths and limitations, and I present the major trends in children's activities.

A note on terminology is needed at the outset of the exposition. For the purposes of this book I accept the definition of "children" that was incorporated in the 1989 United Nations Convention on the Rights of the Child (CRC). The CRC, the most widely ratified international law ever, was formally ratified by each of the countries of our study, and it clearly defines "children" as persons below the age of 18. The fact that "childhood," "adolescence," and "youth" are also culturally and historically specific constructs does not escape my notice. However, when I use the term "children" to refer to persons ages twelve through seventeen, I mean this in its international legal sense, and not its cultural, historical, or psychological sense. At the same time, I often will refer to "adolescents" and "youth." These terms (except in the case of Peru) carry no precise legal meaning, and so I use them to refer to the social-psychological condition of persons in the twelve-to-seventeen-year age group. Obviously, the issues I explore here are even more pressing for children who are younger than twelve. However, I am limited in our ability to contribute useful new insights about this younger group, because national surveys in most countries do not clearly inform us about the economic activities of young children. Even when they do, as in the case of Peru, we might question the veracity of parents' responses about the work performed by the very young: A stigma has been attached to child labor, making household surveys poor instruments for understanding the activities of the very young.

The terms "work" and "child labor" are less clear-cut or standardized than "childhood." Some advocates have attempted to define children's work as any productive activity (including domestic chores that may not generate or add value to a product). Some have attempted to define "child labor"–a term that by now carries a pejorative association–as only that subset of "work" that is exploitative, detrimental, or harmful to children; other work is tolerable, possibly even beneficial. Conceptually, it is clear that all work is "work," including cleaning, cooking, and caring for infant sisters and brothers. However, as will be described later in this chapter, the general national insights offered through using high-quality survey data are constrained by the instruments used to collect information. These surveys record activities by children that may or may not generate income to them or to their families; remunerated work like street vending and unremunerated work, like family farming, are both recorded. However, work that is not aimed at generating or adding value to a product is not recorded as an "economic activity" in these data sources. Thus, for practical reasons, when I refer to children's work I mean children's economic activity. Whenever possible, however, I use the term "activities" to refer to the entire range of possible allocations of children's time, including schooling, work, their combination, or "other." This last category, although opaque, includes domestic labor by many children, especially that performed by girls. Finally, I should point out that I make no a priori assumptions about the ultimate harm of child labor; the purpose here is to document its prevalence and tendencies, along with the politics of its regulation. Thus, I use the term "child labor" to refer to all children's economic activity, beneficial or not. But we should recognize that the survey instruments do not allow us to detect labor that is not classified as economic by national surveys of each country.

THE HISTORICAL CONTEXT FOR THE STUDY OF CHILDREN'S WORK AND SCHOOLING

The worldwide proliferation of labor laws regulating children's activity, since the nineteenth century, was accompanied by three well-known economic and demographic tendencies: increased labor force differentiation and specialization within nations; a fertility transition, which led to smaller numbers of children growing up in the households of developed nations; and increased global economic integration, with an emerging world market for the products of children's labor. Family trades, family small businesses, and the dominance of agriculture provided the bulk of employment opportunities for adults until the nineteenth century. Earlier, most children worked side by side with family members. The industrial revolution increased the opportunity cost of children's time outside of the domestic economy. By the mid–1800s, the activities of Welsh children were dedicated primarily to *non*-domestic labor in support of the family economy, which had come to rely quite heavily on children in textile mills (Smelser 1991).

The first effective arguments for the education and protection of children emerged as a reaction to the grim working conditions in Britain. England's 1802 Moral Health Act limited children to a twelve-hour workday, and in 1842 the Law of Mines prohibited work underground for persons younger than eighteen. In 1840 the first minimum age was established in Britain, for half-time work in textiles (it was set at age eight). Because Britain's economy had become so dependent on children, the campaign for universal education of the 1870s met opposition from manufacturers as well as families. The key role being played by child labor was obvious to those who profited by it, and exploitative relations delayed and truncated the construction of "childhood" as a protected class. For example, in an environment where parliamentary investigation found a "vicious demand for young girls", reformers proposed raising the age of sexual consent from twelve to fourteen. But the House of Lords refused to pass this bill, which would have also made children unable to enter into legal contracts until that age (Horn 1995).

In the United States a hundred years ago, one out of six children aged ten to fifteen was employed outside the home. For example, Modell (1979) found that the children of Irish immigrants contributed between 38 and 46 percent of total family labor income in two-parent families, while native-born children contributed 28–32 percent, as children entered the work force in an attempt to pool risks in a very uncertain world. It was against this backdrop that Marx and Engels predicted the destruction of the traditional family through the power of capitalism: "The bourgeois claptrap about the family and education, about the hallowed co-relation of parent and child, becomes all the more disgusting ... by the action of modern industry: all family ties among proletarians are torn asunder and their children transformed into simple articles of commerce and instruments of labor, (In Tucker, 1978, p. 487).

With more specialized job opportunities available, the numbers of children working side by side with adults began to decline. The educational opportunities represented by apprenticeships in trades began to disappear, while at the same time mechanization in farming lessened the need for children in agricultural work. Concurrent with the tendency for age-segregated employment there was a downward trend in family size. Even prior to the widespread use of modern contraceptives, the birth rates for most countries began a rapid decline. With smaller sibship sizes, family resources were concentrated on fewer children, and families became able to forgo the opportunity costs of their children's time. From Blake's (1989) "resource dilution" perspective on this transition, families who could afford to do so invested in their children's education, and they chose to send them to school rather than to paid jobs. An alternative perspective, emphasized by many economists (cf. Becker 1991), argues for the simultaneity of joint parental decisions to regulate fertility and to invest greater resources in each child. In either event, the families living in the countries with the greatest economic growth experienced the smallest family sizes and could afford to be supportive of child protection laws. Eventually, families in wealthier nations were willing to accept laws proscribing exploitative work, perhaps partly because the families in these countries had fewer children and could focus on the long-term investment in each child.

A third tendency sets the stage for our investigation of child labor and schooling in Latin America. Since the 1980s, increasing trade between wealthier and poorer countries has globalized the production of many goods that are manufactured by unskilled labor, including children. Young people have always worked to support themselves and their families. In the past, however, the products of their labor did not compete on the international market with goods produced by adults. Today the movement toward economic integration has forced labor leaders to join with child advocates in the developed economies and to consider the welfare of children in poorer nations. In North America, a resulting tension from of this globalization surfaces in the public battle over the importation of athletic shoes and soccer balls.

Together, these trends have, perhaps as never before, led to an alliance between organized labor and children's welfare advocates, whose common efforts led to creation of an International Child Labor Office within the U.S. Department of Labor. U.S. House Resolution H.R. 2678, "The International Child Labor Elimination Act of 1997," culminated a call in the United States for regulation of the products of children. This also forced the labor ministries of many developing countries to testify before the U.S. Bureau of International Labor Affairs about the specific steps their nations were taking to protect children from exploitative labor. Evidence was collected in the congressionally mandated Labor Department report, *By Sweat and Toil of Children*, which featured Mexico and Peru as case studies (and in which Peru was grouped with a small number of other nations allowing twelve-year-olds to work). Finally, in 1999, President Bill Clinton signed Executive Order No. 13126 prohibiting federal procurement of goods that may be produced using forced child labor, and he also signed ILO Convention 182, pledging to eliminate the worst forms of child labor. But from what moral ground may one nation, or even an international organization, designate which activities are legitimate and illegitimate for children in another nation? Within a particular nation, with what authority may some parents dictate the age of employment for other parents' children?

THE TERMS OF DEBATE: CHILDREN'S RIGHTS VERSUS SOCIAL WELFARE

Arguments over the moral basis for regulating childhood have been derived from different philosophical traditions, which are reflected in the language used by legal instruments and political actors to effect policy change in the countries of this study. One tradition, loosely associated with Immanuel Kant, bases regulation on the justice of *principles used* to guide action. Another tradition, associated with John Stuart Mill, is most concerned with the *consequences* of regulatory action for the well-being of children and of society as a whole. Purdy (1992), summarizing each perspective, traces arguments for justice to a presumed sufficiency of reason by children, assigning them a judgmental capacity that is not qualitatively different from that which we normally presume for persons once they cross the age of legal majority. Like adults, children have the capacity to define their own best interests. This capacity demands rights to specific protections from interference in personal choice—what Berlin (1964) called "negative liberty." Moral autonomy further requires entitlements from society that allow citizens meaningfully to exercise their freedom to choose—what Berlin called "positive" liberty and what MacPherson (1973), more sympathetically, termed "developmental freedom." One central problem for equal rights arguments about children's activities is with the comparability of capacities for judgment over individuals' life courses. Proponents of equal rights for children (e.g., Cohen 1980) argue that protections and entitlements for individuals are required by even a minimal awareness and planning capacity, a level that most children surely possess, especially those who are of the ages that concern us in this book. But Purdy (1992, pps. 178, 215) insists that the capacity for reason must be compared at different chronological ages. Doing so forces us to conclude that children have *less* capacity than older persons to access the information needed for informed decisionmaking. Thus, the question of child labor can be regulated without necessarily violating the principle of equal rights. As Purdy states, "Granting immature children equal rights in the absence of an appropriately supportive environment would be analogous to releasing mental patients from state hospitals without alternative provision for them."

From an alternative perspective, the *consequences* of child welfare and labor policies are most important, and language from this viewpoint is used by many economists and labor leaders. For example, the ILO's Declaration on Fundamental Principles and Rights at Work, states: "Child labour is detrimental to development, since it means that the next generation of workers will be unskilled and less well educated. In today's increasingly globalized economy, this has especially negative consequences, since . . . a skilled and educated labour force is critical to economic development, increasing incomes and social progress." Two ILO economists (Anker and Melkas 1996, p. 15) summarize the consequentialist argument for intervention in the choices that are made by parents and children: "While poor families may be rational in their feeling that child labour is necessary for survival, child labour is not in the society's best interest—nor in the family's best interest in the long run. Most children working full-time are unable to either attend school or to progress adequately in school." World Bank economists make a similar argument: "Premature and extensive engagement in work prevents children from accumulating human capital and having higher earnings in later life, while economic growth is adversely affected by lower rates of productivity growth. In many instances, child work is the result of capital market failures: when households cannot afford education for their children and cannot borrow for this purpose, although the long-term benefits would be high" (Fallon and Tzannatos 1998, p. 5).

While the consequentialist argument is widely invoked, there also are Kantian-based evaluations that are less concerned with the outcomes of public policy action than with determining a just basis for it. This perspective seeks to avoid the major weakness at the foundation of consequentialism, which in English is summed up in the adage that "one person's meat is another's poison." As guides to action, these theories are limited by a subjective conception of good ends (O'Neill 1996, p. 32). It is possible–indeed it is often quite likely–that what is subjectively experienced by a child as necessary for self-actualization may *not* be necessary. Or, the child's self-actualization could deprive others of their own felt needs. Interpersonal comparisons of utility are off limits to most economists. Meanwhile, a "right" has been compared by the legal philosopher Ronald Dworkin to a trump card in a game of bridge. Rights "trump" welfare consequentialist considerations of policy outcomes, which may weigh the total good produced by various alternatives under the assumption of an equal capacity for moral autonomy, though not necessarily its exercise (Freeman 1992). Regardless of the total good that may be produced, there are some actions and some situations that are unjustifiable. Regardless of the potential for economic growth, nations may not enslave a people, and parents may not prostitute their children.

A rights-based argument for education and against child labor does not deny the economic and welfare rationales offered by the ILO and World Bank. But such rationales are *unnecessary*, from this perspective. Rights-based rationales, as I will discuss in

Chapter 3, are ascendant among education leaders, including those in the countries compared in this book. "The discourse about the value of education for social and economic development is very old," commented two architects of Chile's school reforms in the 1990s. "What is new is that education has begun to *be* development" (Garcia-Huidobro and Cox 1999, p. 8). Into this muddle, the 1989 U.N. Convention on the Rights of the Child plunges at full throttle, attempting to finesse a compromise by incorporating language of both rights *and* consequences. One of the jurists responsible for drafting the convention has asked rhetorically, "How much would it cost a state to fully implement the CRC? Not only is it impossible to answer but the question is not even helpful. A more appropriate question is: what is the cost to the state of ignoring the rights of children?" (Van Bueren 1999, p. 704).

Ignoring children's rights became increasingly expensive for a state's legitimacy after 1989. The CRC gives member states the responsibility to ensure that free primary education is compulsory for *all* children, with the goal being "the development of the child's personality, talents and mental and physical abilities to their fullest potential." Article 32 of the CRC continues:

1. States Parties recognize the right of the child to be protected from economic exploitation and from performing any work that is likely to be hazardous or to interfere with the child's education, or to be harmful to the child's health or physical, mental, spiritual, moral or social development.
2. States Parties shall take legislative, administrative, social and educational measures to ensure the implementation of the present article. To this end, and having regard to the relevant provisions of other international instruments, States Parties shall in particular:
   a. Provide for a minimum age or minimum ages for admission to employment;
   b. Provide for appropriate regulation of the hours and conditions of employment;

c. Provide for appropriate penalties or other sanctions to ensure the effective enforcement of the present article.

But is the CRC an effective or even a coherent defense of children as persons with rights? Adam Lopatka (1992, p. 49), the Polish chair of the U.N. working group that drafted the CRC, retrospectively presented his views on the moral foundations of the convention: "The child is not the property of his or her parents nor the State, the Church, or anybody else. Each child is an individual person whose personality and identity should enjoy universal recognition and respect. In all actions concerning children, the best interests of the child should be a primary consideration."

The CRC language is not consistently faithful to either a consequentialist or rights perspective. Although couched in the language of rights, the architects of the CRC have also kept a careful eye on the consequences of rights for the needs of children. In part, this amalgam seems to have been created out of strategic and practical concerns to implement the agreement. This is most apparent in UNICEF's 1999 report, *The State of the World's Children*, which states that "what were once seen as the needs of children have been elevated to something far harder to ignore: their rights." But problems have been found in the moral basis as well as practicality of this view. O'Neill (1996, p. 132) discusses a prevalent weakness of universal welfare rights, such as rights to education and development free from exploitation. In her view, such manifestos of social rights as the CRC obscure the connection between rights-holders and obligation-bearers. Without an institutionalized responsibility, the rights proclaimed are not properly "rights" at all, she argued, but merely ends seen as desirable by their proponents. "Proclamations of universal 'rights' to goods or services without attention to the need to justify and establish institutions that identify corresponding obligation-bearers may seem bitter mockery to the poor and needy, for whom these rights matter most," argues O'Neill (1996, p. 133). The poor "may come to conceive of themselves as citizens, or as citizens-to-be, who can insist that justice is violated and claim what is owed to them. But, at worst, a premature rhetoric of rights can inflate expectations while masking a lack of claimable entitlements." In practical terms, the language of human rights, as applied to children, is particularly unsuited for a global economy, argue two Australian legal scholars. Children's rights advocacy, like human rights law generally, may be "caught within its framework of state responsibility for human rights violations" and thus be unable to demand redress where the violator is not a state but, rather, "a globalized economic institution or a transnational corporation" (McCorquodale and Fairbrother 1999, p. 763).

A careful reading of the CRC suggests that children were not actually considered autonomous moral agents by the drafting committee. Instead, precisely because they are incapable of defending their best interests, or even *knowing* which types of work activity interfere with their development, children are subject to regulations established by adults (nor were children ever consulted over the wording of the convention itself). Rather than granting children rights identical to those of adults, the U.N. document bases its arguments on the developmental consequences of actions oriented to children, especially actions that can affect their unique, individual interests (not necessarily those of their parents). Children's presumed interests are to promote their own actualization. As actors rather than subjects, children's rights in the framework of the 1989 convention depend on what Feinberg (1980) has called the "right to an open future."

Ambiguities within the CRC's language–offering something to child advocates of diverse philosophical orientations–are apparent to its staunchest supporters. Thomas Hammarberg, writing for the International Save the Children Alliance, states, "Children, especially when very young, are of course vulnerable and need special support to be able to enjoy their rights in the fullest. The combination of these two thoughts is the drama of the Convention: how can we grant children equal value and at the same time guarantee them the necessary protection?" Resolving this dilemma is possible only by accepting the integral protection offered by the CRC and its principles of nondiscrimination, best interest, right to survival and development, and rights of children to express their views.

UNIVERSAL STANDARDS VERSUS CULTURAL SPECIFICITY

Even if we were prepared to finesse, compromise, or postpone a debate between the welfare economic and rights orientations outlined above, additional whirlpools of theoretical dispute remain. Attempts to forge a consensus position, as in both the 1989 CRC and the ILO's Convention 182, face unsettled conceptual issues over universality and specificity, issues for which no compromise has yet been suggested. These issues sometimes hinder the policy implementation. Who has legitimate authority to determine the best interests of a particular child? What international authorities are entitled to decide the interests of children within a particular nation? And who decides what types of labor are "intolerable?" No longer the exclusive concerns of their parents, children first became the co-responsibility of their immediate communities. More recently, shared responsibility for childrearing has been given to (and taken by) nation-states. And finally, in the years covered by this book, the regulation of children has been attempted by global organizations and by international law. This trajectory has not been uncontested, and advocates for family rights see a need to guard against the usurpation of parental prerogatives by the community and nation (for a review see P. Abbott 1981). There also is resistance against the nation-state by the advocates of local or "indigenous" practices of distinctive communities. In the English-language literature, discomfort with the homogenizing effects of school institutions on local culture is found in the seminal work of Ivan Illich (1970) and Ronald Dore (1976). In Latin America, such critiques of schooling were voiced early on. In one of the region's first explicit sociological treatises, Joaquín Capelo's (1902, Vol. 4, p. 119) *Sociologia de Lima,* the author laments the confusion by Peruvians between the very different terms, "education" and "instruction." This "has resulted in the role of *student*, which is considered quite lucrative," and which "creates numerous persons who live many years at the expense of their families as true parasites, producing nothing and consuming time and money," Capelo wrote. "It is one of the occupations of the current age which most damages society and retards the progress of civilization." A more recent and sociological view of the matter, developed from the work of John Meyer, is offered by Bruce Fuller (1991, p. 139), who observes, "The Western tradition is to accept certain differences, then to define uniform individual rights which encourage youths to join nation-wide organizations and to affiliate with a single national culture. The individual buys this lexicon of rights and the promise of broader economic choices by surrendering social links to local community. Mass schooling ... plays the key role in re-socializing children away from local loyalties." More radical critics of the Western "right" to schooling go so far as to advocate local resistance to this conformity to the spirit of modernity and its isomorphic institutions. "Human rights are ... social constructions," write the Mexican and Indian authors Esteva and Prakash. "They are cultural inventions, and not natural discoveries. Human rights are but the formal, juridical expression of a specific mode of being and living. It is defined by the kind of man, woman and child who has appeared on earth only very recently: Homo oeconomicus, the possessive individual. First born and brought up in the West, this modern 'person'–in individual self–is now threatening the whole world with the plague of endless needs, legitimized under the moral mask of human rights" (Esteva and Prakash 1998, pp. 121–122).

Asian nations, in the Bangkok Declaration of April 1993 (as a preliminary to the World Human Rights Conferences), stated that, "While human rights are universal in nature, they must be considered in the context of a dynamic and evolving process of international norm-setting, bearing in mind the significance of national and regional particularities and various historical cultural and religious backgrounds (cited in Alston 1994, p. 8). One of India's U. N. representatives stated, "We have to recognize that while constantly upgrading human rights, the countries of the South, rather than aping Northern models, must work out their own norms and standards suited to their social, cultural, and economic conditions" (ibid.). Esteva and Prakash (1998, p. 151) go so far as to compare studying for school examinations with torture, both of which are said to ruin children's lives.

Responses to advocates of cultural specificity echo the ethics critique of moral relativism generally: The very ability to make categorical assessments of a metanarrative, whether it is considered a narrative of progress or domination, assumes the capacity for universal applications of a particular value (for a comprehensive review of the debate, see Tilley 2000). "Postmodern" critique of children's advocacy departs from an "ahistoric present orientation that rejects all conceptual models as totalizing and views plans for the future as coercive and utopian. The emphasis is on atomistic individualism, privileging agency to the neglect of structure. The rejection of metanarrative and totalizing discourse leads to an extreme relativism that trivializes conventional indicators of development such as access to health care and education" (Loker 1999, p. 16). Even critical ethnographers, with good reason to question the assumptions by Western child advocates about the evils of wage-pay, also question the veracity of the bucolic vision of family work, for example, in the case of girls in southern India. Exploitation outside of the world market-economy, within the realm of the family, is equally if not more likely than in the formal sector (Nieuwenhuys 1995). The Brazilian diplomat José Lindgren Alves (2000, pp. 499–500), recognizes the postmodern critique of the Universal Declaration of Human Rights, which he agrees "is neither a magical formula nor a sacred decalogue." But, granting that its assumptions are "outdatedly metaphysical, it must nonetheless be cherished and kept" as a human achievement. "To dismiss it as ineffective in a multicultural world would mean to abandon the search for human improvement."

In the CRC, arguments based on rights and welfare consideration are *both* present, and the final rational for regulation is never resolved. Similarly, alongside of its liberal individualist language, the convention also acknowledges traditions and cultural values as legitimate sources of regulation of children. Tensions from these competing perspectives surfaced in the drafting committee's debates over the child's freedom of choice of religion, over the rights of the unborn, over female circumcision, and–of particular importance for our focus in this book–over whether or not a child has a "duty to respect his parents and to give them assistance, in case of need." This duty was proposed as a CRC article by Senegal, and it found support from most other African nations. However, ILO representatives immediately pointed out that adoption of this article would provide U.N. legitimization for child labor, and the proposal ultimately was not adopted. Instead, the value of filial piety was incorporated into the text of other articles as one aim of education. The contradictions between liberal individualist and traditional collective orientations can be melded, compromised into a more freighted and, perhaps, a "richer" document than that originally presented by any single nation (Johnson 1992, p. 112). But latent tensions remain.

ON THE GROUND IN LATIN AMERICA

At the same time that education is coming to be seen not only as the means to development but as "development itself"—as Chilean leaders now believe—there remain broad social projects assigned to schooling. As much as in the development heyday of the 1960s, schools continue to be seen by many as part of a nation's investment in its future, alongside other social investments such as health. Also, as discussed below, alleviation of poverty and redistribution of income are long-term goals for most nations. Governments seek to achieve these goals by focusing scarce resources on the most disadvantaged sectors of their societies, including resources for education. And, the provision of schooling is thought by many to be an effective and noncoercive means to remove underage workers from the labor force. For all these reasons, we must consider child labor and education in the context of social welfare policies in Chile, Peru, and Mexico and as part of the context of understanding the evolution of school/work alternatives that have been available to children there since the mid–1980s.

Reviewing the history of Latin America's attempt to lead economic and social growth over fifty years, Sheahan (1999, p. 166) argues that persistent dualisms in access to education are to blame for broader inequality in employment and income. Eliminating the inequality of education will be the first step toward a more equal society. Birdsall and Londoño (1998, p. 112) observe that simple growth models based on human capital accumulation assumed away any distributional problem. There was an implicit assumption that investment in education would naturally "trickle down." This ignored the fact that persistent poverty reduced the expressed demand for school opportunities. Equitable growth will not naturally occur, in part, because of the social deficits created during the recessions of the 1980s. According to Samuel Morley (1995, p. 196), "The 1980s left a backlog of unmet needs in education, health, infrastructure, and private investment. It added 40 million to poverty rolls. Latin American governments face the daunting task of consolidating their progress while reducing poverty and attending to the unmet social needs left by the 1980s. This will not be an easy task."

The consequences of investment in education–the main concern from an economic perspective–are complex and multidimensional. The most immediate and simplest consideration is with the individual or "private" returns on the investment in education. By all available accounts, education has remained a very sound investment around the world, and specifically in the countries that are studied here. For example, in Mexico, regardless of the estimation method used, analyses of the survey data I use have indicated that the returns for each year of education are between 9 and 16 percent, with the greatest returns accruing to rural Mexican women, whose incomes without education would be very low (Bracho and Zamudio 1994; Abler, Robles, and Rodriguez 1998). The overall benefits of education to individuals accrue eventually to society. After taking into account the public investment in schooling, the net value of each year of school investment can be expressed as a "social return." By this measure, the social benefits to education are, as much as ever before, a sound investment, though more so at the level of basic education than at the tertiary level.

There is a second dimension that complicates the economic view of educational investment: the changing level of income inequality and the role of education in this inequality. The investment value of education may rise or fall not only because the productive capacity of educated workers changes, but also because there are secular changes in the distribution of incomes of those who are more educated relative to those who are less educated. A recent example from Mexico is germane here. Building on the work of Cortés and Rubalcava (1991), Lächler (1999) used Mexico's 1984 and 1994 Encuesta Nacional de Ingreso-Gasto de Hogares (ENIGH84 and ENIGH94). Over these ten years, the real income of Mexican workers made modest gains overall. For example, the average hourly wage rate of 5.62 pesos in 1984 grew to 6.88 pesos in 1994 (in 1994 pesos). However, this growth was found *only* among those with at least twelve years of education, that is, among Mexicans who had completed the media superior level of studies. For those with only primary or secondary education, wage rates actually *fell* during this same period. When total average annual income was calculated, the same results were apparent: Gains were experienced by those with at least twelve years or education, and especially those with university education. Obtaining basic education became ever more critically important during the years of my study, because it served as the entry way to further education, attainment of which became absolutely essential to prevent *loss* of income.

A third dimension for the consideration of the welfare consequences of education relates to opportunities. Concern with schooling has been motivated not only by an imperative to improve the quality of life of the current generation, but also the quality of life of future generations, through giving children an opportunity to improve their situation relative to their parents. The "social mobility concern" accounts for much of the populist support for education expansion and reform. Behrman, Birdsall, and Székely (1998) studied twenty-eight Latin American countries with available household data sets. At several points in time in each country, they looked at the impact of family income and parent's education as determinants of the lag or the "gap" experienced by children in their age for school year. The overall relation between family background and school gap was used to construct an index of social mobility for each country in various years. By this measure, Chile demonstrated the greatest overall mobility, Brazil had the lowest, and Peru and Mexico were in a middle group of countries. The investigators further discovered a positive relation between the extent of mobility and each nation's primary school spending (but not, interestingly, spending on higher education). Investing in education may make more permeable the social strata that regulate the opportunities for mobility.

IS THERE ANY PROBLEM WITH CHILDREN WORKING AND ATTENDING SCHOOL AT THE SAME TIME?

This book is about the reasons that children's time and energies are allocated to the home, the school, and the labor force in Latin America. The main purpose is to describe the determinants of these allocations and to examine the political and social factors responsible for changes in children's daily activities in Chile, Peru, and Mexico. However, a few words at least must be said about the *consequences* for children of their time allocations. Development economists of every inclination agree that formal schooling, at least to the secondary level, is essential in order for children to have at least the chance of earning a living wage as adults. Even in countries where the quality of schooling is acknowledged to be low, educational researchers find that the "credential effect" from school attendance is powerful (Schiefelbein 1997). That is, even when schools impart few real skills, the clear signal that school completion sends to employers is of a job candidate possessing the requisite commitment and trainability for work. Therefore, from the viewpoint of children and families, a decision to attend full-time schooling (without working) is ultimately a smarter decision than is the decision to pursue full-time employment (without school attendance). Many studies concur that the individual economic benefits from secondary schooling will more than repay the investment in children's time (for a review of the international evidence see Psacharopoulos 1994). The investigations of my colleagues (Abler et al 1998), using household survey data from Mexico and Peru, support that conclusion, as well: Workers who complete secondary schooling earn more than workers who stop after primary school. The individual returns from secondary education are higher than most children's alternative investments of their time and energy.

Many welfare analysts, and all children's rights advocates, would want to eliminate any type of child labor that prevents children from completing the compulsory school level that is mandated in their societies. But what about the *combination* of work with school attendance? Is *that* necessarily harmful to children? The question is especially interesting in the case of Mexico and Peru because many adolescents–even those who report regular work–also attend school. Much of this book is devoted to the policies and the sociology of the minority who have been left behind, that is, to children who are prevented from attending school and who will be marked for life as a consequences of child labor. But first we should consider the less-certain issues surrounding child labor by young people who also attend school. Knaul (2000) constructed retrospective histories of labor force entry and schooling for Mexican workers. She compared the earnings of persons who had begun to work prior to finishing school and those who delayed working until the completion of their schooling. Although combining work with schooling was more advantageous, in terms of earnings, than dropping out of school altogether, Knaul also found that early labor force entry had a significant negative impact on earnings, even taking into account that each group was self-selected and a distinct population. She concluded (p. 24) that "the combination of work and school is part of a cycle that perpetuates inequalities and intergenerational poverty," since poorer families will be those most likely to require earnings and assistance from their children after the school day.

A related question is whether there are any measurable learning gains for adolescents associated with early work, and whether such gains are offset by a loss to the working student's cognitive growth from schooling. This issue is of long-standing concern for U.S. policy makers and families (for a review, see Greenberger and Steinberg 1986), but it is quite new in Latin America. To address these questions, at least in one Latin American country with a problem of child labor, we can summarize investigations based on the Third International Math and Science Study (TIMSS). This world survey of student achievement by thirteen- and fourteen-year-old students was sponsored by the International Evaluation

Association in 1995. Much of the variance in academic achievement between nations can be explained on the basis of international differences in the rates of after-school employment (see Post and Pong 2000a, 2000b). This suggests at least the possibility that part of the international difference in academic achievement could be attributable to student labor rates. In this case, it would be in the self-interest of each nation to scrutinize the employment/achievement relation of its students so as to develop integrative policies that promote national competitiveness.

Within the limitations of its cross-sectional design, and the absence of a parental component that gathers precise information about students' family backgrounds, TIMSS data allow us to investigate this comparison. The survey methodology included a negotiated list of common questions asked to students in all countries. Of interest to us here is the item that was translated and asked to eighth-grade students: "Outside school, how much time per week do you spend at a paid job?" Although there was no family background information asked directly of parents in the TIMSS, information about family characteristics can be obtained from the student responses to questions about parental education and the number of books in the home.

There are clear associations between a nation's average academic achievement and the national proportions of eighth-grader students who work for pay during the school week. Figure 1.1 includes, on the left side, a weighted scatter plot that illustrates this relationship. Each triangle and each circle in Figure 1.1 corresponds to a nation. Figure 1.1 highlights Colombia, the only Latin American nation participating in the study that dared to release its results. For comparison, we also highlight the United States.

The upper left panel of Figure 1.1 shows the relationship between student work-rates and national math achievement for boys. The lower left panel illustrates the same relationship for girls. In both the presentations and in our calculations of linear regression coefficients, we have weighted more heavily the nations with greater numbers of secondary school students. Thus, in Figure 1.1 the area of each triangle and each circle is proportional to the number of a nation's secondary school students. For exam-

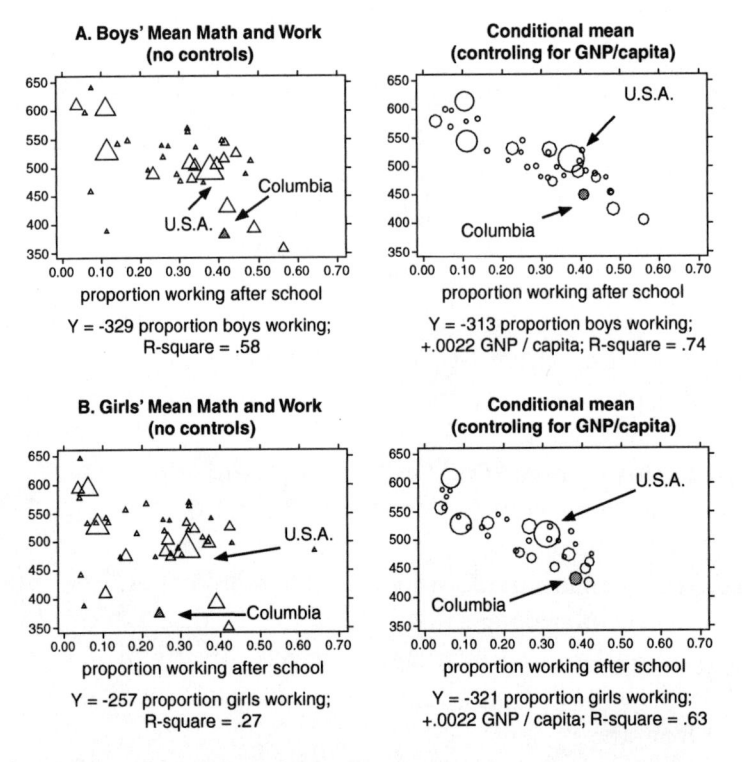

FIGURE 1.1 — Data panels

A. Boys' Mean Math and Work (no controls)
Y = -329 proportion boys working; R-square = .58

Conditional mean (controling for GNP/capita)
Y = -313 proportion boys working; +.0022 GNP / capita; R-square = .74

B. Girls' Mean Math and Work (no controls)
Y = -257 proportion girls working; R-square = .27

Conditional mean (controling for GNP/capita)
Y = -321 proportion girls working; +.0022 GNP / capita; R-square = .63

Source: Post & Pong (2000a; 2000b). Analysis of TIMSS data. National-level correlations are weighted by size of each school system's secondary school student population. The area of each triangle and each circle is proportional to the number of secondary school students in each nation.

FIGURE 1.1 International Relationship Between Rates of Adolescent Student-Employment an Average Math Achievement

ple, the triangles for Colombia and the United States are larger than the triangles for Iceland or Kuwait. This weighting allows us to observe the aggregate impact of part-time work without treating each country as an "observation," (students, not nations, were randomly sampled in this study). By weighting the national means of achievement and labor rates, this strategy allows us to observe the overall relationship underlying international differences in achievement.

The upper left and lower left of Figure 1.1 presents the simple scatter plot of each nation's average mathematics score in TIMSS and its proportions of eighth-grade students who responded that they had worked for pay during the school week. We also estimated the slope for these relations: −329 for boys and −257 for girls. We further calculated the R-square statistic as .58 for boys and .27 for girls. The relationship is less pronounced for girls than boys because in Colombia, as well as Iran, the Philippines, and South Africa (countries of lower math achievement for girls), there are much smaller percentages of girls than boys who reported working for pay. The explanation for this could be found in religious restrictions on girls' activities (Iran) or in the family economies of poorer nations, which often incorporate daughters into household labor and assign domestic responsibilities rather than paid work outside of the home. In either case, we found similar results for international correlations of part-time labor rates with science scores (not reported here). The regression coefficients (significant at the .001 level for boys and girls) confirm what is apparent at first sight: There is a close, inverse relation at the national level between a nation's rate of student employment and a nation's overall level of mathematics achievement.

In thinking about the underlying reasons for this association, we have to consider the possibility that the apparent inverse relationship is not a causal relation in either direction. Rather, both the level of student achievement and the rate of student employment may be co-determined by national-level characteristics of the education system and the national economy. Families in richer nations can usually forgo the earnings from working children. Families in these richer nations are on the whole better able to invest resources in their children's educations because they face no credit constraints to their investments. At the same time, richer nations can afford to employ full-time teachers, to offer students free texts, to maintain school libraries, and generally to supply a richer environment for learning as compared with poorer nations. The theoretical interpretation being sketched here, of co-determined rates of student employment and academic achievement, implies that the bivariate relationship see on the upper-left and lower-left quadrants of Figure 1.1 could reflect the fact that students in poorer nations tend to work more and to achieve less, but they may *not* necessarily achieve less *as a result* of working more.

We sought to investigate the possibility that national achievement is related more to national wealth, which may increase achievement indirectly by decreasing the rate of student employment. To do this we used each nation's per capita Gross National Product, as reported by the World Bank in 1994. We entered this figure simultaneously in a second regression. We found that GNP per capita partly determines a nation's mean mathematics achievement (and is also statistically significant at the .001 level). However, the effect of this indicator of national resources does not eliminate or "explain away" the effect of the rate of student labor. On the contrary, the inclusion of GNP per capita in the regression equation *increases* the impact of student labor rates, especially the impact of girls' employment rates. Thus it cannot be the case that student employment rates merely channel the effects of national wealth. To illustrate this relation, on the right side of Figure 1.1, we have plotted not the actual means of student math achievement, but the *conditional* means, based on the regression reported below each figure. That is, in this figure we present the relationship between national employment rates and math achievement, net of the effect of national income. What we find is that the slope of paid labor rates is actually steeper among girls, after taking into account national wealth. This indicates that the lower academic performance of Colombian students, and students in other nations with high rates of student employment, may be attributable to the child labor. Further investigation confirmed that working students in Colombia are less proficient in math and science than nonworking students, even after taking into account and controlling for these students' family environments. This finding would hardly surprise Colombian educational psychologists and child labor researchers, such as Salazar (1996, p. 175), who writes, "The nature of the work that children carry out, especially in rural areas, is hardly conducive to successful study. Children have to fight exhaustion to concentrate in class, and they have very little time to study or do their home-work. In short, the burden of work makes a burden of school, compromising children's motivation and performance."

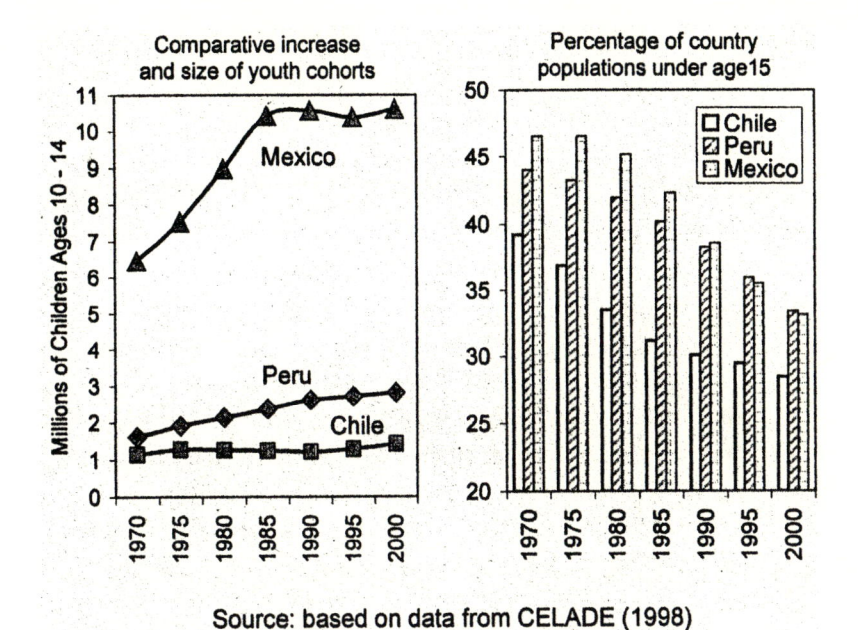

Policies and Realities for Working Children in Latin America 25

Comparative increase and size of youth cohorts

Percentage of country populations under age 15

Source: based on data from CELADE (1998)

FIGURE 1.2 Demographic Trends in Chile, Peru, and Mexico

A COMPARATIVE CASE STUDY

In their sheer demographics, Chile, Peru, and Mexico each presented very distinctive opportunities and challenges to their political leaders and child welfare advocates. Figure 1.2 illustrates two of the most important basic differences that confronted lawmakers and educators in each country.

When compared with the two South American cases of our study, Mexico is a far larger country with many more children and, as we will see, it has a more extensive and complex educational apparatus. Mexico's population growth rates–among the highest of Latin America until the 1970s–meant that its population of adolescents surged upward until the mid–1980s, after which time it leveled off. This growth also meant that, for many years, large proportions of Mexico's population consisted of school-age children. Educating these young people represented both a precious social investment, and also a weightier responsibility, on the population of working Mexicans. Fewer adults contributed to the economy for each child and more school spaces had to be provided somehow each year simply to maintain steady attendance rates. The size, the growth, and the relative share of Mexico's younger population all have important implications for what it has been politically possible to offer them and for the sluggish response of the population to new school opportunities. After the mid–1980s, as the number of children at last leveled off, Mexico became better able to meet the needs of its young people. Mexico's National Population Council forecasts that school-aged children will represent declining proportions of the population until at least the middle of the twenty-first century. This "demographic bonus" (CONAPO 1999, p. 21) has profound implications for the social investments that will be possible in the present and immediate future, as Mexico follows the same tendencies as Chile.

By contrast with Chile and Mexico, Peru's school-aged population is expected to rise until at least 2010. Peru's population of children, while not matching the high growth rates of Mexico, continued growing steadily through the end of the twentieth century, by which time Peru overtook Mexico for first place in terms of the percentage of the population under age fifteen. This means that any Peruvian government, regardless how resourceful or effective may be its policies for children, for many years to come will play the game of catch-up: It must generate and distribute greater and greater resources merely to provide the same levels of services, offer the same protections, and make the same investments in the young as had been possible in the 1960s. Peruvian education will continue to require greater absolute infusions of resources simply to offer its children the same opportunities as were offered in the past. Chile, well before the critical contemporary period that is the subject of this book, entered a fertility transition, a time when its population growth-rates peaked and began to decline. Progressive family planning policies in the 1960s, together with comparatively high levels of women's education, female labor force participation, and older ages at marriage, all contributed to the enviable demographic experience of Chile in the 1980s and 1990s. From the beginning to the end of the 1980s, the number of children aged ten to fourteen actually *de-*

clined by 50,000. This meant that any leadership, no matter how low their policy priority for youth, would not have to expend greater resources simply to offer children what was previously offered. As we will see, this period happily coincided with Chile's return to democratic government, and with a very high priority for youth after 1990 by President Patricio Aylwin and his coalition successor, Eduardo Frei, in 1995. This "arrival present" for the elected leadership–the fruition of family planning investments and historically high levels of women's education–combined with Chile's smaller population to offer child welfare advocates a much more responsive and manageable problem to work upon, as compared either with Mexico or Peru.

The demographic context for our study is important in another way, beyond the strain of the numbers of children on the possibility to provide services or regulate under-age labor. Although large numbers of children place strains on social spending, children are easier to prioritize when they comprise large elements of the population. When 40 percent of all members of a society are under age fifteen, then children will be a more natural focus of public debate and government attention than is the case when the social welfare of the elderly, and attention to retirement, become pressing policy matters. Child welfare advocates will see their "constituency" decline further in coming years, in numbers if not in importance.

During the period of this study, the political economy of Chile, Peru, and Mexico responded to domestic pressures and new international fiscal constraints. In Chapter 2 and Chapter 3 we discuss the consequences of these changes for social welfare and education policy, but here we must first survey the general panorama. Berry (1997) has shown that the overall 3 percent annual growth in per capita income between 1950 and 1980 brought about a gradual decline in Latin American rates of poverty. Had this growth rate continued, then by the year 2000 there would have remained only a small percentage of families living under the poverty line drawn by Oscar Altimar (1982), even in the absence of major progressive redistributions of income. This was not to be. In most Latin American nations, including Mexico and Peru (and in Chile several years earlier), severe recessions and foreign debt crises led to falling income and a set of responses by the region's governments that are described as "structural adjustments." Government responses included the opening of national economies to more private investments, while reducing state sponsorship of many basic services, such as utilities, mining, and pensions. Except for the single case of Costa Rica, in all of the nations studied by Berry, income inequality grew, perhaps as the result of the initial recessions or, as Berry argued is more likely, as a result of the ensuing structural adjustment. The Gini coefficient of primary income increased between 5 and 10 percentage points. As state provision of basic social services contracted, growing numbers of the poor were left especially vulnerable. Labor reforms decreased job protection, and the real value of official minimum wages declined in Mexico and Peru.

A recession of historic proportions affected each of the nations included in this study, first reaching Chile in the years just after the violent 1973 coup lead by Augusto Pinochet and then again in 1982. Instead of fixing the exchange rate to stop inflation, Chile devalued its peso, and exports increased rapidly, which lead to increased employment. Starting in 1985, real wages began to recover. At the outset of the period of our Chilean case study, labor protections had been crippled, but taxes on business had also been increased to finance social spending programs in a complex negotiation. After the transition to democratic government, led by the Christian Democrat–Socialist coalition, Chile adopted a "competitive plus-social model" (Sheahan 1997, p. 19). Poverty was reduced when, rather than simply restrain inflation, the government also took greater responsibility for production, employment, and export.

Under military dictatorship, the Chilean state could act with a high degree of autonomy in its programmatic cuts (Stepan 1985). In contrast to Chile and Mexico, Peru's attempt at stabilization in the early 1980s largely collapsed (Nelson 1990). Peru's economy weakened in the late 1970s and again in 1982, after which a new more competitive model (Sheahan 1997) was introduced by the military government. Then, in the late 1980s, the heterodox adjustment policies of the Aprista Alan Garcia government led to hyperinflation and precipitous declines in family welfare, especially among the poor (Glewwe and Hall 1992; Paus 1991; Pastor and Wise 1992). Mexico, following a precipitous decline in oil revenues in the early 1980s, became deeply indebted to foreign banks. Mounting interest payments triggered a downsizing of many social programs.

What was the net impact of these changes in economic context on the ability of each society to forgo children's earnings and invest in education? A summary answer to that question is suggested by the indicators shown in Figure 1.3. This figure presents two important macroeconomic indicators for the countries of this study: the purchasing power-adjusted per capita income and the inflation rate by year. Figure 1.3 shows that, by the end of the case studies of this book, neither Mexico nor Peru had fully recovered from recessions of the early 1980s. However, Chile had more than rebounded: Its combination of economic growth and a very low rate of population growth brought impressive real increases in income, relative both to its own history and to Mexico and Peru. These increases persist even after adjusting for differences in purchasing power. Peru's situation was unique, among the three countries, in its hyperinflation during the APRA government, when the ability to plan public education or welfare budgets was destroyed in the face of daily doubling prices.

INFORMATION SOURCES AND THE LIMITATIONS OF HOUSEHOLD SURVEYS

This book results from five years of intensive fieldwork and collaboration with Chilean, Peruvian, and Mexican investigators. It draws on interviews, examination of national and regional finances and enrollments, and bibliographic research. Apart from the policy analysis in this book and its comparative study of the debate over children in three Latin American nations, the project also offers new insights based on a study of national surveys that

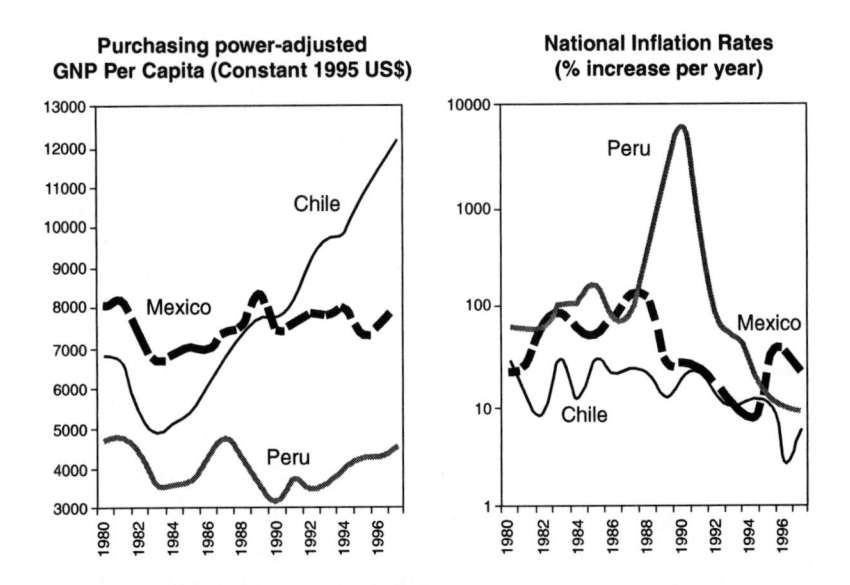

FIGURE 1.3 Economic Indicators for Chile, Peru, and Mexico

have been conducted since the mid–1980s in each country. Since the work relies so heavily on these national surveys, it is important to be candid about their limitations as well as their strengths. One limitation with national surveys, which attempt to estimate the parameters of the population beyond the small sample of selected families, is that they depend on an accurate sampling frame. From what list will households be randomly selected? In some rural areas of Latin America, where not all homes have postal addresses and fewer still have telephones, it is difficult to create a definitive list of all households, or even communities. But this is exactly what each nation attempts to do, basing its surveys on inventories of communities from the last national census.

When surveyors know and can quantify the extent that certain areas or socioeconomic strata are under- or over- represented, they can correct matters by subsequently weighting the data during the analyses. However readers should be aware of the very rough approximations of sampling frames to the true populations. During the early 1990s, for example, Peru experienced tremendous anarchy and Sendero Luminoso terrorism in parts of its interior. Although I originally planned to make use of a Peruvian survey from 1991, I decided to suspend this part of the analysis because not all parts of the country had been adequately represented and, thus, results from the 1991 survey were not comparable with either earlier or later years. Another problem with the sampling frames used here is that, even when they can be assumed to be faithful as representative of households, some populations of working children–the most extreme and exploited cases–may not live in households at all. Working children of "the street" sometimes live apart from parents (though not often, at least in the three countries of our study). Children who do not ordinarily reside in the household that is selected for a national survey will be invisible in the data used in this book. No information was gathered in these surveys about the education, activity, or general well-being of children living on their nations' streets.

A different form of bias in national surveys occurs because of the intimacy and sensitivity of the questions that are posed by strangers. The typical household survey is based on a selection of addresses rather than a selection of telephone numbers: A knock is heard at the front door. The door is opened, and a representative from the national government (although frequently only an underpaid university student) presents a credential and asks to speak with the household's head. In the course of several hours of questioning (sometimes necessitating a follow-up visit), the household's informant (who frequently is *not* the head of the household) is asked to inventory all of the persons who normally reside in the household. The respondent is then asked to identify the relationship of each resident to the person who has been named as the household head, including the exact conjugal relationship. The interviewer asks whether each resident is literate and how far each has gone in school. For surveys like those analyzed in this book, considerable detail is requested about all sources of monetary and nonmonetary income. It might seem that one of the less sensitive or controversial areas of the questionnaire would be the daily activities of each person. Did a given resident attend school last week? Did she engage in any work for pay, or perform any unpaid work? On closer examination, however, we must be aware that even these "objective" questions of fact can lead to some reluctance on the part of parents. How can respondents be assured that interviewers will not identify to authorities those parents who allow their children to work or to leave school, when laws forbid child labor and compel school attendance? More subtly, parents may feel ashamed of their children's activities and so feel a loss of face by admitting to an educated stranger what their children really do for most of the day. An example from Chile will make the point. As we will see, Chile's reported rates of child labor have been consistently low in the period of our study (1987–96). However, Julio Cortés (1999) reports on independent school surveys that reveal far greater rates of students who say they work when they are individually questioned about their after-school activities. Another example comes from UNESCO's 1997 "Evaluation Laboratory of Educational Quality," which tested the achievement and questioned the activities of third and fourth graders in several countries (including Mexico and Peru, which decided against releasing the results). The survey is considered reliable on many measures. In Chile, there was a very substantial gap in the achievement of children living in rural and urban areas. Urban municipal school students also performed significantly behind their peers who attended private subsidized schools, though much of this difference would be explainable on the basis of family background (McEwan et al. 1998). But one of the most intriguing findings is the high rate reported for economic activity among very young children. By contrast with surveys of *parents* (such as the Chilean CASEN survey used in this book), the survey of *children* yielded an estimate of 18 percent who "worked outside of the home" on a "typical day." This same difficulty also surfaces in the United States. The U.S. Department of Labor, in its quarterly household surveys during the late 1980s, found an employment rate of approximately 15 percent among persons who were age fifteen and who were students at that time (U.S. Department of Labor 2000). We must somehow reconcile this estimate with the results of the U.S. National Longitudinal Survey, in which approximately 25 percent of tenth graders reported regular paid employment during the 1990–91 school year. There are three clear possibilities: Chilean and the U.S. parents are minimizing the extent to which their children worked outside the home; adolescents from those countries exaggerate the extent of their employment when they were asked directly by researchers; or both.

Many types of survey biases, although potentially serious, can be discounted when surveys are "internally valid," that is, when they make sense internally and yield consistent results in repeated applications. Imagine, for example, a society in which parents were sensitive to legal restrictions on child labor and who therefore underreported the incidence of work by their children younger than the legal age. In this case we would find, upon inspecting parents' responses, that there was a sudden "jump" in economic activity exactly at the year in which child labor became legal, and school attendance was no longer mandatory. When we find no such jump at the onset of the legal age for work, but a smooth curve (as we do in our results, see Figure 1.4), then we have reason to believe that—on the whole—parent's responses were not biased.

But, even when parents are consistent, how are we to reconcile the differences between their responses and those of children? Perhaps it is the case that, while parents are tempted to underreport their children's work activity, it is even more likely that children exaggerate and overreport their work. Repeated surveys, conducted with independently drawn samples, "triangulate" and mutually support the population estimates of each individual survey. The fact that parents are fairly consistent in the average reports of children's activities gives us some reassurance that the estimates are measures of a reality. Furthermore, in some cases we can verify the accuracy of surveys we use based on *other* surveys, conducted by other offices or ministries than those which fielded the surveys we use for our discussion. In Mexico, a national census was conducted in 1990 and a bi-census (or "conteo") was conducted in 1995. Both investigations lead to estimates of the school attendance rates in the twelve-to-seventeen-year-old range that are very similar to our estimates based on Mexico's ENIGH in 1992 and 1996. Recent work by Levison et al. (1999), based on Mexico's survey of urban employment, yields estimates of the urban child labor rate (around 12 percent working exclusively, and a further 6 percent combining work with school) that is remarkably consistent with the non-rural populations represented in the ENIGH. Chilean estimates based on the CASEN are very consistent with Chile's census reports of school participation. In Peru, a national survey of households was completed in 1996 (the ENAHO), and it points to school participation rates that are similar to those reported in this book based on the ENNIV in later years. Also, as will be discussed in Chapter 5, at several points in the periods of our country case studies, we can rely on official reports of the numbers of students enrolled. We must be cautious about interpreting changes in these numbers, since they may reflect changing rates of repetition as much as changing rates of attendance. Nonetheless, in all three countries, my estimates of school participation rates are quite consistent with official ministry reports in Chile and Peru and with secretary of public education reports in Mexico.

TRENDS IN CHILDREN'S ACTIVITY SINCE THE MID–1980S

With these cautions in mind, let us first turn to what the national survey data tell us about the large-scale tendencies in children's school attendance in Chile, Peru, and Mexico. Figure 1.4 graphs the percentages of children, ages twelve to seventeen, who attended school in the past week during three different years of the survey application (I selected only months when schools were in session). These percentages are shown separately for girls and boys, because one part of the investigation in Chapter 5 will be to show trends in gender equity between and within each nation.

To the unaided eye, several tendencies appear in Figure 1.4 which, while perhaps obvious to many readers, should be emphasized because they are so central to the interpretations developed later in this book. In the top panel we observe the national percentages of Chilean girls and boys who attended school in the week prior to each survey in 1987, 1990, and 1996. The year of 1990 marked the end of seventeen years of military dictatorship and, as will be described in Chapter 3, the beginning of a government that was fully committed to the social programs that had

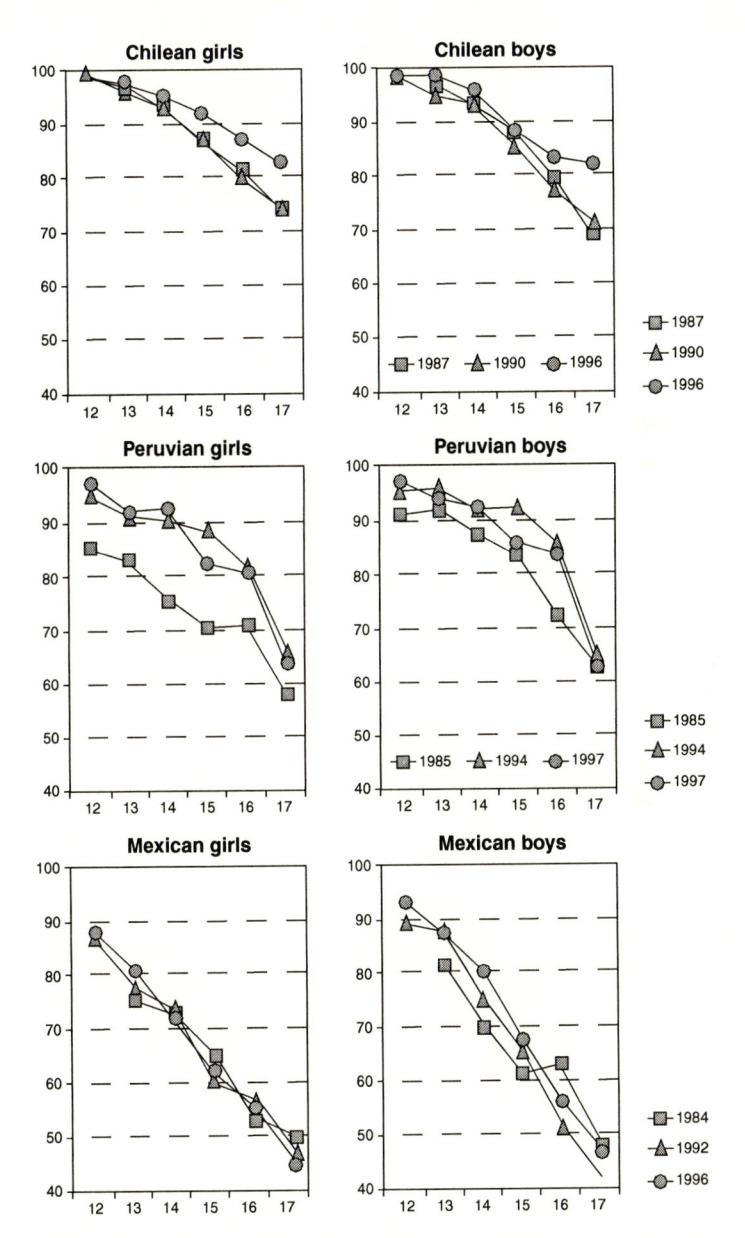

Source: weighted tabulations of individuals living with at least one parent in CASEN 1987, 1990, 1996; ENNIV-1985, 1994, 1997; ENIGH-1984, 1992, 1996. ENNIV-85 excludes summer vacation months.

FIGURE 1.4 Percentages of Chilean, Peruvian, and Mexican Children, Ages 12-17, Attending School Since 1980s

suffered under Pinochet. Although causality is difficult to establish based on the indicators of Figure 1.4, the Chilean trend is clearly consistent with the renewed commitment by the coalition government after 1990. While there were essentially *no* changes in school participation rates from 1987 to 1990, after this time children began to remain in school until older ages, even though only eight years of schooling were compulsory during the entire period of the Chilean case study. Girls, who had slightly higher rates of schooling than boys, even in 1987, increased their rates over the 1990–96 period and maintained their slight advantage.

Peru's trajectory is more complex. Between 1985 and 1992, the Peruvian economy collapsed, plunging millions of children deeper into absolute poverty. Real public spending on education also declined, as we will see in Chapter 3. Then, after 1992, conditions began to improve, as the government slowly increased education funding. Economic growth and rising education funding continued from 1994 through 1997. In this context, we can observe increases in school participation both for boys and, especially, for girls from 1985 through 1994. Girls, who in 1985 were underrepresented in Peruvian schools, had attained parity with boys in terms of participation rates by 1994. Few statistically significant changes occurred in school participation subsequently from 1994 through 1997.

In Mexico, a third historical reality is apparent when comparing across three survey years. For girls, it is remarkable that *no* major changes in school participation rates are seen over a twelve-year period during which, as we will see, economic conditions and school law varied considerably (compulsory school was extended from six to nine years in 1993). As we will see in Chapter 5, this national stagnation for girls reflects, in actuality, opposing tendencies for girls in poorer and more affluent communities of the country. Overall, boys increased slightly their rates of schooling. This reflected their improvement, relative to girls.

It is harder to estimate children's economic activity than their school attendance. In the first instance, there is little ambiguity involved in the question asked about each household resident: "Did X attend school last week?" By contrast with the concrete understanding of school attendance, many respondents do not consider

Policies and Realities for Working Children in Latin America 37

all work to be "work." Especially for the non-remunerated work that is most common in sustaining the family economy, the household head who responds to interviewers may not consider a child's activity to be one that generates or adds to the market value of a product. Yet this is the murky definition of work used in most household surveys, including those we rely upon in this book. Boyden, Ling and Myers (1998, pp. 20–21) critically discuss the inherent problem of using household surveys that force respondents to categorize children's activities as either "economic" activities or not. We must take care to remember that many activities that are not "economic," as defined by national surveys, are still valuable and contribute to the family economy indirectly. Cooking, cleaning, and the care of younger siblings are the most prominent examples of activities that, in addition to being non-remunerated, are usually not considered to be work in the three countries of our study. When it is possible to gauge the extent of domestic labor, it is not surprising to find that girls have more housework responsibilities than boys, even when girls also attend school (INEGI 1998a; Levison et al. 1999)

Despite the difficulty of clearly delineating economic from "noneconomic" activity, it is important to use the information gathered in these surveys to assess the trends in each country and to determine why certain children are likely to attend school, to "work," to do both, or to do neither. For clarity, I describe children's activities at two time points in Figure 1.5. In Chile, we select 1990 and 1996, the years of the coalition government when most changes occurred. In Peru, we use the earliest and latest surveys available: 1985 and 1997. In Mexico, prior to 1992 the survey did not distinguish individuals who worked part-time while attending school. Thus, we select 1992 and 1996, two survey years when this detailed information is available. As in Figure 1.4, we present our graphics of children's activities in Figure 1.5, first for girls and then for boys.

In the case of Chile from 1990 to 1996, for both sexes there was an obvious reduction in the percentage of children who worked rather than attended school. This was accompanied by increases in exclusive school attendance. For both years, and for

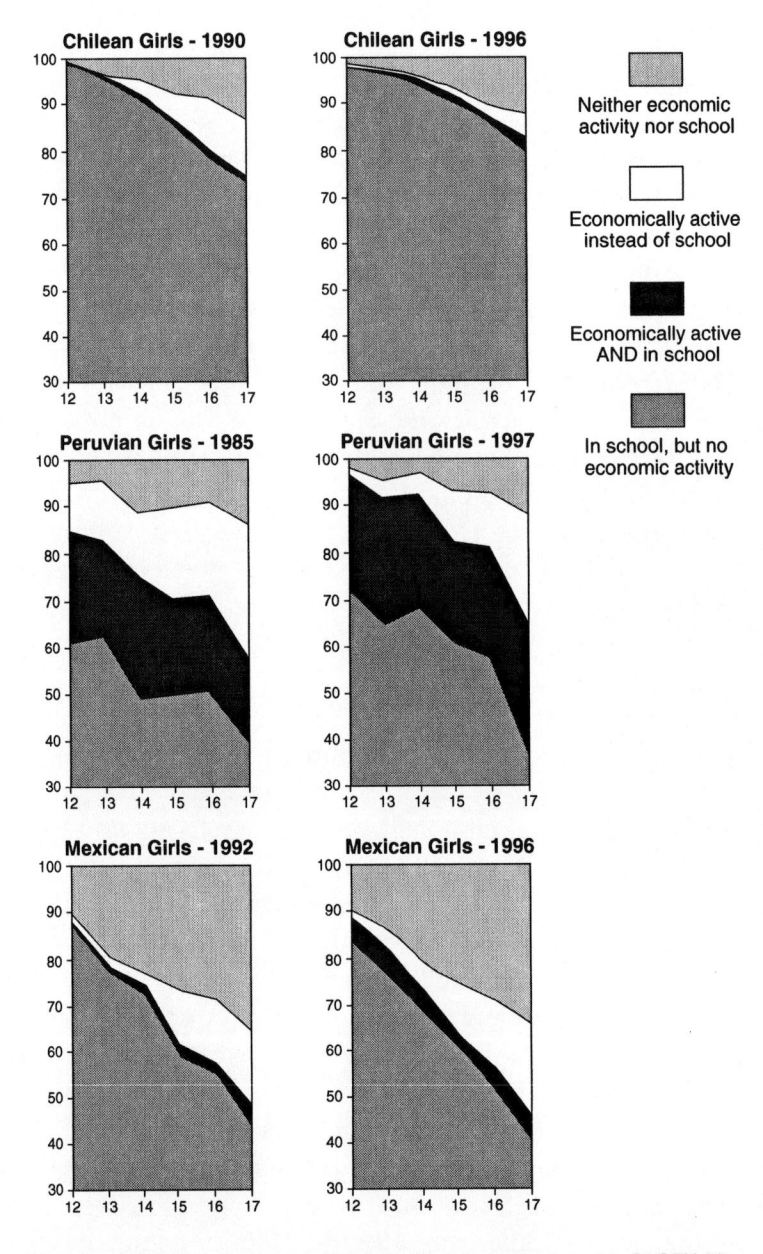

38   *Policies and Realities for Working Children in Latin America*

Source: weighted tabulations of individuals living with at least one parent in CASEN-90, CASEN-96, ENNIV-85, ENNIV-97, ENIGH-92, ENIGH-96

FIGURE 1.5   Trends in Activities of Girls and Boys, Ages 12-17

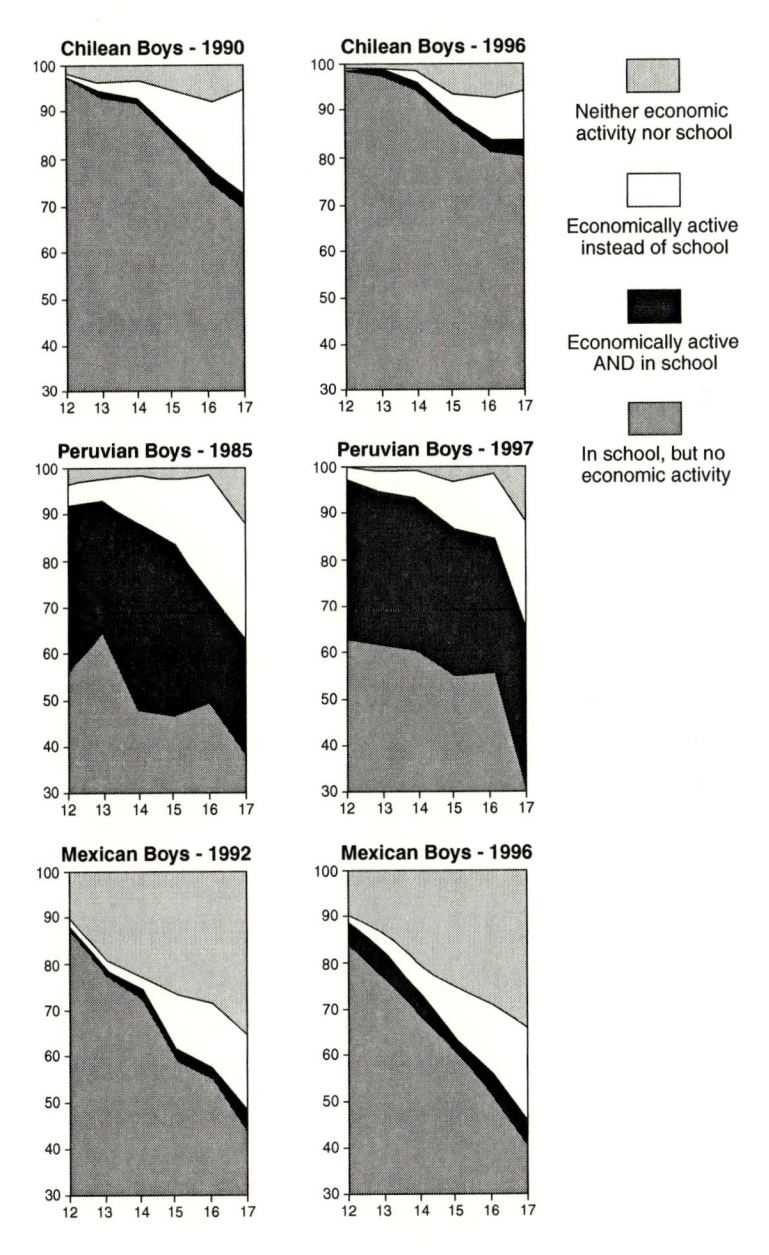

Policies and Realities for Working Children in Latin America 39

Legend:
- Neither economic activity nor school
- Economically active instead of school
- Economically active AND in school
- In school, but no economic activity

Chilean Boys - 1990
Chilean Boys - 1996
Peruvian Boys - 1985
Peruvian Boys - 1997
Mexican Boys - 1992
Mexican Boys - 1996

Source: weighted tabulations of individuals living with at least one parent in CASEN-90, CASEN-96, ENNIV-85, ENNIV-97, ENIGH-92, ENIGH-96 both girls and boys, there were very small percentages of workers who were in school, and there were even tinier percentages of students who were economically active. Notice that the category on which we have no direct information–"neither economic activity nor school"–is larger for Chilean girls than for boys. It seems quite likely that the gender difference in these "neither" rates is attributable to the fact that girls take on more domestic responsibilities than boys, such as cooking, cleaning, and caring for siblings. Because these efforts are not included as "economic activities," girls appear more often than boys in this category, a finding that also surfaces in the other countries of our study.

As we previously saw, the case of Peru is far more complex; this can be appreciated in comparison to Chile. Many economically active Peruvian children (the majority, in fact, of younger workers) also attend school. By the same token, many students work part-time. The reasons for this will be deferred until Chapter 2, but suffice it here to note that this feature of Peruvian childhood is found for both sexes, and in each year. Unlike Chile, where economic activity and schooling appear to be mutually exclusive, in Peru there is a great deal of overlap. From 1985 to 1997, when overall school attendance increased significantly (especially among girls), it is important at the outset of this study to emphasize how this was accomplished. By contrast with Chile, where work-rates diminished to make way for schooling, in Peru the two categories were absorbed into one another. In 1985, roughly half of the economically active girls were in school. By 1997, the majority were in school. The percentages of girls who were in school *exclusively* grew modestly over the twelve-year period. The percentages of girls who worked while studying grew even more. At the same time, the percentage of girls who worked exclusively declined. But girls' overall rate of economic activity did not change substantially, because more students also worked. For Peruvian boys there are parallels with the tendency for girls. Like girls, Peruvian boys also combine schooling with working. The rate at which they tended to pursue schooling *exclusively* increased even more modestly among boys than it did among girls over the 1985–97 period. More boys attended school in the latter year, but this happened because many workers combined their work with schooling.

Mexico's tendencies in activity rates for children are distinct from both Peru and Chile. Compared to boys, large proportions of Mexican girls are in the "neither" category, and this difference is larger for Mexico than for either of the other two countries of this study. As in Chile, in 1992 only a small proportion of Mexican girls who were in school also worked. What is remarkable is that this percentage grew over the 1992–96 period (and the change is statistically significant). As a result, for boys as well as for girls, a greater proportion of young workers attended school, although still not so great as in Peru. Still more noteworthy is the fact that, as seen previously in Figure 1.4, the total school participation rates barely budged from 1992 to 1996. What *did* increase was the rate at which students worked. Even with this increase, schooling and economic activity appear to be mutually exclusive categories. Although this exclusivity was less pronounced in 1996 than in 1992, Mexican children continued to work to the exclusion of attending school.

Chapters 4 and 5 discuss the effects of poverty on the activities of children in each country, and over time. However, suffice it here to remind readers that the summaries presented in Figure 1.5 gloss over substantial differences in children's activities between income groups and region. For example, overall in Mexico in 1996 there were an estimated 7,363,000 children (63 percent of all twelve-to-seventeen-year-olds) who attended school without any reported economic activity. But this overall distribution varied by income. Among the *poorest* fifth of children aged twelve to seventeen, there were only 990,000 children (41 percent) who attended school without working. By contrast, among the richest fifth of children twelve to seventeen, there were 1,907,000 children (83 percent) who attended school and did not work. In other words, more than twice as many children from the top income quintile attended school full-time than from the bottom income quintile. Rather than narrowing, this gap actually appears to have *widened* over the 1990s in Mexico. The gap also grew wider in Peru. In Chile, by contrast, a small gap between the activities of the rich and poor appears to have diminished even further. Appendices A1-A3 provide detailed population estimates for each activity and each year for Chile, Peru, and Mexico.

At least in the case of Mexico, it is possible to triangulate and confirm the information presented in Figure 1.5 with another national survey, the 1995 Mexican National Employment Survey (Encuesta Nacional de Empleo, the ENE). The ENE makes it possible to estimate the numbers of persons who: a) attend school; b) report economic activity outside the home; and c) report some type of noneconomic domestic work, including activities that would not even be defined as "work" by the Mexican, Peruvian, or Chilean surveys used in our own study. Based on the ENE, Mexico's National Institute of Statistics, Geography, and Information (INEGI 1998a) investigated the full range of activities of persons aged twelve to nineteen, including all possible combinations of the three major activities. INEGI's results are not directly comparable with our own findings, because we more narrowly focus only on children between ages twelve and seventeen (when children are most likely to attend lower and upper secondary school and to live with their parents). Nonetheless, the findings from INEGI provide additional confirmation of the basic findings in analysis using Mexico's household survey on income and expenditure. The findings from the employment survey (see Figure 1.6) reveal percentages of students who work after school that are very similar to those seen previously in Figure 1.5. Findings from the ENE also are quite consistent with those from the ENIGH about the overall percentage of young people attending school.

Beyond their confirmation of the tendencies seen from the ENIGH, the results from the ENE are important in their own right, for they better inform us of what children are likely to be doing when they are reported neither to be economically active nor in school. As we can see in Figure 1.6, there are clear differences in these alternatives, between boys and girls. Very few boys are reported to engage in domestic work of any kind, either alone or in combination with employment or school. In 1995, girls who did not attend school (including those aged eighteen and nine-

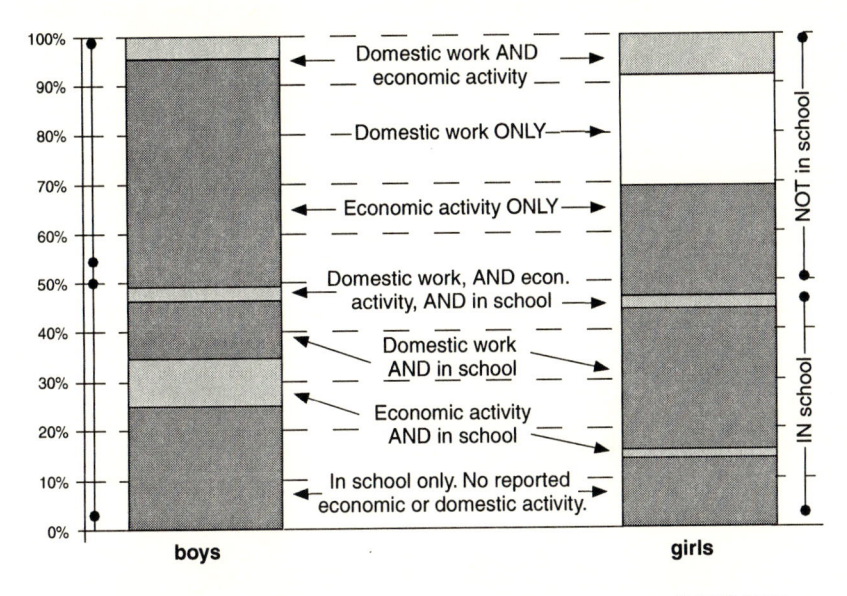

Policies and Realities for Working Children in Latin America 43

[Figure: stacked bar chart comparing boys and girls, y-axis 0%–100%, with categories: Domestic work AND economic activity; Domestic work ONLY; Economic activity ONLY; Domestic work, AND econ. activity, AND in school; Domestic work AND in school; Economic activity AND in school; In school only. No reported economic or domestic activity. Right axis: NOT in school / IN school.]

Source: recalculated from National Employment Survey tabulations (INEGI 1998)

Figure 1.6 Full Range of Activities of Mexicans, Ages 12-19, in 1995

teen) were about evenly divided between economic activity and domestic work. Figure 1.6 also highlights a further gender difference, one that will be discussed in greater detail in Chapter 5. Note that, while similar percentages of girls and boys attended school in 1995 (a little less than half of those aged twelve to nineteen), only 15 percent of girls were reported to attend school *exclusively*, as opposed to 25 percent of boys. Boys were more likely than girls to be economically active after school. But girls were far more likely yet to perform domestic work. Closer investigation of Mexico's employment survey, focusing on children ages twelve to fourteen, reveals that 60 percent of economically active boys work in agriculture, as well as 33 percent of girls who are economically active (INEGI 1998b).

To interpret the overarching trends within each country, and their inter-national divergences, we now turn to a discussion of child labor in each nation.

2

The Nature and Politics of Child Labor

As we have seen in the previous chapter, global and regional economic trends have proved insufficient to eliminate child labor or universalize education to the official obligatory levels in Latin America generally or in Chile, Peru, and Mexico in particular. What should be done depends, of course, on one's perspective on the nature of the problem. In the three nations of this study—just as throughout the world—a variety of perspectives are taken by researchers and policymakers who debate child labor, educational opportunity, and the actions to be taken. These "perspectives" are not abstract viewpoints suspended in air. At one level, interpretive differences inhere in their institutional foundations, where they help to legitimize the legal and organizational arrangements concerned with the general public welfare. In the next sections, I will compare the Chilean, Peruvian, and Mexican institutions that directly regulate children's activities, and I will discuss recent welfare policy actions that may indirectly play a role in determining what children do in each nation. But first, in this section, I consider the ideological debates over children in each country because, at another level, choices about children's rights and welfare are moral choices rather than merely the reflection or legitimations of state capacities and interests.

WORKING CHILDREN: AGENTS, VICTIMS, OR SYMPTOMS?

Different perspectives on child labor reflect divergent conceptualizations of the child-family-state relationship, as well as differences between welfare consequentialist versus a rights-based criteria for evaluating policies. We have touched upon these in the introductory chapter. In Latin America, differences in outlook on child labor also reflect growing national and class-based differences in the character of the work that is actually being done by children and adolescents. Even within contemporary Mexico, Peru, and Chile, the qualitative experience of working differs markedly between the populations of destitute urban children, rural farm children, and children of the middle-class, whose earned incomes go toward their own consumption demands. Latin American child labor appears in a broad panorama, one in which advocates for children have different objects in view as they characterize child labor.

Three vantage points on this broad panorama have particularly attracted researchers and policy advocates; these vantage points also are implicit in the institutional responses to child labor. For simplicity, we label these points as those offering a view of working children as *agents* of their own development and of social change; as *victims* of exploitation by adults and the world market; and as *symptoms* of family poverty and the uneven development of the world economy. We should recognize that most commentators and reformers are capable of simultaneously viewing all three perspectives on child labor, but these labels are useful for highlighting some essential differences in contemporary Latin American social policy discourse.

Children and Adolescents as Agents

From one perspective, labor is seen as an integral part of the human condition. Working children express their humanity, creativity, and ingenuity as they struggle not only to survive but to surmount life's obstacles. Like their parents, children confront the universal problem of scarcity. Their resolution of this problem, at best, develops children's dignity and furthers their capacity for personal and social action. Child labor reflects the agency of young people, from this vantage point, because work is not in and of itself degrading or detrimental to human development. Rather, it is the *condition of work* and the paucity of alternatives open for working children that may damage children who work, for example by closing off their options for schooling, harming their health, and stigmatizing them as pathetic untouchables. One of the clearest and most effective proponents of this view is the Peruvian-based MANTHOC (Movimiento de adolescentes y niños trabajadores hijos de obreros cristianos, or "Movement of adolescents and children workers of Christian laborers"). This movement of working children and adolescents takes the following position:

> We see children's work as a phenomenon worthy of more than general and superficial ethical censure or the sporadic, charitable gestures of some kind soul. For us, working children form a social group, and precisely because they work and have the status of workers, they can transform themselves into a collective subject, a movement and an organization which represents a new part of popular movement.... Without disregarding the condemnation of the violent, unjust and inhuman aspects of children's work, we set our hopes on the recognition and appreciation of working children's capacity for organizing themselves, putting forward proposals and taking up antagonistic positions. We set our hopes on their social protagonism, on the fact that working children could represent not only a pathological episode of Third World folklore, but an aware and active dynamic of the movement for liberation and social change (Schibotto and Cussiánovich 1994, p. 92).

From this perspective, children, though they can be exploited, also can be change agents. Attempts to measure social progress by "protecting" them, by the removal of children from the workforce, are misguided; what human or social progress can be achieved by ensnaring children ever more tightly in the nets of liberal welfare institutions? Protecting children from immediate exploitation is possible, perhaps even necessary, but it risks greater and even more insidious exploitation. Alejandro Cussiánovich, founder of MANTHOC, (1995, p. 19) argues that "The ideology of 'protection' has served throughout the history of childhood to cover and legitimate the separation of children from their social reality, and their internment in institutions under the pretext of offering them protection." The Colombian advocate and historian Cecelia Muñoz (1996, p. 104) similarly argues the case for children's agency:

> If we recognize that it is through work, thought and language that mankind has transformed the environment, for better or for worse, we have to conclude that work is an important component of the human identity. Why then should we prohibit children from working? . . . Perhaps it is time that we make an effort to change our negative perception of children's work, translating its unrecognized value, like that of women's work within the home, into positive values associated with cooperation as well as into monetary value.

Supporting the contention by Muñoz, studies even of the children assumed to be the most desperate—"street children"—reveal that the majority live in nuclear families and are not abandoned. For example, in 1992 and 1995, UNICEF (1996) undertook a head count of children found to be spending their days on the streets of Mexico City. UNICEF distinguished between children it termed to be "in" the street and "of" the street. The 13,400 total children found working or living on the streets represented a 20 percent increase over the number UNICEF found in 1992 at the same observation points of the city. However, 66 percent of these children lived with both parents, and 40 percent stated that they attended school. Of the total, there were only 1,850 children who actually lived in the streets of Mexico City, surviving by begging (25 percent), cleaning windshields (20 percent), and selling goods (10 percent), among other activities.

An incisive case study of working children on the outskirts of Mexico City by Rosaura Galeana (1997) reached the conclusion that child labor was not, in and of itself, detrimental for children. From her interviews, she found that most of her informants were in control of their labor decisions, except in cases where they had been systematically marginalized by the school. In essence, the difficulty for these workers was that "The educational institution ... takes little importance or denies the reality of children and adolescent workers, worrying more about their existence as 'students' than as social agents with a history" (p. 111). Galeana found instances where working children tried to attend school but were informed by teachers that they must choose between working and schooling (an institutional response that is especially likely in the case of Mexico, where schools receive no financial incentive to enroll additional students). This response is denigrating to children, she argues, because "the experience with work represents an important means through which children are socializing themselves and preparing themselves for life" (p. 123). Galeana concludes that part of the child's existence is:

> negated when their history outside of school is sanctioned or ignored by those who view as disqualifying all that is not related to the school uniform and to uniformity. It is not so much a question of whether working knowledge is better or worse than school knowledge. Rather, it is a question of institutional legitimacy and the implicitly ethnocentric attitude that is imposed on other forms of reasoning, behavior, and living that are beyond the parameters of the educational institution (p. 125).

In Mexico, an opposition of the roles of "student" and "worker" has deep historical roots. For example, in 1875 Mexico's minister of justice and public instruction, José Díaz Covarrubias, wrote that "obligatory education is not made more difficult by the question of child labor and pauperism; the problem consists only in supervising vagabonds and correcting the vices of the ignorant classes" (cited by Latapi 1993). In the late nineteenth century, as in the community studied by Galeana, the natural clientele for schools was not considered to be children who worked.

Qualitative investigations of working children in Latin America often confirm a level of maturity and calculation that surprises middle class reformers or child advocates from the North. And yet, there are signs that working children, from very young ages, know precisely what they are up against. Galeana's conclusion from Mexico appears consistent with the results of direct study of the desires of working children in Peru and in Chile. In Peru, Alcarcón and Vega studied a purposeful sample of 500 street children working in Lima during the early 1990s. They found that the majority of the sampled children lived and worked with both parents and that over 90 percent had attended school recently. This is consistent with what we know from Peruvian survey data, introduced in Chapter 1, about the large proportions of children who work while attending school. Most of the children studied by Alarcón and Vega had been held back at least one year in their studies. When these workers were asked what type of support they would most like to receive from Peru, their answers were striking: Half of the respondents demanded help with their educations. Of much lower priority for these children, it would appear, were help with the conditions of their work (9 percent); their health (8.6 percent), or nutrition (7.2 percent). For these children, work was not in itself something so onerous that schooling was impossible, nor was their exploitation from this work such that children referred to it when they were solicited for a list of demands (Alarcón and Vega 1995). These results were also consistent with the agency expressed by children in an earlier study by Alarcón (1991). Only 16 percent of working children in Lima who were interviewed in 1990 believed that their employment interfered with their schooling.

Based on the results from Chile's 1996 CASEN, in 1998 the International Program for the Elimination of Child Labor (IPEC), part of the International Labour Organization, sponsored a revisitation of 800 Chilean households, selecting homes where there were working children and adolescents in the 1996 survey. The goals of this revisitation were to characterize the employment and school situations of working children through more intensive, in-depth interviews; to describe their home environments; and to discover the underlying perceptions, values, and expectations associated with child labor as they differed between parents and the children themselves.

The revisitation led to some unexpected results. In the words of the authors (MORI 1998), "an important part of the labor behavior of the population studied can not be explained simply by the theories and paradigms which have previously been used to explain child labor." First, the study confirmed that most working children attend school. Second, poverty explained little of the motivations of children. Only 9 percent of the children and 28 percent of the parents stated that the children worked out of necessity; less than one third said they worked to support the family (this contrasts with two-thirds of the working "street children" in Mexico, in the UNICEF study cited previously). Finally, and most provocatively, the study found that children were not subject to their parents' decisions; they were agents. Only 11 percent of working children reported that their families had asked them to work, and nearly three quarters of the parents stated that, if it were up to them, their children would only study and would not work. Parents of working children expressed great concern about their children's school experiences, as could be seen from the fact that 92 percent asked to see their school grades and 79 percent knew their children's friends from school.

Working children—students and non-students alike—were highly instrumental and strategic in their behavior. They stated in the majority of cases that earning money was their primary motive. Nor did Chilean working students feel pushed out of school, as did the Mexican informants of Galeana (perhaps because Chilean schools receive funding depending on the number of students they enroll). In fact, most working children who were in school had a very high evaluation of their school experiences. On a seven-point Likert scale, 95 percent of employed students rated their teachers and school experience on the favorable side of the scale. Students were asked which they enjoyed more: work or school. By nearly five to one they favored school over work. And yet all of these children had decided that they wished to work. The authors conclude that there is an emerging "culture" of work that penetrates children's lives from outside of their individual family economy. The rising consumptionist mentality creates a desire for acquisition on the part of children, leading them to the labor force even when their school experiences and perceptions are positive.

Since 1988, a Latin American mobilization of working children has developed, with a first congress held in Lima and, eventually, with participation by children's movements from other nations. Children leading these organizations—with the assistance of MANTHOC organizers—left little doubt about their capability to advocate for themselves when necessary. Subsequently, a world conference on child labor was hosted by the Netherlands in 1997, and children representing the Peruvian working children's movement attended. The Dutch minister for development cooperation welcomed Peru's delegates by declaring: "We should not discuss child labor without involving the children themselves in the decision-making processes. An adult sitting behind a desk cannot for a moment imagine what it is like to be an undernourished, overworked child, stretched beyond the limits of its physical strength. We need inside information and this can only be gained by involving the children themselves. Children are, moreover, perfectly capable of assessing their own situation and coming up with solutions." But labor organizations were not entirely convinced that NGOs representing working children ought to be represented in discussions and they urged that such groups not be included in the next venue for the discussion of a new convention, scheduled to take place in Oslo later that same year. Peruvian organizations of working children responded by convening their own congress in Lima, this time *without* support from the ILO or UNICEF.

The final declaration of the 1997 Dutch meeting included the demand that the United Nations insert a new clause in the Convention on the Rights of the Child, one which would provide for: "(a) Recognition of the right to work as a human right based on the dignity of the child. (b) Recognition of children's civil capacity which overcomes the traditional civil incapacity. (c) Recognition of their organizations, giving them the necessary legal function according to the right to association stated in the Convention on the Rights of the Child. (d) Enlarge the functions of the Committee on the Convention on the Rights of the Child to incorporate reports from the working children and adolescents' organizations on violations of the rights of the children and make the national legal bodies implement the resolutions adopted." Partly in response to the challenge represented by this position, UNICEF organized a seminar in Bogatá as a forum for debate over the strategy and assumptions of the child rights movement. The international advocacy for working children that has been most visible in Latin America has been Rädda Barnen (Swedish Save the Children), and this organization presented its alternative to the views of the ILO and UNICEF. Jaime Jesús Pérez, the Peruvian representative of Rädda Barnen, offered one of the most succinct critiques of the dominant position (UNICEF 1998, p. 45). Campaigns to remove children from work see a child only as a "future citizen, assumed socially to be without a present . . . the paternalism and verticalism of adults castrates the potential of the child, and fails to recognize the responsibility of the society as a whole in the defense and promotion of their rights."

Child Labor as a Social Disease

A competing perspective to that of childhood agency, and one that clearly distresses those who view children as protagonists, concludes that much of the work being done by young people is exploitative. Child labor is not a free exchange of labor for money or necessities, under this view, but reflects an unequal and asymmetric power relationship with adults and with the adult economy. Such work is degrading because it lowers rather than elevates the potential capacities of working children. As such, child labor not only reflects poverty but violates human values. It is even, at one extreme, pathological. Like those who view children as protagonists, a perspective on children as *victims* counts on support from empirical work.

Gabriela Scherer (1995) and her colleagues undertook intensive participant observation and intervention over a year with street children who lived in the area surrounding the Observatorio subway station in Mexico City. Under the most extreme and precarious material conditions and emotional deprivation, these children survived for and through robbery, drug traffic, and prostitution, but also through non-sex work that was de-skilled and exploitative in character. None of the children studied had achieved a fixed salary or regular hours through their work, nor was any type of negotiation observed with their patrons, either sexual or not. No collateral health benefits or medical assistance derived from their work, which apart from prostitution and drugs also included making trips as porters in the wholesale market, washing dishes, and carrying boxes of drinks or barrels of garbage. Of the thirty-eight children ages thirteen to seventeen who were followed closely in this study, only two had been able to complete primary school. Of the entire group of fifty-five studied (ages ten to twenty), only thirty-four could read and write.

A similar perspective on street children in Lima is offered by Ordóñez and Mejía (1995). In a purposeful sample of one hundred working children, merely eight of those studied had *not* had some type of morbidity associated with working, such as skin problems, pulmonary problems, malnutrition, or gastro-intestinal problems. And yet these were children who tended to live with parents and to go to school, just as in Alarcón's earlier study. Of those who did not attend school, few attributed their absence to their jobs (also similar to Alarcón's study). It appears that the mere fact these working children had active parents and attended school did not protect them from the health problems noted by the researchers. And the health problems found in this comparatively privileged group are consistent with my own observations of working children in the central market of Lima during field visits in 1995. Market children had been unable to attend school but were, instead, being served individually by the "Street Teachers" program of the National Child Welfare Institute with support from UNICEF. Among these street children, not formally enrolled in regular schools, exhaustion and lack of hygiene were evident, along with the wheezing and coughing so common in Lima's humid winters.

Equally clear dangers for children are present outside of Latin American cities. Since the mid–1980s, Peru has become Latin America's largest producer of gold, and the eighth largest producer in the world. According to the U.S. Department of Labor, the United States imported $16 million nonmonetary gold and gold scrap from Peru in 1994 and gold necklaces valued over $30 million (U.S. Department of Labor 1997). The participation of Peru in this international market was accomplished primarily through large, modern extraction industries with international capital. However, the growth was also accompanied by a notable increase in unregulated "artisan" production. The implications for children were stark. In the mountains of southern Peru, since the mid–1980s, the population of Santa Filomena grew from nothing to 1,500. Without electricity, sewage, or any place for garbage, the inhabitants lived without access to the most basic health services. Children from the ages of eight entered open pits into the rock, where they assisted those over twelve years old hammering holes into the rock face for the placement of dynamite charges. After detonation, young children carried heavy loads of ore out of the mine to be processed by hand into artesianal gold. Dangerous quantities of mercury are produced through this process, and the majority of children aged one to twelve tested for high concentrations of mercury in the urine. Only eighty of the children from ages six to seventeen attended any school at all, and all who did so attended sporadically, without leaving behind the exhausting work of the mine (Cooperacción 1999).

Labor reformers and child advocates in Latin America have also viewed agricultural labor as exploitative of children. In a survey of seasonal child workers in the Mexican state of Sinaloa, Guerra (1994) reported these hazards. In 1993, the children received an average of N$115 / week (approximately US$ 19). Most children (75 percent) worked more than nine hours each day, seven days a week. Only 60 percent attended any school at all, or could read and write; 40 percent were illiterate. The families of these children lived in plywood shacks without plumbing, electricity, potable water or sewage systems and were constantly exposed to herbicides and fertilizers as their shacks had no floors but were set upon the fields.

Another observation of working children as victims documents their employment in the artesianal production of bricks. In arid regions of Latin America, such as the Peruvian coast, the construction of shanty towns for migrants from the highlands has been made possible due to a supply of bricks produced using child labor. For example, the International Labour Organization has studied the conditions of children working in Huachipa, where children must meet quotas set for entire families. Of the 3,000 inhabitants and participants in the artisianal production of bricks, 700 are children, according to the ILO. From the age of six, these children are involved in filling brick molds with heavy clay, then passing through the drying rows of bricks and turning each repeatedly until the bricks dry in the equatorial sun. Infectious diseases are common from the close contact with the mud. Clean drinking water is scarce. No creativity or self-fulfillment is possible from the routine, repetitive motion in turning the tens of thousands of heavy bricks.

The essential injustice characterizing most child labor in Latin America, from this position, is that it prevents the full development of children's potentialities. Children become the means to an end determined by adults, with few chances to actualize themselves or control the conditions of their growth. Reviewing the conditions of Peruvian working children during the 1980s, Boyden (1991, p. 40) argues that exploitation by adults is one of the gravest risks because so few children are actually self-employed. Rather, most deliver their earnings to adults and take their orders from them; the interests of these adults may not necessarily coincide with the best interests of the children who undertake the hazards of working. In a more recent investigation, Ordóñez and Mejía (1995, p. 59) wrote, "Child labor on the streets is a form of under-employment in the present and probably a means of 'preparation' for under-employment in the future." Investigators of child labor in Colombia corroborate this view. Salazar (1990, pp. 18–20) found that Colombian "children work in conditions of subordination and exploitation, similar to those which characterize the work of women in the Third World: their remuneration is inferior, even in those cases where their tasks and hours of work are equal to that of adults." Muñoz and Palacios (1980, p. 210) see child labor as part of reproduction of capitalist exploitation; it "represents the science of exploitation, of family mistreatment, of the value of work, of the possibility to exchange work with money. Initially the child offers work without receiving any remuneration; later, the child sells it."

Some of the most eloquent testimony of exploitation and the pathological character of child labor came from a march of working children all over globe, sponsored by the International Programme on the Elimination of Child Labour (IPEC). This "Global March Against Child Labor" led children from all continents to converge on several cities, among them Santiago. The record of their demonstration is replete with testimonies of the pain caused by early work for family or others. Their joint declaration states:

> We, the boys and girls meeting in Santiago, representing Argentina, Uruguay, Colombia, Peru, Bolivia, Ecuador, Brazil and Chile, declare that: the governments of our nations must listen to us, the children; they must understand our reality; child labor exists, and it damages us physically and psychologically. Child labor takes no account of the value and dignity of children. All children like to read, play outside, share, listen to music, go to school, help in the home, play and take care of their younger brothers and sisters. But there are things that disgust us and hurt us, such as exploitation through hard labor; the lack of physical space to develop. Often our parents won't listen to us, and it is so hard to reach our dreams. We form part of a system that puts us down. We want child labor to disappear from the face of the earth, and for there to be new laws that respect our rights, that say fifteen years old is the minimum to work. Yes to the right to education! No to exploitation!

Phenomenon or Epiphenomon? Child Labor as a Symptom

By far the most widely shared perspective on child labor among social science researchers and development agencies also offers the widest panorama: Child labor is but one small element in the condition of poverty and the traditional responses to it by families who are excluded from opportunities to participate in modernity. At a macro-level, child labor is symptomatic of uneven development. A position paper from the World Bank, for example, argues that "poverty is the major cause of harmful child labor in developing countries. In poor households children may contribute a significant proportion of household income, which means that because such households spend the bulk of their income on food, income from child labor may be critical to survival" (Fallon and Tzannatos 1998, p. 10). Because poverty is reduced unevenly, there is increasing inequality. Relative scarcity becomes more pronounced and new needs are created with the encroachment of the world economy.

Microeconomic approaches similarly view the alternatives to families as manifestations of perceived budget constraints and the relative prices of labor for children and adults (for a comprehensive review see Basu 1999). The "problem" of child labor emerges as a paradox out of the contradictory effects of this encroachment: On the one hand, there is a moral consensus that childhood should be economically priceless; on the other, there is an individuated relationship of children with the market and the uncontested value of commerce. Nieuwenhuys, in a comprehensive review of anthropological contributions (1996, p. 238) states, "The moral condemnation of child labor assumes that children's place in modern society must perforce be one of dependency and passivity. This denial of their capacity to legitimately act upon their environment by undertaking valuable work makes children altogether dependent upon entitlements guaranteed by the state. Yet we must question the state's role—as the evidence on growing child poverty caused by cuts in social spending has illuminated—in carrying out its mission."

In a classic study of working class Mexican neighborhoods during the 1960s, Lomnitz (1977) argued that poor children were part of a reciprocal exchange system among extended family members. Thus, the application to marginalized communities of the concept of a labor "market" for children was misleading because the supply of child labor was governed not by market forces, but by the norms of reciprocity, of the pooling of resources so as to reduce the uncertainty and insure the survival of the extended family. Gonzalez de la Rocha (1994) found that the labor resources of children constituted a prime means for the poor to survive the economic crisis of the early 1980s in Guadalajara, but certainly not the only means. The allocation of free time and responsibilities among sons, daughters, mothers, and (when present) fathers, was a collective, integrated response to scarcity. In this sense, children should be considered neither as individual victims nor as individual agents. In the populations of six poor neighborhoods on the outskirts of Mexico City, Oswald (1991) similarly found that increasing the work of children constituted one of the responses by parents over the 1987–1988 period, but that this was not nearly so common as was a reduction in consumption. Bar Din (1998) studied the nutritional, cognitive, and emotional development of children in an extremely impoverished rural area of this state, one similar to those depicted by Oscar Lewis and Juan Rulfo. She found that the nuclear families are in themselves "dysfunctional" (p. 60) but that the community and its social network are the only way to ensure the minimal development for children. In this context, meaningful work, by integrating children into a wider circle of the community, may be the only way to prevent alienation or perpetuating the culture of poverty. In the neighborhood she studied, the efforts of the community were focused on the school through supporting its teachers and building a house where children could eat.

Mexico's National Council on Population (CONAPO) has warned of the detrimental consequences of poverty and inequality for children in the most marginalized areas of Mexico and has created a classification system to identify the areas of the country most at risk of being left behind in the country's unequal development. The research director of CONAPO, Rosa María Rubalcava, wrote that "it is necessary to deepen the study of the mechanisms which promote the transmission of poverty between generations. The decisions put into practice by the population in order to compensate for the lack of income are often irreversible, affecting especially the weakest. When a daughter or son leaves school it is extremely difficult to reenter the path of education" (CONAPO 1999, p. 160).

The view of working children as the "epiphenomenon" of a more fundamental relationship between families and the larger economy continues, in new language, the historical materialist traditions of Marx and Engels, and also the neoclassical economic explanation for human behavior of Gary Becker. The contribution to the demographic study of children's activity in Latin America offered in this book can similarly be situated within this broad perspective. At the same time, we must recognize that the language of "social scientese" has become a lingua franca in many countries. In conversations with legislators, poor parents, working children, and government officials, many informants made reference to poverty as the lamentable cause of the need for children to work. "Structural adjustment" (el ajuste) and "neoliberalism" are terms familiar to every high school student. An economic view of human behavior is further legitimated in the ILO's 1999 Convention No. 182. Its preamble includes the conviction that "child labour is to a great extent caused by poverty and that the long-term solution lies in sustained economic growth leading to social progress, in particular poverty alleviation and universal education." Numerous policy evaluations of working children include this view as well. For example, a World Bank summary by Fallon and Tzannatos (1998, p. 3), sees the structure of production—especially the proportion of workforce in agriculture, as determinant of rates of child labor. A study sponsored by OXFAM and UNICEF in 1985 concluded that "the contribution made by minors to the domestic economy is crucial, and therefore any notion of abolishing child work without first improving family income and general security of employment for adults is entirely inappropriate" (Boyden 1991, p. 42). As mentioned in the first chapter, poverty grew substantially for many Mexican and Peruvian families during the mid–1980s. From a macro-level perspective on national development and economic growth, child labor and school-leaving might simply be manifestations of a larger problem.

Discussion: A Critical View of Child Labor Perspectives

At this juncture, the purpose is not to reconcile or "balance" the preceding perspectives–as though they had weights one might compare. Rather, here the goal is to highlight details of the panorama that are visible, and invisible, from each vantage point. A perspective on child labor as symptomatic of the family economy under conditions of poverty offers little hope for change without an end to scarcity. It also ignores the fact that, as emphasized by Alarcón (Salazar and Alarcón 1996, p. 125) children in the poorest families are *not* those most likely to work. "Although poverty is an inevitable factor for the existence of child work, it is insufficient to explain the entire phenomenon" (p. 125). And, as we will show in Chapter 4, child labor rates in Peru held steady in the face of one of the steepest declines in real income over the 1985–97 period, much worse than the effects of recession in Mexico. As Alarcón writes (p. 151), "Poverty is no excuse for families to exploit or abuse their children. Being poor does not mean adults are entitled to exploit or abuse their children. Being poor does not mean adults are entitled to mortgage their children's future. Parents have the first responsibility in safeguarding their children's present and future lives." From a macro-level perspective, too, poverty seems at best only a partial explanation for the persistence of child labor. The same World Bank study cited above, finding steep declines in child labor rates as nations achieve per capita incomes of US$1000, also notes that *further* declines are arrested after this point. That is, beyond the threshold rate of lower middle income countries, there appears to be little relationship between national wealth and the incidence of child labor. At least past this point, we can conclude, children's activities are not simply reflections of national poverty.

Survival strategies of the family; historical materialism; neoclassical family economics: these approaches provide important analytic tools for the discussion of international tendencies in child labor and children's schooling. Yet they also carry a danger when applied in too facile a manner to policy, for they may easily become justifications for inaction, as they have in Peru (Alarcón, personal interview). It is not difficult to adopt unenforceable legislation; to affirm the dignity of work; even to extend compulsory education. It is a far more costly proposition to launch a campaign committed to the elimination of child labor. Myron Weiner (1991), interviewing education and labor officials from India during the 1980s, found high comfort levels with social science explanations for the most discomforting and hazardous work by Indian children.

We should seek a balanced view of the economic contextual, legal, and school-level influences on child labor. We might, for example, support the consensus document of the Grupo de Iniciativa National, an *ad hoc* consortium of fifteen Peruvian non-governmental organizations, because their perspective recognizes there are still unanswered questions, parts of the terrain that need further to be explored: Should children work, even when this is not for their survival? Do children have a right to work when this is the means to their survival? Is work formative? The Peruvian consortium emphasized its "belief in the multicausality of the factors that interact in the problem [of child labor]. From our point of view, there is a relation between economic policies and models that generate basic needs among much of the population; poverty, which must not be idealized; the rising of violence that generates, with the deteriorating levels of life, family disintegration and an unfulfilling educational system that is inadequate for the social reality" (GIN 1996, p. 107). For those who seek incremental progress through social policy, a danger with the sense of child labor as epiphenomenal is that it can engender a sense of fatalism and despair over the possibility of change. Helplessness may pervade the outlook on the school, as in the case studies of Chilean working students during the 1980s by Gajardo and de Andraca (1988, p. 283), who write: "It is evident that, within its present structure and organization, the school does nothing but contribute to strengthen social and economic inequalities.... Against the exigencies of work, it can do little in terms of retaining children in school ... and it can do little to insure the acquisition of knowledge among children who remain in school."

To view children as the passive instruments of adults, and as victims of unequal power who must rely on society to defend their best interests, seems at first sight justified where children are being aggrievedly exploited and put in harm's way. But, aside from the work hazards publicized by the ILO in Peru and elsewhere, for example, in handling liquid mercury in the Santa Filomena gold mine, what about the far more common agriculture, fishing, or pastoral activities? Do Mexican or Peruvian children who herd sheep prefer in every instance to sit (or stand, when chairs are unavailable) in a rural school? If these children are to be considered "victims," then it is likely that education ministries are partly culpable. In the next chapter, I review the quality of the schools that have been supplied to children in Mexico, Peru, and Chile. It is unnecessary to go so far as to claim, with UNICEF's Peruvian representative Ann-Lis Svensson, that "deficiencies in the school system are the principal cause of child labor." However, suffice it to say that few children in North America or Europe would willingly forgo work for schooling in the overcrowded, understaffed, and demoralizing conditions experienced by most public school students in Latin America. Furthermore, we must acknowledge that, at least in some cases where the state has been unable to protect working children, there are eloquent testimonies of the ability of children to fight back. One seventeen-year-old Peruvian delegate to the 1997 Amsterdam conference on child labor represented 120 working children from a Peruvian mining region. According to this young worker,

> There they exploit all children, youngsters and adults, old people, everybody: without any mercy. There is no protection, the food is bad, they only give us "churito" or rice, meat only once a week, no milk and we have to work all day "changando", breaking

stones to look for minerals. If you are lucky you find gold and you earn money. If not, they simply do not pay you. In this place there is no safety, no protection at all, you could be buried when there are collapses. They do not pay you in money but in material, sometimes with the mineral you find. . . . I believe that the only way to get protection is by organizing ourselves as working children and youth and make people respect our rights as children and adolescents. By organizing ourselves we get stronger and we develop ourselves, just like other people.

Where child welfare has been, in practice even if not by law, abandoned to non-governmental organizations, with what authority can the state claim a monopoly over actions to protect children?

A view of children as agents of change, rather than as subjects of domestic or international exploitation, provides valuable insight to their testimonies and to the evidence gathered by qualitative researchers in several countries. However, one limitation with the aforementioned studies is that their authors typically have focused only on the populations of working children and cannot be sure how the evaluations in their testimonies differed from those of non-working children. The distinction is crucial because social psychologists have long emphasized that subjective evaluations of personal circumstances may be conditioned, even distorted, by the subject's perceptions of their alternatives (Festinger 1962). A common term for this condition—"sour grapes"—refers to the subject's re-evaluation of their desires in light of their possibilities (Elster 1983). Is it possible that working children who are interviewed in Chile, Peru, and Mexico feel that work is their own choice because of the pain involved in the opposite response, that is, admitting that they were forced to work rather than to attend school exclusively? This possibility is not so far-fetched, and it has been discovered in at least one previous study of educational choice (Gambetta 1987).

A limitation in the view of children as agents is that it ignores developmental stages of growth. While it certainly is the case that adults and children make their worlds, their powers to do so increase over the early years of their lives. Even those who would de-emphasize the passivity of working children and adolescents and advocate for the rights of children to participate in decisions over their labor and education, also see the necessity of a "dynamic self-determinist" view of agency (Eekelaar 1994), one in which children's self-interests are changing with their personal development and growth. Protecting children's best interests does not mean according them the legal autonomy of adults, and this protection is compatible with a view of children as having rights. It is clear that very young people have few alternative paths to resolve the problem of scarcity, as compared with older persons. Before some age, it makes little sense to speak of children as the protagonists or "agents" of their futures, let alone the future of society. Peruvian law attempts to address the developmental dimension by codifying a distinction between "children" (ages eleven or younger) and "adolescents" (age twelve through seventeen). One may quibble with the age brackets used in Peru's *Código*, but the point here is to highlight that even under this law—strongly supported by MANTHOC—there is a recognition that young children depend on adults for their protection and that below some age they can hardly function as protagonists. Could the ages at which children learn to act as agents on their own behalf depend on the general expectations of them in their societies? If agency and responsibility are socially rather than biologically determined, then is it appropriate for adults to raise expectations that twelve-year-olds can or should act as instrumental, calculating adults? When is it appropriate to delay the development of protagonism; when is it better to promote it?

One final observation about the perspective of children as protagonists rather than as instruments of adults is that this view has been presented by adults as part of a broader purpose. Such a strategy has been denied by Cussiánovich, founder of MANTHOC (1995, p. 21): "*protagonismo* is not the invention of those who work with child laborers: it is of the children themselves, an historic protagonism although not registered in written history or registered in the weak memory of those who every epoch and place try to reject the public character of childhood as a social phenomenon, and its potential for change." But the history of the movement tells a different story. The movement originated in the repression of trade unionism under Peru's military in the mid-1970s, and when the first signs of the neoliberal economic orientation were emerging. In the words of MANTHOC's leaders:

> At that time it was already possible to glimpse a not too-far-off future with no job security, widespread use of short-term contracts and hence a weakened union organization. Not only would there be few young workers in the factories, but these would have little opportunity of belonging to a union. New generations of workers and leaders had to be produced, and their education as workers could not wait until they had grown up. The practical conclusion, the feeling at this juncture, was to put our efforts into supporting working children and adolescents (Schibotto & Cussiánovich 1994, p. 15).

A labor movement that puts children on the front lines in the struggle against international capital may or may not be in a strategic position to highlight the deficiencies of the new global order, wherein the outsourcing of production provides so few opportunities for secure employment by adults. But the point here is that, from this perspective just as from others, children are also being viewed as the instruments of a grander scheme, in this case a struggle against the more general exploitation of workers. Hart, Himes, and Lansdown (UNICEF 1998, p. 46) cogently argue that in an authoritarian political context it makes indisputable sense for non-governmental organizations to lead campaigns for the right of children to defend themselves against exploitation. But with the consolidation of democratic institutions in Latin America, it is to be hoped that it also will be possible to collaborate with governments and to accept the legitimacy of international law, which (contrary to the claims expressed by working children's movements) do not give children the "right" to forgo education so they may work in peace.

THE INTERNATIONAL LEGAL AND
INSTITUTIONAL FRAMEWORK

Divergent perspectives on children's work are not mere abstractions. They surface weekly in the international debate among national governments, political parties, trade blocs, NGOs, church groups, and labor unions. In Chapter 6 we will further consider the dynamics of this debate and will interpret its ultimate effects on child welfare in Chile, Peru, and Mexico. But, before drawing conclusions about the debate's effect on children, we must first understand the legal institutions that have resulted from that debate and so condition family choice. As we have seen, the frameworks that guide changes in labor and education policies for children reflect contributions from both a consequentialist, welfare economic perspective, on the one hand, and from a human rights orientation, on the other hand. The debate to define international norms of activity for children is unresolved today, in part because the participants in the debate use different criteria for evaluating policies. International agencies and national advocates invoke competing perspectives. Consequentialists and rights advocates speak from distinct rhetorical traditions. They often speak past each other, rather than to each other, as separate arguments are used to set the terms of the debate. Another component of the institutional framework for child education and labor policies is, obviously, the perspective of the actors on the benefits and dangers to children of their alternative activities. As previously mentioned, there is sound empirical support for a view of working children as agents, victims, or symptoms of a larger problem. And these three perspectives are reflected in the arguments by actors on both the international and national level. We should begin with the presentation of the international legal institutions and the norms embodied there, although it will be clear that the precedence of international law has not always determined the outcomes for national policies in Latin America.

In early reform attempts worldwide, the utility for the family and the consequences for children weighed equally as criteria for evaluating child labor and school absence. In 1911 in Chicago, the reformers Edith Abbott and Sophonisba Breckinridge wrote that "the ignorant and discouraged parent, weary of the desperate struggle with poverty, may be excused from wanting some help from the children he is trying to support" (p. 9). But Abbott and Breckinridge approached child labor and education using the consequentialist rather than rights-based criteria: "The necessity of work must be estimated not by the poverty in the home but in terms of its educative value [in] their later industrial life and their fitness for citizenship" (p. 30). There was a constant tension between the apparent interests of parents—who sought to maximize family well-being by pooling labor and encouraging child labor—and the emergent social service profession, which advocated for education over working as in the child's individual best interest (Stadum 1995). According to Zelizer (1994, p. 57), the subsequent transformation of children into treasures too precious for labor reflected, in part, the resolution of a moral conflict. Yet, even in the United States, the conflict between the interests of the family and of the child is unsettled. Just as in Latin America, parents continue to make trade-offs in allocating their children's time depending on family needs and do not give absolute priority to children's rights to educations (for a recent review and evidence, see Blair 1992).

From a world trade perspective, the persistence of child labor among trading partners has been seen as a type of unfair competition because it violates the "core labor standards" that have been won by labor organizations in developed nations. What standards qualify as "core" labor standards? The Organization for Economic Cooperation and Development (OECD) has developed a list of five standards, among them the elimination of child labor (the others are the prohibition of forced labor; freedom of association; the right to organize and bargain collectively; and nondiscrimination in employment). But, like human rights norms, there is no universally accepted or legitimated body charged with policing core labor standards. In 1947, the first General Agreement on Trade and Tariffs (GATT) was signed, with one of its goals being to ensure that "relations among countries in the field of trade and economic endeavor should be conducted with a view to raising standards of living and ensuring full employment." The hope at that time was that an International Trade Organization (ITO) would be created to monitor labor standards. But this never occurred. The GATT's successor, the World Trade Organization (WTO), similarly has avoided monitoring labor standards as one of its responsibilities. It was this avoidance that generated massive protest at the November 1999 WTO meeting in Seattle. The Americas already have a pilot monitoring capability, at least in principle. The 1994 North American Free Trade Agreement (NAFTA) dealt explicitly with labor standards and included a labor supplemental agreement known as the North American Agreement on Labor Cooperation (NAALC). Under the terms of the NAALC, trade sanctions can be levied against nations that permit child labor. As symbolic support for the elimination of child labor, the United States also began to threaten trade sanctions against other nations that violate the ILO Convention 182 for the elimination of the worst forms of child labor.

Children's Rights and Freedom for Development

Children's rights were first introduced under the belief that parental authority could not protect children from the predations of the new poverty and the growing market for their labor. In 1923, a coalition of children's advocate organizations was united as Save the Children International Union. Its Children's Charter was later adapted by the League of Nations in its 1924 Declaration of the Rights of the Child. The league's declaration anticipated later protections and conventions by specifying the rights of children to training to earn a living and the right to be protected against exploitation (Knutsson 1997, p. 34). These positive liberties implied increased responsibilities on the part of states, although the declaration did not directly address states but, rather, "men and women of all nations." The principles motivating the 1924 declaration did not dissipate with the demise of the League of Nations. In 1946, at the same time the new United Nations created the International Children's Fund (UNICEF), the Temporary Social

Commission of the Economic and Social Council (ECOSOC) declared that the 1924 declaration should become binding once again. In 1948, the U.N. Declaration on Human Rights by the General Assembly reflected the commitments of nations to universalize primary education by making it free and compulsory. While an official commitment to free primary schooling had already been well-established in many nations (including Chile in 1920, Peru in 1905, and Mexico in 1934), the U.N. declaration sent a message that education was not merely another welfare benefit, a service, or a shrewd public investment. Rather, education was affirmed as a social right and a positive liberty. It was therefore incumbent on governments not only to respect but also to enable children to become more fully developed through education.

In 1950, the ECOSOC initiated the process for formal adoption of a new Declaration on the Rights of the Child. This was achieved at last in 1959 (Mower 1997, p. 13). By then, the norms of protection for children were expanded: Children must "not be admitted to employment before an appropriate minimum age." The child should "in no case be permitted to engage in any occupation or employment which would prejudice his health or education or interfere with his physical, mental, or moral development" (DRC, Principle 9). As a declaration (rather than a treaty convention), this document may have had suasive powers, but it had no legal authority over U.N. members. The introduction of a treaty convention following the 1979 U.N. "Year of the Child" was proposed by Poland, under one interpretation to highlight the social rights and positive liberties enjoyed by children in nominally socialist nations (Alston 1994). The United States tacitly opposed a new convention by placing guarantees on individual freedom in the wording of the convention. But at the end of the Cold War, language acceptable to the United States and to the eastern European countries was adopted (as of the year 2001, however, the United States had signed but not formally ratified the 1989 Convention, and today the United States remained almost the only country not to have ratified it).

Under international law, ratification of the 1989 convention obligates nations—including Chile, Peru, and Mexico—to implement it. The CRC protects human rights with a special emphasis on children. It recognizes children as individuals in need of special protections and with needs that must be satisfied by their governments. In legal terms, children are recognized as autonomous subjects with the status of persons and subject to international law. Article 32 of the CRC guarantees the "right to be protected from economic exploitation and from performing any work that is likely to be hazardous or to interfere with the child's education, or to be harmful to the child's health or physical, mental, spiritual, moral, or social development." By protecting children's development, the CDC helps to define the essence of childhood as a period of progress and actualization. Autonomously developing children, if protected from interference by potentially exploitive institutions, will be able to realize the potential of their humanity. Consequently, in the aggregate, societies also will realize their fullest potentials. Furthermore, "exploitation" is defined in terms of "the relevant provisions of other international instruments." This could be interpreted as obligating even nations that have not yet ratified ILO Convention 138, or that are not members of the OECD, as having a duty to abide by its age standards, simply by virtue of having ratified the Convention on the Rights of the Child.

If events subsequent to 1989 had continued on a "natural" path, according to the UNICEF regional head, Emilio García Méndez (1999, p. 80), then the availability of the convention would have remained a "nice instrument for international law" and would have had few political repercussions or been little publicized in Latin America. Prior to 1990, legal codes had legitimized social service policies and had seldom taken a visionary or leadership role. But after the adoption of the U.N. convention, Brazil changed the outcome expected by child advocates and jurists. There, the convention formed the basis for profound constitutional reform and expanded duties to children in response to grassroots mobilizations to implement the spirit of the U.N. instrument. Brazil's 1988 constitution reflected demands by a grassroots movement by 1.4 million children and adolescents, who signed a petition in support of protections that were codified in Article 227: "It is the duty of the family, of society and of the

State to assure children and adolescents, with absolute priority, the right to life, health, nutrition, education, recreation, vocational preparation, culture, dignity, respect, liberty and family and community solidarity, over and beyond making them safe from neglect, discrimination, exploitation, cruelty and oppression." With the ratification of the U.N.'s 1989 convention, Brazil codified its policies, and the positive freedoms they bestow, through its 1990 Statute on Children and Adolescents (ECA, in Portuguese). Among other important features, the ECA prohibited employment below age fourteen, stressing the incompatibility of working and school (Boyden and Meyers 1995).

Brazil's modifications were only the start of a movement that has linked national groups with the spirit of international law. Subsequently, a 1991 Constitutional Constituent assembly put child rights into Colombia's constitution; based on these new rights, in 1991 a juvenile code was enacted that closely followed the terms of the Brazilian statute. With the prestige and momentum of the new convention and the rights perspectives embodied in the new Colombian constitution, added force was given to criticisms of the Colombian Instituto for Family Welfare, founded in 1969 and charged with "protecting" minors through improving family welfare. (Turbay and Acuña 1998).

A world movement was beginning to gather momentum. At the end of the Cold War, a world summit met in New York in September of 1990, with participation by heads of state or ministers from every nation. The summit affirmed the commitment to ratify the U.N. convention and went on to list the problems besetting the world's children that must be addressed. Among these, the summit declared that "over 100 million children are without basic schooling, and two-thirds of them are girls. The provision of basic education and literacy for all are among the most important contributions that can be made to the development of the world's children."

The world movement to free children from labor based upon human rights concerns includes not only U.N. organizations. The world's oldest regional multinational cooperative, the Organization of American States, includes the Inter-American Children's Institute (IACI), founded in 1927. Under its charter, the IACI is responsible for promoting child-oriented public policies in the Americas; articulating the relationship between the state and civil society; and publicizing the problems affecting children and young people. Within the parameters of a very modest budget, the IACI has allied itself with national-level actors and has promoted efforts by NGOs and government programs; it had about one hundred ongoing agreements in force during the 1990s. Since the 1989 Convention, IACI has been one of Latin America's most vocal proponents of a human rights perspective on child labor and education and has publicized these issues, especially in South America.

The United Nations organizations primarily concerned with children—UNICEF and UNESCO—operate high-profile programs in Latin America and in the countries of our study. Both have become major proponents in diffusing the norms behind the social and economic rights that are described in the 1989 convention. UNICEF's plan of action interprets the convention as recognizing: "the right to survival; to develop to the fullest; to protection from harmful influences, abuse and exploitation; and to participate fully in family, cultural and social life. Every right spelled out in the Convention is inherent to the human dignity and harmonious development of every child. The Convention protects children's rights by setting standards in health care, education and legal, civil and social services. These standards are benchmarks against which progress can be assessed. States that are party to the Convention are obliged to develop and undertake all actions and policies in the light of the best interests of the child."

Labor Regulation and Welfare Approaches: the ILO

Paralleling the movement that expands the *rights* of children to development, free from exploitation or interference, another world movement also bears on this investigation of adolescent activities: the movement to regulate work by children and adults because of the social *benefits* of doing so. At the conclusion of the First World War, labor representatives from nine countries forged a convention aimed at achieving lasting peace through social justice. When integrated into the peace treaties, this convention culminated in the International Labour Organization, which was composed not only of member nation-states but also of workers everywhere, represented as workers rather than as citizens of any particular country. From the outset of the ILO, the abolition of child labor was seen as a necessary step to improve the welfare of working adults, their families, and, indirectly, the welfare of children (Lauren 1998, p. 97).

Historically, the efforts of the ILO to regulate child labor continued to reflect a strong syndicate interest: where adult workers did not need to compete with underage workers, parents were better able to press wage demands on their employers and on their governments for the standards necessary to obtain a living income. Consequently, parents would become less dependent on the labor of their children. The first important multinational convention on child labor was adopted by the ILO at the time of its founding in 1919, when the age of fourteen was set as the minimum age for employment by industry. New conventions on minimum ages were adopted in subsequent years: in 1920 for sea labor, in 1921 for agricultural labor; in 1959 for fishing, in 1965 for underground work. The watershed came with ILO Convention 138, in 1973. This replaced all previous ILO conventions with a general proscription against underage work by children everywhere and in every sector.

Apart from the fact that none of the three countries in this study had ratified Convention 138 during the period covered by this investigation (Chile did so only in 1999), there is another important point which bears emphasis here and which helps to explain the lukewarm reception given to that convention (it has been ratified by few countries where child labor is prevalent). Under the convention, formal education, rather than labor, is considered the key to children's development. Article 2 of the convention stipulates that the minimum age for employment should be no less than the age at which compulsory schooling ends and, in any case, not less than fifteen (age fourteen in developing countries). But few child advocates would wish to criminalize children's violations of the principles behind Convention 138, in part because some see working children as change agents who are entitled to protection, dignity, and respect. Another reason for the failure of Convention 138 to spark a mobilization for ratification is the view of child labor as symptomatic of poverty, and a respect by lawmakers for the survivalist savvy of the families who confront austerity when governments do little for the poor. In conversations with leading researchers and lawyers in Mexico and Peru, we were continually reminded by informants of the creative possibilities for work outside of school (interviews with Smelkes, Yañez).

There have been two chief responses by the ILO to the general failure of nations to implement or ratify Convention 138. One came in 1992, when Germany helped the ILO establish the International Programme on the Elimination of Child Labour (IPEC). Originally, the narrow mission of IPEC was to convince *governments* (not families or employers) to progress toward the goals of Convention 138. In 1992, only six nations worldwide formally had entered the IPEC (one key early participant was Brazil). But, since 1992, this ILO lobbying of national governments has been accompanied—more accurately we should say it has been accomplished—by indirect alliances with local non-governmental organizations and direct demonstrations of ways to eradicate child labor. There has been a snowball effect in Latin America. Over the succeeding years, as more and more nations contributed funds to IPEC (the United States contributed $30 million in 1999), its programs expanded. During 1999, the IPEC included over 1,000 separate programs conducted in collaboration with governments and non-governmental organizations.

IPEC operates in countries where national authorities enter a formal agreement to let it do so. It then seeks to establish a national directorate for the eradication of child labor, one which IPEC helps to lead but which is autonomous and counts on broad-based support. In 1996, both Chile and Peru entered such formal agreements. As will be discussed in Chapter 6, the fates of these two national directorates took widely different paths and serve to indicate the differences between the autocratic management of Peru and the political pluralism of Chile during the 1990s (as well as the obvious difference in child labor rates:

Chile's was already very low). Suffice it to say that the IPEC has become a major force in both countries in modeling the interventions. Examples of IPEC projects in Peru include channeling donations from Spain to purchase an electric winch in the Santa Filomena gold mine and training families to manufacture and market noodles as an alternative to the mine.

In Colombia, the IPEC helped the government formulate a national action plan, and indirectly its presence energized national coalitions and led the government at last to ratify Convention 132. But IPEC did not end its work with the ratification of the convention. It helped support a grassroots mobilization in the form of the Colombian March Against Child Labor (which sent children to Chile as part of the Global March). IPEC persuaded labor unions, employer associations, and regional governments each to include the elimination of child labor in their plans. Colombia's Ministry of Labor and Social Security agreed to include new modules in its national household surveys so as to detect changes in the incidence of child work. In Chile, the IPEC has similarly spearheaded a broadbased coalition of unions, churches, employers, and educators to draft a new legal code for children. It is noteworthy that Mexico is one of only a few countries not to have signed cooperation agreements with IPEC. Its reluctance to do so will be better understood after reviewing its official responses to the ILO's second major contribution to the debate in Latin America, the introduction of Convention 182.

The second chief response by the ILO to the failure of nations to ratify Convention 138 was to introduce a new convention on the most intolerable forms of child labor. By the mid–1990s, ILO experts had become increasingly realistic about the prospect of eradicating underage labor as defined in Convention 138, an objective that was conspicuously absent both from the agenda set by the 1990 world summit for children and from the 1989 convention. In the debate leading to Convention 182, Mexico contended that the definition of what types of labor are intolerable should be left up to each nation and that universal definitions were unlikely to garner much support. The United States replied that it was not willing to make to make the consideration of intolerable labor place-specific. Rather, the standard should be comprehensive and universal. The definition of child labor should reflect the ILO's own Declaration on Fundamental Principles and Rights at Work, according to the United States, and the declaration clearly states, "Child labour is detrimental to development, since it means that the next generation of workers will be unskilled and less well educated. In today's increasingly globalized economy, this has especially negative consequences, since, as pointed out in the present report, a skilled and educated labour force is critical to economic development, increasing incomes and social progress."

During 1997, a compromise document was drafted and presented at the 1998 ILO session. This draft again was circulated for comment. Once again, Mexico argued that the preamble to the convention should indicate that member states themselves were responsible for suppressing the most intolerable forms of child labor and that this was best done by progressively enhancing the economic and social circumstances of each member state. Any reference to the elimination of child labor was to be avoided, in Mexico's view. Only "intolerable" forms of child labor had to be eradicated. Peru held that the convention should refer only to children, not adolescents. The U.S. view was that the convention should focus on types of work that are intolerable at any age. Mexico (with India) held that deciding which forms of labor should be considered hazardous must be made independently by member states, that these states should collaborate with employers and workers' organizations, with the assistance of experts of their own national legislation. By contrast with Mexico, nations such as Chile and Peru (and the United States) believed that the recommendation should take full account of international standards for this decision. Other significant changes were made in the final document as a result of these negotiations. The relationship and priority of the new convention with Convention 138 was considered. Chile emphasized that the two instruments were complementary rather than overlapping. Originally, the target of the new convention, and its title phrase, referred to "intolerable" forms of child labor. However, a more generic "worst forms" of child labor was decided upon after extensive debate.

The U.N. Committee on the Rights of the Child had a voice in the debate, which it used to highlight one of the clearest differences between Conventions 182 and 138, as well as with the 1989 U.N. convention. While the draft document refers to the "health, safety and morals" of the child (as in Article 32 of the CRC), the proposed convention failed to give much importance to education. A UNICEF background paper (1997, p.2) previously insisted that "Any work activity which interferes with a child's right to education is intolerable and must be eliminated. All best efforts must focus on preventing children from entering work that will impede or prevent their education as well as removing those who are currently working under harmful conditions and ensuring that they are provided with an enabling educational environment." The NGO subgroup drafted a document for consideration by ILO delegates which stated that, in addition to eliminating the most exploitative and intolerable forms of child labor, "Milder forms of labour as a means for child and family survival can only be tolerated if they do not deprive children of education. The formula 'work and education' would therefore be the only one acceptable as a transition to a generalized elimination of children's work. It must be recognized, however, that inadequate teaching and disrespectful treatment lead to pupil's lowered self-esteem, loss of interest and, finally drop-out, thus furthering children's early entry into the job market."

In fact, representatives of the Global March Against Child Labor, as well as ILO officials and the representatives of most developed countries, drafted a clause that added to the existing criteria of worst forms of child labor, "all work that, by its nature and by the condition in which it is performed, systematically deprives children of their access to basic education." Such wording would have brought the new convention very close to the coverage of Convention 138. But this was exactly the problem, in the view of most delegates from developing countries. Had Convention 138 been universally adopted and implemented, there would have been no need for a new convention. Therefore, the only remaining references to education are peripheral, and access to school opportunity is not part of the criteria used to define the worst forms of child labor. Developing nations agreed to include references to education in the document's preamble, which states that "the effective elimination of the worst forms of child labour requires immediate and comprehensive action, taking into account the importance of free basic education." Education was again included in Article 7, where nations ratifying the convention agree to "ensure access to free basic education, and, wherever possible and appropriate, vocational training, for all children removed from the worst forms of child labour."

A Summary and a Synthesis

At this point it is useful to summarize, and attempt to synthesize, the previously discussed theoretical justifications for regulating childhood and the associated views of working children. We must situate the stance and the movement by several important international actors in order to ground our later discussion of national legal codes and movements on their foundational concepts. Of course, the value of all dichotomies and schema is their oversimplification of reality; frameworks are meant to be broken through the discussion they provoke and the conversation they initiate, hopefully with progress and engagement of differing perspectives.

With this in mind, a highly stylized framework would situate the justifications for regulating childhood by non-family members as belonging either to the class of a) "human rights" arguments or b) "welfare consequential" arguments. The first view is most visible in the Convention on the Rights of the Child (though, as discussed in Chapter 1, the CRC is a compromise document that also includes social welfare perspectives). From this perspective, children's rights trump other considerations, in the view of its advocates, and the "best interests of the child" override other competing concerns. Alternatively, most economists, labor leaders, and social development proponents take the protection of children as a means to a greater end: economic growth, redistribution, or even the conservation of traditional values and institutions. These two general orientations toward regulating children's

The Nature and Politics of Child Labor

view of child:	Concern to regulate children's work and schooling is from perspective of:	
	Human rights	**Welfare consequences**
Potential agent of actualization and social progress	**Rädda Barnen** Because governments are unreliable as their advocates, children must mobilize for own self-interest. They have a right to work when school quality is low. Schooling can be improved, made more compatible with work in response to children's demands.	**I.D.Bank; W.Bank** Utility-maximizing household firms generate and distribute welfare to children. Governments should increase productive capacity by expanding supply of schooling and create disincentives to employers (including parents) who prevent children from attending school.
Potential victim of adult abuse and social pathology	With legitimation of authority from CRC, local N.G.O.'s can lobby for social clauses in trade bills and special judicial treatment for those under 18. Children need entitlements and ombudsmen. Removal of abused minors from exploitative parents. **UNICEF**	Exploitation reflects unequal power or information constraint on free choices. Solutions lie in empowering families through demand-side subsidies. Min. age labor laws are needed to protect families, but governments should first target "intolerable" labor. **I.L.O.**
Potential symptom of poverty and of social inequality	Renegotiations of national debt; pledges by North to channel resources to South; pledges by Latin American nations to spend min. 20% on social programs. Regional development strategies for indigenous peoples; extension of schooling to all regions.	Survival strategies of families depend on children when other resources are depleted. Solution is greater government or donor supply of minimum basic nutritional and educational needs for redistribution of opportunity. **E.F.A.; Jubilee; 20/20**

FIGURE 2.1 Conceptual Framework on Children, Rationale for Regulating Their Activities, and Situations of International Advocates

activity can be crossed with the three views about the nature of children's work that have been discussed in this chapter: children as agents, victims, or symptoms. This cross tabulation yields six coherent positions in which it is possible to situate major organizations and political actors (see Figure 2.1)

Each of the six cells in Figure 2.1 contains distinct arguments and rationales for actions protecting or empowering children through regulating their work and schooling. At the top of the figure are the orientations that make individuals (rather than governments) the main agents of their self-actualization (from the perspective of rights) or their maximization of utility (from a welfare and consequentialist perspective). Both approaches, if not directly subversive of national law or national identity, at least are not directly founded on citizenship. The ILO and Save the Children were founded with constituencies of *workers* and of *children* rather than the citizens of any particular state. To promote children's well-being, the World Bank and the Inter-American Development Bank (IDB) lend not to individuals or NGOs but to governments; however, their chief concern is not with the effect of their loans on governments, but on poor children. In Latin America, the best-known Save the Children organization is that of Sweden, Rädda Barnen (discussed previously). Its position differs from that of the ILO, the World Bank, and the Inter-American Development Bank by virtue of its priority of human rights over social welfare. Rädda Barnen supports grassroots mobilization in countries fraught with weak government and revolving personnel at the top (the typical tenure of Peru's average minister of education has been measured in months rather than years). Their efforts, and those of the NGOs it supported, have probably contributed to Peru's distinctive pattern of children's activity (seen previously in Figure 1.5), in which working children attend school and many students simultaneously work.

The ILO's position covers more than one cell in the framework offered in Figure 2.1. Originally, the ILO lobbied governments directly to monitor and restrict underage labor. Similar to the economic orientation of the World Bank and the IDB, the ILO historically has relied on families to promote their own best interests with a minimum of interference. The advent of IPEC and the adoption of Convention 182 signaled the movement of the ILO to a more critical view of child labor as an urgent concern. Focusing on the "worst forms" of exploitation highlights the pathological aspects of work by children, with an implicit assumption that the detrimental consequences from this abuse can not be eliminated without emergency government action. The movement of UNICEF from a "needs-based" to a "rights-based" orientation has been clear over the last decade, moving it closer to the position of Save the Children, and further from the positions of the

World Bank and the Inter-American Development Bank. As a coalition of U.N. member states, UNICEF by charter works with governments rather than directly with non-governmental organizations. However, the Convention on the Rights of the Child provides UNICEF with an indirect legitimacy to encourage the advocacy of NGOs, which appeal for ultimate moral authority to the CRC rather than to the legal codes of their nation. In the bottom two cells of Figure 2.1 are positions that see children's activity as symptomatic, as the side effects of inequality of political power and welfare mal-distribution. Among numerous occupants of these conceptual cells would be The Education For All movement, the Jubilee 2000 movement, which urges loan forgiveness, and the Twenty-Twenty movement, pledging greater support for social programs from both the North and the South. Since their inception, these movements have, like UNICEF, begun to incorporate the language of children's rights alongside arguments to protect children's welfare.

CHILD LABOR LAWS AND ENFORCEMENT IN CHILE, PERU, AND MEXICO

Protections for children in Latin America preceded the multinational campaigns that dominate in today's debate. As early as the 1681 Laws of the Indies, children under the age of eleven are mentioned as being prohibited from certain types of work. During the nineteenth century, Mexican minors under fourteen were prohibited from working without the permission of parents (Dávalos 1996, pp. 295–99). In 1917, two years prior to the ILO's inception, Article 123 of Mexico's constitution was devoted to labor issues, stating that "every person has a right to a dignified and socially useful work; to bring this about, the creation of employment and the social organization of work will be promoted according to the law." While few Latin American countries had ratified Convention 138 by the 1990s, all had ratified the U.N.'s 1989 Convention on the Rights of the Child. In so doing, Chile, Peru, and Mexico each obligated themselves to adapting their laws to safeguard the human rights of children. The constitutions of Chile, Peru, and Mexico provide the legal means for the implementation of treaty conventions. Article 50 of the Chilean constitution gives the president power to issue laws required to comply with treaties that have been ratified by the Chilean legislature. Article 133 of the Mexican constitution states that international treaties ratified by congress automatically constitute the supreme law of the state (thus circumventing the process of mobilizing political support for new laws).

Even apart from ratification of the CRC, the constitutions of Mexico and Peru (but not that of Chile) establish government authority over the activities of children. Federal authority over child labor was established by Article 123 of the Mexican constitution, which originally was designed to protect minors under the age of twelve years. In 1962, however, to comply with the terms of Mexico's membership in the International Labour Organization, "child" labor was regulated for persons under the age of sixteen, despite the fact that until 1993 Mexico did not obligate children to attend school beyond the primary level. Even today, this 1962 revision of the constitution continues to guide the formulation of other existing labor laws, including Articles 173—180 of Mexico's 1970 Labor Law. Today Mexican law clearly "prohibits" the use of work by persons under the age of fourteen. However, persons ages fourteen and fifteen can work for up to six hours each day. Throughout the period we study in Mexico (1984–96), the law made no attempt to criminalize child labor. In theory, fines from 3 to 115 times the prevailing minimum monthly salary could be levied against employers who profit from underage workers. In actuality, this sanction is rarely if ever applied, and Mexico has no specific agency delegated to monitor even formal sector employment to prevent abuses of the law.

The Peruvian constitution of 1993 provides a special article on child labor, Number 23. Far from prohibiting work by children, through this article the Peruvian Republic gives implicit protection to working children. The article states that "no labor relationship can limit the exercise of constitutional rights, nor lower or ignore the dignity of the worker." Of the three cases in this study, Peru is the only country to criminalize *abuse* of child labor (while not criminalizing children who work). Article 128 of Peru's Criminal Code thus states: "Those who expose any person under their authority, dependency, guardianship, or supervision to situations that could endanger [the child's] life, either by depriving him of food or basic care, either subjecting him to excessive or inadequate work, or abusing the means of correction or discipline, will be sanctioned with one to four years of imprisonment." There are no recorded cases of parents having been prosecuted under this ambitious statue for allowing their children to work.

As the dimensions of Peru's recession and the impact of the "Fuji-shock" became known, lawmakers from the left coalition (Izquierda Unida—IU), NGOs, and the archbishop of Trujillo all lobbied to create a new legal framework for children. The architect of the bill, Ana María Yañez, was an outspoken labor lawyer with views on working children close to those of MANTHOC. During a period in which Fujimori's "self-coup" had suspended the Congress, this bill gained support from the presidency and some international support from UNICEF and was in part justified as a response to Peru's 1990 ratification of the U.N. Convention on the Rights of the Child. With minimal public discussion or debate, Yañez obtained a presidential decree legalizing the Code on Children and Adolescents (el Código, D.L. 26102) in December of 1992. She recalled the inappropriateness of prior laws on working children, which prohibited employment by those under fourteen, in accordance with the ILO's guidelines. Such laws only served to push child labor underground, making it impossible to pinpoint abuses or to insure minimal protections for workers (personal interview).

Peru's Código is noteworthy both for what it does and for what it does not do. Unlike the U.N. convention on children's rights and the 1999 ILO convention on the "worst forms" of child labor (in which all those younger than eighteen were considered children), Peru's Código defines childhood and adolescence as separate age categories: children are said to be those ages eleven and younger, while adolescents are considered persons from twelve through seventeen. Different standards are applied to each group under this Peruvian law. The overarching aim is to decriminalize and destigmatize child labor, offering children who work legal protections from the state. In Article 22, "the State recognizes the right of adolescents to work" when this work does not put them at risk or disturb their regular school attendance. Age restrictions on the authorization to work for pay outside the family economy apply, but the institutions that monitor and authorize this work are not specified in Peru's Código. The responsibility to protect adolescent workers was originally placed in the hands of an inter-ministerial "Ente Rector" which would coordinate policies from the regional governments, municipalities, and the ministries of labor, of health, and of education. Subsequently, in 1997, this responsibility was transferred to the newly created Ministry of the Advancement of Women and Human Development (Promoción de la Mujer y del Dearrollo Humano-PROMUDEH). Through its nineteenth article, the 1992 Código "guarantees" special hours and accommodations by schools for the needs of adolescent workers; it places responsibility on school principals to ensure that work being done by adolescents "does not affect their attendance or academic performance" and "principals must report on the performance of students who work." Since the Código was decreed without participation from teachers or representatives of the education ministry, it is not surprising to find that this feature of the Código is largely unknown. Nonetheless, as we will see in the next chapter, educators in Peru accept its basic orientation.

There is little awareness or application of Article 23 of the Código, which requires municipalities to maintain a registry of nonremunerated family workers. Interviews in the mid–1990s found no evidence that municipalities had ever registered their adolescent workers. Article 63 further specifies that adolescent workers must possess a booklet, provided by whomever has authorized the individual to work, and that this booklet must contain the authorization for the hours to work and the hours in which the adolescent will be in school. Again, provision of booklets for young workers was never institutionalized by the government. No means were ever specified for implementing Article 63.

By contrast with Peru, but similar to Mexico, Chile's regulation of child labor is done through a variety of education and labor codes applicable to youth. Chile's first compulsory education bill, of 1920, prohibited employers from contracting with persons under the age of sixteen unless they had completed their (originally four years) compulsory schooling (Fischer 1979, p. 34). During the period of our study, the Chilean labor code proscribed work by children younger than fourteen. Furthermore, fourteen-year-olds could work only with the permissions of parents. Article 13 of Chile's labor code states that a labor inspector may not authorize the work of underage workers without placing the child's file with a juvenile judge. When authorization for work is granted, the child has all the other labor rights corresponding to adult workers for minimum salary, benefits, and union membership.

INCENTIVES AND WELFARE PROGRAMS THAT AFFECT CHILDREN'S ACTIVITY

Apart from direct legal sanctions touching children's lives by regulating their opportunities for work and compelling their school attendance, governments provide indirect incentives for families to change their behaviors. The most important alternative to child labor, of course, is the school system itself, just as problems with schooling are frequently blamed for the incidence of child labor. We can defer our consideration of school opportunities until the next chapter, but here we can examine additional welfare programs that may indirectly affect children's activity. Schiefelbein (1997) reviews some of Latin America's most commonly used incentives to induce school attendance in place of child labor: cash payments; school feeding programs; payment of direct costs; voucher systems of school finance; apprenticeship programs to give students a salary along with their schooling; incentives to school administrators. During the period of this study, the schools of all three nations maintained some type of school breakfast and lunch programs. Mexico began to experiment with using highly targeted cash payments to parents, and Chile's schools were financed by per pupil subventions. Over the period of the studies, there were substantial differences in coverage of feeding programs and in the application of stipends for school attendance (as in Mexico), and these may have played roles in the activity outcomes that are our focus in this study.

The antecedents of Chilean social policies date to the Congreso de Beneficencia Pública of 1917, which declared that the state had a duty to care for those who were aged, sick, and poor. As Schkolnik (1992, p. 3) relates, the movement that culminated in compulsory primary education also brought with it, following the election of President Arturo Alessandri Palma (1920–24), laws regulating employment, protecting trade unions, establishing the income tax, and setting up the Ministry of Hygiene, Social Assistance and Social Security. Such initiatives were viewed not as charity but as a matter of justice and the guarantee by the state of social rights. By 1925, social spending by the government grew to about 2 percent of Chile's GDP and 12 percent of its total government spending. In 1953 Chile established the National Council for Scholarships and Student Financial Assistance (JUNAEB), with the aim to help poor families meet the indirect costs of sending their children to school, such as school meals. Real government spending for social programs tripled from 1930 to 1955, with the bulk of the benefits being earmarked for well-organized urban working-class families. Under the Christian Democrat government (1964–1970) and Salvador Allende's Popular Unity government (1970–1973), income redistribution became an explicit policy objective. During these years, spending by the government on health, basic education, and social security grew to 42 percent of total spending, and over 10 percent of the country's GDP.

It was against this historical backdrop that Chile's neoconservative military junta altered the normative basis and operation of welfare programs. Economic growth was viewed as the only means to reduce poverty, and the state sought to distort as little as possible the efficiency of the free market, in order not to impede growth. Another basis for reducing the role of the central state was the principle of "subsidiarity." As Schkolnik (1992, p. 7) explains:

The state was to act only to protect individual freedoms, assure respect of contracts and equal opportunity and assume responsibility solely for the production of pure 'public goods' and for those functions which could not be carried out in an adequate way by individuals or private organizations.... 'Equal opportunity' in this context was seen as the absence of interference or discrimination on the part of the public authorities in the free play of market forces. Rigidities and distortions in the social structure and the operation of market forces could be easily removed through direct government subsidies designed to meet the basic needs of vulnerable groups. All other determinants of poverty would then be offset automatically once people reached certain critical minimum levels of well-being in terms of health care, education, and housing.

The orientation of the military government toward social spending had several concrete implications for Chilean families. Focusing on the poorest families rather than universally providing benefits meant an increase in the total value of aid to some recipients, even while the *number* of beneficiaries was reduced. The National Supplemental Food Program and the School Meal Program dated from 1954 and 1964, respectively. Under the military, the criteria for participation in each program was restricted until such benefits went only to families and children who were near destitution, as determined by an indicator of physical household attributes, such as appliances. From 1973 to 1988, the numbers of school breakfasts and dinners dropped from 1.4 million to 480,000; lunches were reduced from 670,000 to 500,000. By the start of the 1987–96 period we study in Chile, the direct incentives that were represented by feeding programs had been restricted to families whose behavior, it was believed, would be most responsive to these incentives.

Indirectly, several emergency employment programs created by the military government also could have played a role in family thinking about children's activities near the start of our Chilean case study. Almost half a million Chilean adults—11 percent of the labor force—were working for one of these programs in 1982 (Graham 1994, p. 34). By 1987, the first year in which CASEN data are available to investigate children's activities, open unemployment had begun to decline and so, too, did the government's support for emergency employment of adults. In 1987, only 104,000 workers were employed in government programs during an average month; in 1988 just 21,000. How might the contemporary employment options for parents have affected their outlook on children's time at the start of the Chilean case study? On the one hand, the compensation for emergency employment was extremely low in Chile, between 25 and 40 percent of the minimum monthly wage (which was US$56 at that time). The phase-out of participation in these programs, at the start of the study, took place along with concomitant increases in private sector work at least to the level of minimum salaries. This would create less need for work by children. On the other hand, it is certainly possible that the elimination of this safety net for the extremely poor—including those without skills necessary for regular employment—may have created a more desperate need for work by children.

After the democratic transition in 1990, the Christian Democrat—Socialist coalition implemented several important changes in Chile's social safety net which could have altered the options seen by parents for their children. Most obviously, the expansion of school-based food programs raised the incentives for school attendance, although this would have had a minimum effect on the higher-income families whose children became eligible. Reforms in the labor code for adults could have had a much more significant impact by preventing arbitrary layoffs and strengthening worker's organizations. The minimum wage was increased for adults, thereby further reducing the need for children's supplemental income.

By contrast to social safety nets of Peru, Mexico, and most other Latin American countries, the Patricio Aylwin administration was fortunate enough to create the Fondo de Solidaridad e Inversión Social (FOSIS) during a period of economic growth and state expansion, not recession and adjustment. Its aims were not palliative but curative of national poverty. Its official principle was the first commandment of development economics: "investment in people," with the population of youth and rural Chile given preference. During the 1990s, Chile's Congress approved annual expenditures of US$50 million annually for the operation of FOSIS, which distributed these funds through micro-projects, with an average value of $US14,000. FOSIS acquired a high degree of legitimacy and was perceived as independent of short-term political interests. The program included a special module aimed at training youth ages sixteen and over in skills for employment. Participants in the program ("Capacitación Laboral de Jovenes," or "Chile Joven") were normally required to have completed their eight years of compulsory basic education. We might speculate that such an investment sends families a message that early apprenticeships in family business or agriculture are not necessary because, for those who do not plan to attend university, other forms of training will be available.

In Peru, school breakfast programs had been supported by Lima's socialist mayor during the early 1980s. By 1985, school-based feeding programs were institutionalized within the Ministry of Education, and these may have created incentives for schooling (even if children simultaneously worked). In the first years of the APRA government, as well, there were important poverty programs that could have affected the allocation of children's time. First, modeled after the Chilean military's temporary employment programs, APRA created the Program of Temporary Income Support (PAIT). Unlike Chile's program, however, workers in this program received the official minimum wage. At its height, about half a million workers were employed in this program, most of them female (Graham 1994; Graham 1991).

Created by presidential decree in 1991, Peru's poverty alleviation program, FONCODES, had the goal of offsetting the drastic effects of structural adjustment. Its ambitious mission was to improve the quality of life of the poorest poor, generating temporary employment, attending to basic needs in nutrition, health, education, and infrastructure. Three types of projects received financing from FONCODES: social infrastructure (drinking water, sewage systems); economic infrastructure (reforestation, irrigation, rural electrification); production (support of new artisanal crafts, beekeeping, fish farming). Like the predecessor safety net programs of the APRA government, FONCODES has been severely criticized for its usage to achieve political goals by Alberto Fujimori. Graham (1994) describes how Fujimori's close political allies were originally given control over which projects would be funded. Many problems with implementation also have been apparent. According to a team of researchers who studied areas of Peru that had very high rates of extreme poverty (Vásquez et al. 1999), "Social programs barely reach the Peruvian households in extreme poverty. Problems of asymmetry in information generate a high probability of lack of use of the programs." Thus, six years after the inception of Peru's targeted assistance programs, and after a per capita increase in social spending from US$56 to $177 over the 1990—1997 period, 15 percent of the population was officially said to live in extreme poverty, with incomes of less than one dollar a day. In part, the difficulty of FONCODES is reminiscent of Peru's income distributive history discussed by Webb (1977, p. 102), in a classic study of Peruvian inequality, which concluded that targeting would be difficult because of the dispersion of the poor, who remain politically fragmented. Even among districts of Peru that did receive FONCODES funding for school construction, econometric studies have found no evidence that greater expenditures increase the probability of attendance by secondary-school-aged children (Paxson and Schady 1999, p. 20).

The other key safety net provision of the Fujimori government was the Programa Nacional de Apoyo Alimentario—PRONAA (National Program for Nutritional Support). This program attained greater autonomy than those operated directly by the Ministry of the Presidency. Instead, the PRONAA was operated by the newly created Ministry for the Promotion of Woman and Human Development (PROMUDEH). By 1996, there remained nearly 26 percent of children under five years of age who were chronically malnourished. But the PRONAA lacked institutional autonomy, and often was micromanaged by the president and his close advisers (Portocarrero et al. 1999).

It is noteworthy that no new attempts were made by Fujimori explicitly to provide disincentives for children to work or to link benefits with school attendance. Schools were "out of the loop," as PRONAA shifted its support to free-standing institutions not linked with the Ministry of Education. In one respect, the absence of state action is not surprising, given the social mobilization of working children's groups (which originally mobilized for self-protection because they despaired of meaningful protection by the state). Government inaction also is consistent with its strained relations with the ILO, as we will see in Chapter 6. The government's disinclination to provide a social safety net was seen by Graham (1994) to be a result of the low expectations of the state after the Garcia-provoked economic crisis, and the shell-shocked public sensitivity after the anarchic war against Sendero Luminoso terrorism. Whatever the reasons for Peru's actions or inactions, we could conclude that 1985–97 changes in children's activity are unlikely to have resulted from social programs under either the Garcia or Fujimori regimes.

During the 1970s, Mexican programs for poverty alleviation were conceived to promote infrastructural development with the goal of augmenting local and national productivity. For example, the Program for Integrated Rural Development (PIDER, in Spanish) invested federal resources in agricultural and manufacturing initiatives. Building community institutions to sustain development was also a priority of such programs (CONAPO 1993). Later, in 1978, the federal government created the Coordination of the National Plan for Deprived Zones and Marginalized Groups (COPLAMAR). Its objective was to attend to productivity, increase employment, and distribute basic welfare services to Mexico's least developed regions. Nutrition education, health campaigns, and food subsidization were some of the means COPLAMAR used to accomplish its objectives.

By the 1980s and 1990s, such programs as those administered under PIDER and COPLAMAR began to give greater emphasis to basic education. In 1985, President Miguel de la Madrid (1982–88) stated that education would be the highest priority of his administration (Mexico 1985). In 1989, Carlos Salinas de Gortari (1988–94) declared that education was an "irreplaceable condition for social and economic modernization" and would also receive the highest priority from the federal government (Mexico 1989). However, in Mexico as throughout Latin America, there were both political and resource constraints to state involvement in education (Nord 1994).

During the 1980s, income inequality worsened in Mexico (Lustig 1990; Cortés and Rubalcava 1994; Knaul and Parker 1998). However, at just the time that poverty alleviation came to emphasize education, the federal government was less able to afford massive intervention to promote school attendance or eliminate inequality (Prawda 1987). The process of Mexican decentralization (discussed in the next chapter) reduced the federal ability to lead new intervention programs. In place of universalistic, across-the-board educational investments, in Mexico, just as in many other Latin American nations, "targeted assistance" (*ayuda focalizada*) became the preferred approach. The state's role became more selective, focusing on compensatory help for particular populations (Levy 1991; Dresser 1992; Graham 1994; Grosh 1994). In 1988, Mexico created the National Program of Solidarity (PRONASOL) directed specifically at states and counties considered to be underdeveloped or marginal based on several demographic criteria. PRONASOL aimed to combat poverty primarily through providing jobs. Education appeared alongside of other basic services such as health and nutrition, sewage systems, electricity, and land title reform. In the context of this broader mandate, three specific PRONASOL programs, initiated in 1991, emphasized school construction in rural areas and dropout reduction in primary school.

Mexico's National Council for Educational Development (CONAFE) expanded upon the work of PRONASOL by further focusing *within* marginalized areas on early school leaving and grade repetition. In a series of programs, CONAFE subsidized scholastic supplies and texts, as well as teachers who accepted placements in rural and indigenous communities of Mexico. As one part of these programs, need-based scholarships from the federal government's Secretary of Public Education were provided to families who sent their sons and daughters to school. The states of Oaxaca, Guerrero, Chiapas, and Hidalgo were the focus of this program, the Programa para Abatir el Rezago Educativo (PARE). An innovative feature of this program was its experimental character. Apart from a "treatment" set of communities and families, there also was a "control" group. For most rural children, participating in the PARE program increased the probability that they would remain in school (Lopez Acevedo 1999, p. 13).

Building on the success of PARE, Mexico's most ambitious example of targeted assistance for education arose only at the end of our study period, in the 1997 Program for Education, Health, and Nutrition (PROGRESA). PROGRESA is noteworthy because, of all the targeted social programs relevant to children during the time period of this book, it was most closely designed to attend to the integral needs of children and families living in poverty. The program recognizes the "urgency of attending to rural and indigenous communities in order to extend to them the welfare of the population in general." The program focuses specifically on families in the lowest 20 percent of the income distribution, comprising some 24 million persons. It aims to integrate existing welfare programs of education, health, and nutrition. Similar to previous programs that had been administered by CONAFE, in most respects PROGRESA also treats the family as the fundamental unit of welfare. However, there is one significant departure from welfare programs previously administered in Mexico and most other nations: PROGRESA establishes a different scale of stipends for girls and boys after they complete primary schooling (up to which point equal monetary scholarships are awarded for the enrollments of sons and daughters in poorer families). Larger subsidies are offered for the continuation by daughters to secondary school than are offered for the continuation of sons. Mexico thus follows the examples of targeted programs in Bangladesh and Guatemala, where the World Bank piloted a special subsidization of education for girls (Herz et al. 1991).

3

The Norms and Institutions of Education

To understand why children's energies are divided between worlds of work and schooling, one must appreciate the needs and opportunities faced by families and youth. In the first chapter we observed the general tendencies in the labor force opportunities of Mexico, Peru, and Chile. The first chapter also summarized national trends in population, poverty, and wealth in each country. In some imaginary land, without compulsory education or legal institutions, this background would suffice to interpret the household survey findings presented in Chapter 1 and their analyses in Chapters 4 and 5. But, of course, Chile, Peru, and Mexico each regulate the activities of their younger generations. Thus, it is necessary to appreciate the normative and the legal governance of childhood, in addition to the market forces of labor supply and demand that may determine children's time allocation.

The last chapter reviewed existing national labor laws and their tendencies, as well as the substantive debates over the nature of child labor and the impact of the global norms governing children's activities via ILO and U.N. conventions. In this chapter, I compare the features of the Chilean, Peruvian, and Mexican education systems that contribute to decisions about how much of children's time should be invested in schools as opposed to paid or unpaid work. I first extend the discussion from Chapter 2 on the developmental-consequentialist and the human rights rationales for regulating children. Then, I describe the school opportunities that have been available in each country, highlighting changes over the periods of our studies. I further document each government's efforts to provide school opportunities, as indicated by national spending patterns. Through a review of each school system, I discuss the family and government incentives to get and keep children in school, which are produced by the school finance systems and social welfare safety nets of each nation.

THE RIGHT TO EDUCATION WORLDWIDE AND IN THE THREE NATIONS

Education, at least to some minimum or basic level, is obligatory of the world's children. It is constitutionally guaranteed in most nation-states, including those whose children are discussed in this book (see Figure 3.1). The expansion of social responsibility for education within national charter documents is itself a noteworthy historical tendency over the last 150 years (Boli and Ramirez 1987). No nation today leaves the education of children entirely in the hands of parents. However, the *justifications* for public interventions have shifted over time, and they continue to vary between nations.

Mexico's 1934 Constitution, its first making primary school compulsory, established that public education was to be socialist in orientation and "to create in youth a rational and exact concept of the universe and of social life." In 1946, led by Mexico's secretary of public education and the future head of UNESCO, Jaime Torres Bodet, the goals of Mexico's public education were revised. Eschewing socialism, the purposes were to inculcate values of liberty, justice, and democracy to the Mexican people as a whole (Ornelas 1995, p. 69). Rather than inculcating international socialism, the emphasis in Mexico's constitutions from 1946 until 1993 was on the national. Rather than to focus on the

Min. Age	Chile	Peru	Mexico
below six	*Educación Parvularia:* not compulsory but free in subvented pre-schools.	*Educación Inicial:* not compulsory; free in the state centers & nonformal progs.	*Educación Inicial:* not compulsory; free in the state and federal centers.
6	*Educación Basica:* free & compulsory (4 years) since 1920; muncipalities and other providers use Ministry subventions on a per pupil basis since 1982, with non-municipal providers for growing proportions, especially in cities. Values of all subventions increased after 1990, and subventions to rural municipalities tripled. Also offered by private fee-based school. Teachers are civil servants.	*Primaria:* Since 1905 free and compulsory in schools owned and operated by central gov. There is loose coordination of local units; teachers employed and unionized at national level. Also fee private, and contracted Church schools. Morning, afternoon, and evening session shifts.	*Primaria:* Since 1934 is free and compulsory; since 1993 is administered by state governments, and teachers employees of states, but with all previous benefits. Funded by states but mainly through transfers from Federal SEP, subject to political negotiation during most of period prior to 1996.
7			
8			
9			
10			
11			
12		*Secundaria:* free, but not compulsory until 1993. Previously, attendance is required until age 15. State centers funded by Ministry; no linkage between funding and enrollments despite law decreed to do so in 1992. Schools constructed by Ministry of Presidency without planning by MOE.	*Secundaria:* free but not compulsory until 1993; part of "basic" ed. since then, with management devolved to states. Includes television centers for rural students.
13			
14	*Educación Media:* free but not compulsory. Types are: municipal; ind. subvented; corporate (since 1987); and private fee providers. Offers humanities/science and vocational curricula.		
15			*Media Superior:* includes university preparatory schools & professional/ vocational curriculum.
16			

Note: dark-shaded areas were compulsory over the entire time period of each case study; light-shaded areas were made compulsory during time period.

FIGURE 3.1 Age Sequences and Levels of Compulsory and Non-Compulsory Education in Chile, Peru, and Mexico

well-being of individual citizens or on specific groups, the emphasis was on the cultural and economic independence of Mexico as a corporate entity. Only in 1993—midway through the time period of our Mexican case study—was Article 3 of the constitution amended to read that "Every *individual* has the right to receive education" (emphasis added). Only after 1993, we might infer, did the basic charter for public education come to conceive of a possible distinction between the interests of individuals and those of the nation as a whole. Article 32 of the General Law of Education thus states that "the education authorities will take measures to establish conditions which permit the full exercise of the right to education for every individual, a greater equity of education, as well as the attainment of effective equality of opportunities of access and continuation in education."

Peru's official commitment to public education dates to the positivist view of progress held in common by its governments at the end of the nineteenth and the beginning of the twentieth centuries. President José Pardo promulgated Law No. 162, which made education free and compulsory, writing that "the prosperity, power, in sum the future of the Republic requires that the State totally develop national education" (Peru 1994, p. 21). Thanks to this law, the number of Peru's students and teachers doubled from 1905 to 1908, initiating a trend toward mass schooling that, as we will see, ultimately created a secular religion centered around education. By many measures, Peru is the poorest of the three countries in our study; one might assume that Peru has offered the least commitment to free public education. In fact, the reverse is true. Peru's most recent constitution (1993) raised the compulsory schooling bar to five years of secondary school: to approximately seventeen years of age from the prior fifteen years of age (adopted more than twenty years earlier, and in itself a very ambitious goal during its time). Peru's 1993 modification extends obligatory education longer there than in either Chile or Mexico (or most other countries, including the United States). At the century's end, the thirteenth and fourteenth articles of the Peruvian constitution identified the goal of education as "the integral development of the person .... Education promotes knowledge, learning and practice of the humanities, science, technology, arts, physical education and sports. It prepares one for life and for work, and promotes solidarity."

Chile's constitutional commitment to compulsory education dates to 1925. By contrast with clerical persecution in Mexico, and the secular dominance of public schooling in Mexico and Peru at that time, Chile sought no state monopoly on education, but simply made parents responsible for insuring at least four years of primary schooling. By contrast with Peru and Mexico, during the years of our Chilean study (1987–1996) the education system was regulated by a consistent public commitment and a single charter, a consistency that is remarkable, considering that Chilean politics differed so greatly before and after the 1990 advent of democratic rule under the coalition of Christian Democrats and Socialists. Chile's transformation was certainly more obvious than political changes in Mexico prior to the 2000 electoral demise of the P.R.I., the governing party during the period considered in this book. Yet Chile's age of compulsory schooling did not change over the period of our study. The tenth article of the 1980 constitution states that "Education has as its object the full development of the person in the distinct states of life. Parents have the first right and duty to educate their children. It is up to the State to offer a special protection of this right. Basic education is obligatory, the State having the duty to finance a free system with such an object, aimed to insure access to the entire population."

The ideals that are reflected in each nation's legal and institutional responsibility for education, as the desired alternative to child labor, have been given added legitimacy in recent years by world campaigns that articulate both welfarist and human-rights orientations to compulsory schooling. Just as the ILO and UNICEF have become key players in the campaign to alter national norms of child labor, the United Nations exerts an influence through UNESCO, which led and supported actions by governments.

Founded with the creation of the United Nations out of earlier international education institutes, UNESCO came to play a key role in providing governments and families with technical planning for pedagogical innovation and links to resources to increase school participation. Multinational organizations soon formed alliances through the linkages provided by UNESCO, which helped to legitimize the concerns by actors within those organizations who sought to prioritize education. How did this play out in the nations of this study? In Lima, during 1956, UNESCO organized a conference on the expansion of primary education to greater proportions of children. The meeting was timed so as to coincide with the Inter-American Meeting of Ministers of Education and a meeting of the Inter-American Committee for Culture organized by the Organization of American States. Out of the

Lima meetings, attended by specialists across these American organizations, there was first articulated the developmentalist orientation that soon became the dominant rationale for state action in education across Latin America. One key recommendation from the Lima meeting was that "improvement in living standards and community development in Latin America requires the simultaneous action of full primary education for the entire school age population and of fundamental education for all adults." As part of UNESCO's first major project, in 1963 it placed its Regional Office for Education in Santiago; in Mexico City it created a School Building Center for Latin America and the Caribbean. The year of 1963 also coincided with the return to civilian democracy in Peru. UNESCO's project, together with new development assistance from the United States in the continuing wake of Cuba's revolution, provided a powerful boost to the efforts and legitimacy of school construction by the man who was then Peru's president, the architect Fernando Belaunde. This concern with the economic and social welfare rationales for school expansion has continued, especially through the role of the World Bank and the Inter-American Development Bank. UNESCO's second major project, launched in Mexico City in 1979, pledged Latin American member states to extend compulsory schooling to eight or ten years by 1999.

The terrain changed during the 1980s, however. Facing severe downturns in their economies, despite unparalleled levels of schooling, Latin American educators began to face publics who were profoundly disenchanted with welfarist and economic consequentialist justifications for expansion. Expansion's consequences, to say the least, inspired little confidence in the fruits of continuing along the same path. In particular, the experience of military repression in two of the region's most educated societies, Argentina and Chile, disabused planners of any simple equation of learning with democracy. And soaring rates of open unemployment and underemployment made the demand for higher education appear irrational in some countries, notably in Peru (Post 1985, Post 1991, Post 1994). Alternative justifications for education began to be formulated. For some, expanded education could be a force for alternative development by raising public expectations of a better social order which, if frustrated, would be mobilized for radical change (Carnoy 1982). For others, nutritional supplements and the non-labor market benefits to schooling were stressed (Easton and Fass 1989). But probably the most pervasive and politically significant shift came through the increased reliance on a human rights rationale for educational participation.

In Chapter 2, we saw how the Convention on the Rights of the Child has legitimized a new justification for campaigns to eliminate child labor, beyond the traditional arguments forged by the ILO at its inception. We must also appreciate the importance for school participation of a human rights movement—institutionalized on a world scale most prominently beginning with creation of the United Nations. Calls to provide basic education for all children have deepened over the last half century. "Education For All," the theme of a 1990 conference in Jotiem, Thailand, and of a world movement since then, joined the support of the World Bank, UNICEF, and the United Nations to make opportunities for *learning* (not mere attendance) available to everyone—children and adults alike. Just as UNESCO's first major project had coincided with a return to civilian government in Peru, the 1990 Jotiem conference had a major impact in Chile, coming at the end of seventeen years of military dictatorship. In Chile, as in Peru twenty-seven years previously, international organizations offered reassuring support for the new initiatives of civilian education ministers.

Like the abolition of child labor, the norm of school attendance as a human right became widely shared and quickly invoked by local interest groups. UNICEF has been the most articulate extranational proponent of this perspective in Chile, Peru, and Mexico. UNICEF's 1999 report, *The State of the World's Children*, elaborates the basis for a new approach to the opportunity for education. "What were once seen as the needs of children have been elevated to something far harder to ignore: their rights. Jomtien marked the emergence of an international consensus that education is the single most vital element in combating poverty, empowering women, protecting children from hazardous and exploitative labor and sexual exploitation, promoting human rights and democracy, protecting the environment and influencing population growth." A Swedish diplomat and human rights advocate, Thomas Hammarberg (1997, p. 8), reviewed the character of school systems in many developing countries and concluded that "none of these schools seem to reflect the vision of the United Nations Convention on the Rights of the Child. A school should not be a ranking mechanism which favors or handicaps a child in the race for jobs in the future. Indeed, if the child is respected, it is a fundamental mistake to reduce childhood to a period of preparation for adult life." As a blueprint for a school system based on the rights of children, Hammarberg argued that the convention demands a more child-friendly school. "All the experience so far shows that the child-friendly school also provides the most effective learning. It is in that sense 'productive'. *But that is not the point.* Such a school would be good for children. It will also be an essential building bloc for a society which combines dynamic development with tolerance and mutual respect—a better society" (p. 28, emphasis added).

As seen in Figure 2.1, a rights orientation is ascendant in UNICEF and other advocacy groups. Nonetheless, other researchers continue to emphasize the importance of the negative *consequences* of school dropout for children and society as a whole. School-based researchers naturally look at what working children are leaving behind when they abandon school. Edwards (1995) concludes from her studies of Chilean dropouts that these children are losing contact with the school as a public "ritual," the loss of which distinguishes them from other children who persist as students. "Leaving school today in Chile also signifies abandoning the possibility for daily nutrition, preventive health attention, obtaining school texts, and the lengthening of the work day.... Leaving school is the beginning of a larger process of dropping out" (p. 78).

The years of our country case studies were momentous periods during which there was a general decline in popular and government faith in centrally planned development and increased faith in the rights of individuals to make choices in their best interests. By the end of the 1990s, human rights perspectives on both child labor and education dominated the discussions among officials and popular mobilizations for education. In the face of the severe setbacks encountered by Latin America's children during the 1980s, the environment during the nineties could be expected to compensate for the social deficits and reliance on children's labor.

SCHOOL SYSTEMS IN THE THREE NATIONS

Chile: Demand Subsidy and Rural Development

During the entire 1987–96 span covered by this investigation, Chile's school system was market-based and demand-subsidized, with a unique financing mechanism that had been promulgated under the military dictatorship in 1980. The major elements of this form were retained by the Christian Democrat-Social Democrat coalition after their election in 1990. As in years immediately prior to the 1973 military coup, the school system included eight years of free and compulsory education, referred to as "basic" education, on top of an impressive system of non-compulsory publicly supported preschools, which in recent years have served nearly a quarter of the children under the age of six, and over half of all five-year-olds. Basic education is followed by free but non-compulsory Educación Media ("middle education") in either a vocational or a humanistic-scientific track, for an additional three years. Figure 3.2 outlines the time sequence of education in Chile and compares this with the other countries we study.

Since 1980, the unique feature of Chilean education, in contrast to Mexico, Peru, and most other nations, is that there are a variety of school types that are publicly supported through subventions based on family choice, an arrangement that was originally inspired by the voucher proposal of Milton Friedman. By the end of 1996, 57 percent of basic and middle school students attended schools owned and operated by municipalities, but paid for on a monthly per-student basis by the central government to the municipality. These schools are not permitted to charge fees to their students, and deficits must be covered using other sources of municipal revenues (or by requesting special transfers from the

Ministry of Finance). By 1996, a growing number of families had elected to send their children to independent schools that were owned and operated by private providers, but which similarly received per pupil subventions covering most of their costs (after 1994 such schools at the post-compulsory media level were permitted to charge a co-payment to prevent deficits). In addition to the 33 percent of children who were being educated by these independent providers with public money, slightly less than 2 percent of students attended vocational middle schools owned by businesses or trade associations, and these schools received funding through a contract, rather than per-pupil subsidization. Finally, 8 percent of all students attended private schools that received no state subvention or financing. In exchange, these private-paid schools are allowed to charge very high tuition rates to students in order to finance their operation.

Historical investigations into Chile's 1980 reform have found little evidence remaining from the tightly controlled decisions by a group of University of Chicago graduates in that year, who sought to introduce market mechanisms and competition into Chile's centralized (and unionized) national system of public education (Espinoza and González 1993). Gauri (1998) reports that Chile's budget director, Juan Carlos Méndez, investigated Belgium's decentralized school system and then reported to General Pinochet with a similar recommendation. As an alternative to complete privatization and the use of vouchers, Méndez advocated a transference of the national schools to the control of Chile's municipalities. This was ultimately accepted by the military junta and, in June 1980, a decree law (No. 3.476) established the terms under which municipalities could become the owners and operators of the existing schools. Teachers were free to remain national employees as civil servants, but they were eligible for a large sums in severance pay if they elected to become employees of each municipality. This severance package was attractive to central government planners because of the even greater expense of a scale legislated for teachers in 1978 (the Ley de Carrera Docente).

Over the next seven years (with a brief interval due to budget shortfalls caused by a recession), the central government was able to transfer all of Chile's schools either to municipalities or to other independent "providers" (*sostenedores educacionales*). There soon emerged the essential elements of Chile's school system, which are unique among the countries of this study and in all of Latin America. The central government was to set the curriculum and standards, using a national standardized achievement test; to regulate teacher salaries; and to finance education indirectly through subsidies called "units of subventions." Originally, these subventions were weighted only by the level of instruction and the modality of instruction (basic education for minors, secondary education for minors, basic and secondary for adults). By 1988, an additional subsidy per student in schools of rural municipalities was created. Chile's provincial governments were given responsibility for supervising instruction and enforcing standards. Each municipal school site was expected to limit class sizes to forty-five students, although the actual number is far lower in most rural schools and in cities where subsidized private schools have expanded.

After the return to democracy, education was prioritized to pay back the "social deficit" accumulated under the military, in the words of President Patricio Aylwin. A broadly based national commission for educational modernization was appointed by President Frei, one that included representatives from Catholic and Protestant church groups, unions, university students and rectors. The commission called for greater and more equal investment in education, highlighting the differences in middle-school participation rates by students from families of different wealth. While some critics (e.g., LaTorre 1997) called for positive discrimination in favor of students from disadvantaged homes, the response to inequality under the coalition government was universalistic rather than focalized. After the commission gave a politically pluralist stamp of approval, the education ministry helped rural schools to compete with non-rural schools by tripling the value of the subvention to students in rural areas, in recognition of the difficulty of achieving an economy of scale in low-population rural areas (González 1999, p. 315).

There is a voluminous international literature discussing theoretical arguments for financing schools through subsidies of family demands, rather than via a direct supply (Coons and Sugarman 1978; Chubb and Moe 1988; Levin 1991). Chile represents one of the world's longest-running attempts to introduce market rules to education, and thus there have been numerous theoretical and empirical analyses of the impact of the 1980 deconcentration (Schiefelbein 1991; Espinola 1992; LaTorre 1997; Gauri 1998; Graham 1998; Carnoy 1998). The impulse behind a demand-based finance of schooling, described by commentators from Adam Smith to Milton Friedman, is that the productivity of state-supplied schooling is insensitive to the demand for it. Thus, quality and quantity are not improved by the normal process of consumer choice. More efficient use of resources will result from empowering families to exit schools of low quality and to patronize schools of higher quality. Eventually, the providers of education will innovate, retain good teachers, and develop other features promoting learning. Education providers will be forced to release teachers and to dispense with the organizational features that impede learning, or that lower the quality of the school experience.

In Chile, as in most countries, education was initially sponsored by the state not for its private but for its public benefits in terms of fostering national identity and citizenship and transmitting culture. But in recent decades the private benefits of education in status attainment, income, and political power have been universally recognized. If schooling is a public good that brings private benefits to children and families, then can its quality be improved by allowing a variety of providers to compete for children's time? Yes, proponents argue, so long as parents have equal abilities to choose between schools of varying qualities; have adequate information about the benefits of the educational alternatives; and are equally motivated in their decisions by a common concern for educational quality.

To meet this first condition, Chile developed transparent formulas for the subventions of municipal schools and of independent corporation schools. In addition to class-size limits, the non-municipal subvented schools were restricted in the co-payments they could request from parents, and they were not allowed to discriminate against students based on their ability to pay. To provide parents with access to the information necessary for an informed choice about school alternatives, the government publicized each school's standardized test results in national language and mathematics examinations of students.

Even if Chile's devolved, demand-subsidized education system of education could have been implemented perfectly, it would still have been based on several dubious assumptions. First, for market forces to improve education, parents must be able to move children from one school to another, something not possible in rural Chile, where one-fifth of all children lived at the beginning of the 1980 reform. Low population density and rural-urban migration, along with Chile's below-replacement levels of fertility, mean lengthy journeys to schools in the countryside. Even in the late 1990s there were 3,350 rural schools, offering basic education to 96,540 students, and these were using three or fewer teachers per school (San Miguel 1999). A large number of children attended one-room school houses. In such a context, meaningful competition is impossible due to the distances between schools and the inability to pay teachers when there are few students (although, as noted above, the value of the subvention in rural areas was increased in 1995 to three times that of non-rural subventions).

A still deeper pitfall is that, in a highly unequal society, parents will necessarily have unequal access to information, no matter how universally available it may be. As early as 1885, the Chilean positivist Valentín Letelier argued that "although an individual who knows about the commodities he needs can choose effectively between one good and another, an individual without any instruction lacks the competence to choose between one education and another" [cited in Gauri 1998, p. 16]. This universal flaw in choice-based reforms of school finance would be expected to increase the self-selection of students, and the overrepresentation of children from more informed families in more desirable or more innovative schools. Since home environments have a greater impact on outcomes than school environments, this means that public schools should be expected to become stratified by family background, even in the absence of overt discrimination by subvented schools. This is exactly what has occurred (Rounds Parry 1995). As Gauri (1998, p. 56) observes, families with higher socioeconomic status may apply to better schools; their children may gain admission to more selective schools based on previous academic records; and upper SES parents value education more highly such that they usually invest more time than lower SES families in transportation to a distant school. Theoretically, these processes would lead to a greater gap in the quality between different schools and school types, one which even in principle will be difficult to close.

By the time the coalition government assumed power in 1990, the percentage of Chile's students attending municipal schools had fallen to 58 percent, compared with 78 percent at the time of the reform. Some of the decline was due to growing numbers of students who attended elite, non-subsidized paid schools and to the institution of corporation-sponsored schools in 1987. However, the greatest component in this decline came from the increasing numbers of families who elected to send their children to subsidized schools administered by private providers (González 1999). Not only were differences in family resources apparent between these school types, but some worried about emerging gaps in the performance of children attending municipal and other subvented schools (and the gap with paid-private schools also remained large.)

A distinct rationale behind the subvention of parental demands for their children's schools (though proposed largely after the adoption of the new system) had not to do with eliminating low-quality schools through competition and the exit of clients from them, but with improving existing schools through giving parents a "voice" in schooling, to use Hirschman's classic terms. From an economic perspective, parents' investments of time in choosing schools for their children will lower the marginal costs of additional information, and in the process these sunk costs will facilitate parents' input to teachers and principals. Parental input, in itself, may represent an improvement. Irrespective of parents' educations and income, their involvement in schools will necessarily increase under a demand-subsidized finance system, since they must elect some school for their children. In so doing, they become "stakeholders" (Graham 1998) in a public good, and thus the school system's citizen-owners-users will feel more responsible for its effective stewardship. Not only that, but as proprietors in their children's schools, parents who may have been disconnected or felt disenfranchised from the formerly centralized system could bring a rich network of support and social capital to Chilean schools, just as Catholic schools in the United States benefit from linkages with parents (Coleman and Hoffer 1987).

Whatever the theoretical advantages in terms of increasing parents' stakes in school success, it appears doubtful that Chilean municipal administrators were able to do so. As Chile's former education chief of budget and planning commented wryly, it is hardly a coincidence that one finds no ready Spanish translation for school "accountability" (González 1999, p. 308). Rather than mere linguistic complexity, the difficulty of speaking in such terms reflects deeper differences in traditional orientations of the public and the Chilean state. And the hope that parental choice and a demand-based finance system will increase families' stakes in schooling remains just that: a hope, but one that runs counter to the more deeply seated popular conception of the *Estado docente*, the "teaching state" relation. Chilean families may indeed feel better connected to their children's schools than do families in Mexico or Peru, but there are several reasons why Chile's unique demand-subsidized system fell short of achieving the full potential of this connection. The most important of these occurred in the earlier time period of this study, when the subsidization of demand fell, relative to earlier years of the decentralization. Facing a fiscal crisis, the real value of subventions declined 25 percent from 1982 through 1990 (Baytelman et al. 1999). Municipal responsibility for schools came to resemble an unfunded mandate during the 1980s. Education had become a local responsibility, but there were insufficient resources to offer a quality education. Another important question with regard to demand-based financing is whether the incentives for student enrollments ever were felt at the school level. As González observes (1999, p. 313), Chile's incentives to enroll students derived to administrators of municipalities, but not necessarily to school administrators, whose budgets may not always be linked with their own enrollments in a transparent formula.

Another major deviation from a pure market-based system is that teachers could not be dismissed after they were returned to civil service status with the restoration of democracy in 1990. Nor could they easily be transferred to other municipalities. This exacerbated the underfunding of municipalities, which were obliged to provide schools but were required to find alternative public revenues to bridge the gap. Prior to 1990 as well as afterwards, and even after substantial per-pupil increases, in many municipalities teacher salaries exceeded the total in subventions received from the ministry. This created a need for the central government to bail out bankrupt municipalities (Espinola 1992).

Education deficiencies gave the coalition government an immediate focus upon its arrival to power in 1990. Among the numerous responses to the political opportunity to improve Chilean education, four overarching tendencies after 1990 are especially important for understanding trends in children's activity in the workforce and school. These are, first, a new preoccupation with the improvement of school quality; second, a renewed focus on excluded parts of the population, through attention to rural and low-performance schools and through augmentation of school feeding programs; and third, rapid expansion of public childcare and preschool education. Finally, and related to all of the foregoing, there has been a real increase in the value of subventions per student, and thus increased incentives for public and private providers to attract students. These increased incentives are especially obvious in rural areas, where much more favorable weighting formulas have been applied.

Subsequent to Chile's 1980 decentralization, wide gaps in student achievement scores appeared between school types and urban-rural areas. These gaps persist. UNESCO's 1997 "Evaluation Laboratory of Educational Quality" tested the achievement and questioned the activities of third and fourth graders in several countries . In Chile, there was a very substantial gap in the achievement of children living in rural and urban areas. Urban municipal school students also performed significantly behind their peers attending private subsidized schools, though much of this difference would be explainable on the basis of family background (McEwan et al. 1997. With loans from the World Bank, and later with exclusively national financing, Chile began in the 1990s an ambitious program designed to improve the pedagogy and resources of *all* schools, with one focus being to reduce the gap between the highest- and lowest-performing schools. This is today considered a successful intervention: National scores for Spanish and mathematics exams have increased consistently since 1990, and they have risen both among fourth-graders and eighth-graders. As a result of new curricular choices and new opportunities for student participation, a national survey found overwhelming support by Educación Media students in the methods of the national improvement programs (Mecklenburg 1999, p. 158).

While it may seem that improving school quality is a complementary goal to increasing school participation—the focus of this book—in fact the two are likely to be two sides of the same coin. Parents—even those who keep the faith that education is the surest escape route from poverty—are sensitive to overcrowded, understaffed, inhospitable, or irrelevant schools. A review of the economic incentives for eliminating child labor concludes, "A significant factor in discouraging children from attending school is the shortcomings of the education system. This raises the question whether even replacing the lost income of children would be adequate to keep them in school, and implies the need to improve the educational infrastructure besides providing economic incentives to families and children (Anker and Melkas 1996, p. 33). One of Chile's former education ministers, Ernesto Schiefelbein (1997, p. 37) agrees and highlights the nature of educational quality. "A vicious circle is created by the combination of poor school performance, mainly among low-income students, and a lack of understanding on the part of their parents of the real cost of temporary drop-out. Discouraged by their children's poor grades, many parents feel that school is a waste of time. Consequently they have no qualms about taking their children out of school during harvest or peak work periods. In their opinion, the cost of temporary absence from school is small, especially when compared with the expected economic returns of their child's labor. In fact, the cost is extremely high."

In addition to its effort to improve education, Chile was a pioneer in Latin American school lunch programs, which were created in 1964 and brought free lunches to all students in Basica (Graham 1994, p. 31). But the military government cut eligibility for free lunches, and there are many anecdotal cases of increased hardship for families in rural areas as a result of this. We might speculate that this reduced the incentives for school attendance. The restoration of these benefits under the coalition government could have provided additional reasons for attendance and disincentives for working.

In the broader context of poverty elimination, and with a view of education spending as a social investment, Chile also attempted to improve the education offered to the worst-performing tenth of all schools. This program, called the "P–900" because of the 900 schools originally included, was based on the concept of "positive discrimination," in the words of its director (Sotomayor 1999, p. 71). Although not all of the P–900 schools were rural schools, most were. The program attempted to involve community participation and to change the teaching experienced by children attending the worst schools. Over the 1990—1996 period, the gap in test scores between the P–900 schools and other publicly subvented schools had been reduced by half.

The expansion of preschool education may be indirectly relevant for the activities of adolescents because, as Anker and Melkas (1996) note, even free schools or material support will not effect the activity of girls if the reason they do not attend school is because they are needed at home to care of younger siblings. Preschool education not only affects the children benefiting from it; it also has consequences for those who formerly cared for young children. Schiefelbein (1997) advises that increased preschool participation will be especially helpful in reducing the need for poorer urban parents to depend on daughters to care for younger siblings. And, in Chile, the participation in preschool by children under six increased from 20 to 29 percent of the population, during the 1990- 1996 period.

Money was not the only thing Chile needed to make the post–1990 school improvements of the coalition governments. But money certainly helped, and it indicates the commitment to back ideas with resources. In the context of this study, we must keep in mind that, during the 1987—96 period, the Chilean economy grew prodigiously, averaging above 6 percent. During this period, as well, Chile increased its value-added tax to 18 percent to pay for these programs. Education became the highest priority, growing as a percentage of public expenditure from 8.1 to 15.8 percent, and as a percentage of GNP per capita from 2.5 percent to 3.3 percent in 1997. These large increases entailed expansion of the programs we listed above, as well as growth in the value of the subvention unit across the system and special increases for rural schools.

The young people who are the focus of our study attended both the basic and media levels of the school system. The per pupil expenditures for these levels are provided in Figure 3.2. Note that the denominator in this spending/pupil ratio does not include the number of students attending non-subvented, fee-financed private schools (where 8 percent of students were enrolled). A takeoff in real investment is obvious at the end of military rule. Increased education expenditures, when used to increase the student subvention unit, might be expected to increase the incentives for municipalities and independent providers to attract and retain students. Perhaps they also might raise incentives for school directors to inflate attendance reports, but readers should keep in mind that school inspectors frequently make surprise audits of subvented schools, and that heavy criminal sanctions apply to fraud.

Changes in the resources available for each student are reflections both of changing student demand, in the form of enrollment, as well as changing supply, in the form of funding. There is an important relationship between these two dimensions in the case of Chile. At first consideration, it might seem that spending ought to have been elastic with respect to demand, given the per-pupil basis of funding. It might seem that increases in students

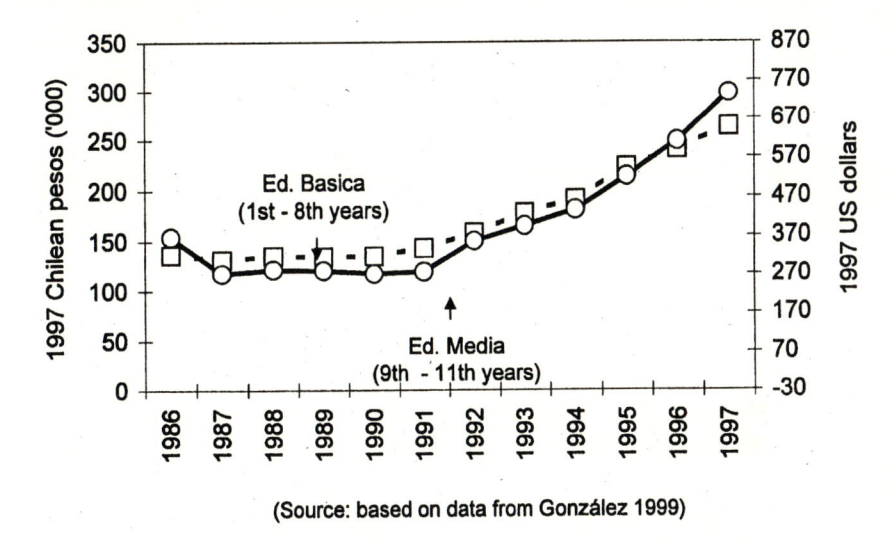

FIGURE 3.2 Chile's Per-Pupil Government Spending in 1997 Pesos and US$

would have been closely correlated with changes in public expenditure. But this was not the case. A different relationship entirely is seen, most clearly with regard to the Educación Media level (typically serving children ages fifteen to seventeen).

Before 1990, enrollments tended to increase along with the modest population growth discussed in Chapter 1. But spending on the media level did *not* rise. This reflects the relatively low priority given by the military to social spending generally, outside of highly targeted programs for the very poor. Categorical programs such as education received less attention, because some government planners expected greater private contributions to education from families themselves, who would make up the difference in government spending (for example, through their increased patronage of fee-based schools). Instead, after 1989, enrollments began to decline. In part, this decline reflected the population trends seen in Chapter 1, as well as a shift from subvented to fee-based private schools. But there was also a slight decline in age-specific attendance rates at this level. Rather than taking the opportunity to reduce programs at this level, or at least to maintain flat spending for media and reap the benefits of Chile's fertility

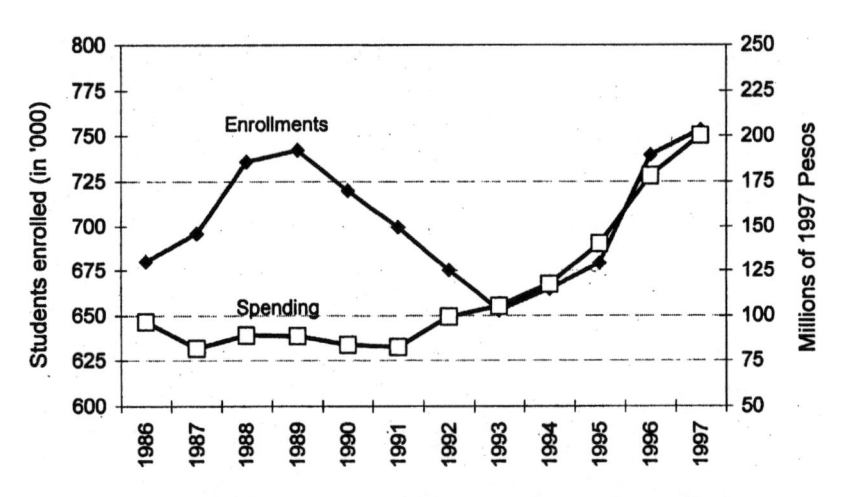

FIGURE 3.3 Chile's Constant Public Spending and Enrollments in Educación Media

transition, the government opted to jump-start student demand. That is, rather than *following* increases in student enrollment, education finance was out in front of it. This reveals an important feature of Chile's state-society relation that has implications for our survey data analysis in the next two chapters and that we will return to discuss in Chapter 6.

Peru: Centralization and Economic Crisis

Analysts of popular culture have long noted a widespread fascination by Peruvians with education as the unique and most secure means to personal ends. Earlier we saw Joquín Capelo's biting critique of credentialism at a time before obligatory schooling had been adopted. According to the great 1920s Socialist writer, Jose Carlos Mariátegui, Peruvians valued education even prior to widespread capitalism and a labor market because of an aristocratic and literary concept of education inherited with Peru's feudalistic economy. Early in the twentieth century, the reformer Manuel Vicente Villarán dryly complained that "All parents prefer [their children to be] lawyers, doctors, administrators, literary figures, teachers. Thus, knowledge is triumphant; the word and the pen are in their golden age; and if this evil isn't soon corrected, Peru will become like China: the Promised Land of lettered bureaucrats." The local faith in social progress through education gained added legitimacy through international efforts led by UNESCO and the U.S. Agency for International Development. School participation exploded through the efforts of the first administration of Fernando Belaunde Terry, which dedicated a year to universal literacy, and whose theme was to "break the exile" of children who had been excluded from primary schools. A 1963 law was implemented and financed that transformed all primary schools (even single-room rural schools) into units that taught the entire six years of the official curriculum. This immediately gave a further boost to enrollments. In 1966, education spending grew to 26.5 percent of all government spending, and 5.1 percent of Peru's Gross Domestic Product, figures which have never again been attained. Much of this funding was used to construct new public universities, and this provided younger students with a fixed goal and purpose to their studies.

Peru's nationalist military government from 1968–1980 also placed education at the center of its reform program. Its 1972 law sought to match the education system with the development needs of Peru and to create a more cohesive sense of national identity among all sectors of the country, including the non-Spanish-speaking indigenous population, which had been marginalized by the dominant cultural orientation of the official curriculum. Six years of primary and three years of secondary schooling were unified, made obligatory, and renamed "basic" education. As part of the development strategy, termed the "Inca Plan," Quechua became a second official language of Peru, and bilingual instruction was included as part of the education reform. A planning council (CONUP) for higher education was instituted, for example, and this monitored the duplication of publicly funded degree programs and had to approve all new universities. As alternatives to universities, technical education programs were offered to the graduates of "basic" education.

The military-led education reform gained worldwide recognition and praise from education planners. For example, the head of the International Institute for Educational Planning, Torsten Husén, called it the most interesting in the world (Barrantes 1989, p. 95). However, the reform fell short of its most important goals. Parents and schools tended to prefer Spanish-language instruction over Quechua, with a result that today there are far fewer Quechua-speakers than prior to the Velasco government. Technical education was perceived as a dead end by many students, who used it only as a stepping stone to universities, which eventually expanded despite promises by the government to rationalize their growth. Most significantly for the contrast with Chile, decentralization programs of the military failed to become institutionalized because of the inherent conflict between autocratic decisionmaking and the potential for bases of dissidence by teachers and community members (for a critical review see Stromquist 1986; Delgado 1981). The units that were originally envisioned to serve as micro-decision-making units—the Nucleos—never were accorded sufficient autonomy to operate as such. Their role did not progress beyond the lowest level of the national bureaucracy, a portentous failing that can be seen, in retrospect, as foreshadowing a similar attempt made in 1993.

When Fernando Belaunde was reelected to power in 1980 under a new constitution, he declared that his five-year term would be officially dedicated to improving education: the "Quinquenio de la educación." In his first year he succeeded in finding funds to increase school construction and support additional teachers. But this only sufficed to match increases in numbers of students and did not approach the resources he had given to education as president fifteen years earlier. A "General Law of Education" (No. 23384) was submitted and approved by Belaunde and his education minister, Jose Benavides Muñoz, which nullified the reforms that had been promulgated under the Velasco government in 1972.

Three modifications of this law may bear on the interpretation of our findings for Peru in 1985. These concern the curricular organization, level of obligatory schooling, and the responsiveness of the school system to needs from the regions. Under the 1982 law, the unified organization of obligatory basic education in three cycles, which had been implemented under the 1972 reform, was redivided into the levels of primary and secondary education. Whereas school attendance was officially obligatory up to age fifteen under the 1972 reform, only primary education was declared obligatory in Belaunde's 1982 law. The "Nucleos" were transformed into service units. Any municipalities that wished to do so were said to be free to establish their own schools, but it was never clear where the funding for these schools would come from, since municipalities had no authority to collect taxes. As a result, during the entire period of our 1985–97 case study of Peru, and by sharp contrast with Chile, there was no attempt to plan or rationalize the supply of school opportunities in accordance with the demands of students. Nor did the government allow political input from families in the prioritization of spending. Finally, whereas the 1972 reform had envisioned a truly bilingual system of education, with equal respect given to indigenous language and culture, Belaunde's 1982 law provided instruction in the indigenous languages merely as a bridge to Spanish. Only in communities where the majority did not understand Spanish would there be initial instruction in the vernacular, but with a tendency for "castellanización progresiva" (progressive transformation to Spanish) with the goal of merging the students' own cultural characteristics "with those of modern society."

By contrast with Mexico, as well, there also was less and less of an attempt to distribute resources in accordance with national needs as determined by central planners. Instead, from fiscal crisis and benign neglect during the 1985–2000 Alan Garcia government, Peru weakened the institutions for central planning that had been established under the Velasco education reform of 1972. During the first years of the Peruvian case study, a strong moralistic attitude was assumed by the ministry, urging greater probity and "volundad" from the nation as Peru improved education. Heterodox economic positions were actually incorporated into Ministry of Education plans (Peru- MOE 1986), and used to justify indiscriminant, across-the-board funding increases during the first two years of the administration. When inflation and the tax apparatus began to collapse after Peru's moratorium on foreign debt in 1987, revenues for education and other social spending also collapsed.

In 1985, the first education minister during the period of the case study had strong credentials linking him with the non-APRA constituencies which Garcia hoped to pull into a coalition. Grover Pango had leadership experience in the national teachers' union, had taught in Catholic schools, and was from the south (APRA's stronghold was the north). In education policy, consistent with APRA's usage of employment programs to support Aprista organizations, decisionmaking grew more insular and less responsive to potential constituencies outside the organization. It was little wonder that the service units of the ministry were ignored as sources of information or decisionmaking. At the time of Alan Garcia's election, there was a strong sentiment among APRA leadership that the lessons of the military law had not been adequately evaluated and a desire, common in the cycle of Peruvian politics, to put a distinctive stamp on the education system rather than to continue with the laws of the previous administration. Grover Pango felt that the 1972 reform failed because of the vertically imposed attempt to implement them. Rather than attempt another legislative reform, however, Pango emphasized, "Educational problems will not be resolved through laws, but through convictions. In our country, law must be the result and not the cause of convictions. Attitudes do not change through a law, especially in the field of education."

Preoccupation with Sendero Luminoso, the abrupt departure the first education minister, and the precipitous fall of Peru's economy all delayed any APRA education proposal. The delay in new education initiatives lasted until 1989, when the civil institutions of the country had almost ceased to function and APRA had lost much of its moral authority. In that year, a new education minister, Mercedes Cabanillas, proposed a new bill of law entirely, one that would have reestablished obligatory "basic" education along similar lines to that of the 1972 law, but without the technical and vocation education modules. The bill, like most proposed in the last year of the ill-fated Garcia administration, languished and came to naught. By the time of Alberto Fujimori's election, in 1990, Peru's education system was in a shambles. Teacher's salaries had fallen to historic lows, and in 1991 a five-month long national strike temporarily reoriented an entire generation of Peru's public school children to alternative activities.

In keeping with the neoliberal orientation he soon embraced, Fujimori anticipated a decentralized system, one similar to Chile's. There is even an affirmation in the 1993 constitution that Peruvian education is, in fact, already decentralized. But, facing intense opposition to neoliberal ideals and the privatization of education, Fujimori never effected a new education law to replace the one that had governed education since the 1982 Belaunde instrument. Intense political opposition from the left made Fujimori vulnerable to charges that his plan would exacerbate inequality and incrementally move Peru away from its cherished ideals of free education for all (for a summary of the arguments see Graham, 1998). In fact, opposition from legislators over education was one issue contributing to Fujimori's decision to stage an "auto-golpe," or "self-coup" in 1992, when he shuttered the congress, suspended the constitution, and called for a new constitutional constituent assembly. But, just as the earlier military government could not ignore popular pressures to restrict access to education, Fujimori could scarcely ignore the widespread sentiment that education must be a responsibility of the state. The result was another example of autocratic populism. Originally, Fujimori sought constitutional reforms and a new set of education laws that would give less control to the central government and more to communities. The most important modification would have been a law issued by presidential decree (D.L.26012) during 1992, a radical modification of the historical relationship of teachers to the ministry (Guabloche 1993). The law stated that teachers were to be employed by schools themselves, which receive funding from the ministry depending upon the number of students enrolled. However, this law had still not been implemented by the concluding year of our Peruvian case study (nor at the time of this writing, eight years later). Instead, the ministry was proposing a new complete overhaul of the system, shortening secondary school to four years and instituting an optional two years of studies for the Bachillerato, similar to the system in Mexico. Like the assertion of a decentralized system in the 1993 constitution, the ministry simply ignored Law 26012. In reality, financing became far more centralized in the later years of our study. Fujimori's concentration of powers were a recapitulation of the tendency during the Garcia government, but with an important administrative twist. Fujimori began to use a new Ministry of the Presidency to replace authority over many programs that formerly had been the domains of less-centralized civil institutions. This trend was accelerated when a close ally of Fujimori lost in Lima's mayoral election. As a high-profile (and far more powerful) consolation prize, the losing candidate was appointed by Fujimori as secretary of the Ministry of the Presidency. During the mid-1990s, much-needed capital investments in school construction were evident to all in every region of Peru. Reminiscent of Belaunde's program, thirty years previously, this plan had overtly political intentions, as each construction site took care to post placards that identified the project specifically with Peru's "Ministry of the Presidency" (rather than Education). Not only was the Ministry of Education not consulted about locations of new schools, it was barely informed. New school construction proceeded with little to no strategic planning, with the too-common consequence of construction near existing schools but no plans to supply teachers.

The net result of the administrative developments under the Garcia and Fujimori governments was that, over the 1985—1997 period covered by our Peruvian case study, children faced a system that was increasingly unresponsive to the demands for participation and less adaptive to changes in the local economy or to normative reform of child labor. Schools were built; teachers were hired; in some cases quality may have been improved when teacher salaries began to reach levels at which a second job was not absolutely essential. But these changes came about largely in response to exogenous changes in the resources available to the government, and then they formed part of a populist political strategy by Garcia and Fujimori. While each administration was sensitive to the pervasive social demand for education, the public apparatus for meeting these demands was top-down and not clearly articulated with the public through any civil institution, neither through local service units nor through the Ministry of Education. In a prescient remark years before she was to be appointed by Fujimori as the first in a rapid succession of ministers of education, one prominent secondary school principal, Gloria Helfer, shared her belief that the entire education system was characterized by "authoritarianism, vertical control, and imposition of relationships from the top." Gloria Helfer saw "directors are over teachers, teachers over students, older students over younger ones: there is tremendous latent violence."

It is important to understand the disintegration of Peruvian education planning in order to appreciate fully the anomaly of the nation's growing rate of school participation. Administrators from past and current Ministries of Education make it clear that resources have never been allocated in a transparent basis (this section relies on interviews with Oscar Collao, Sonia Peralta, Pedro Orihuela, and Henry Harmann). During the early 1970s, each "zone" of education maintained an office of planning and budget. State schools would send reports of their attendance to the zone's planning office, together with the list of their teachers and available classrooms. Each year, as the government would draft its education budget, a commission would visit the office of each zone. The commission would include a statistician, a planning officer, and a budget officer, and their job was to evaluate the needs of each zone and provide a recommendation to the Ministry of Education. The ministry, after facing each "techo prepuestal" (budget ceiling), would then allocate funds to each zone based on its own internal criteria. In practice, the personnel officer of each zone would then allocate the teaching slots to each school based on his or her own criteria. Unlike Chile, Peru never used a formula for allocating teachers based on attendance. Consequently, there was no direct incentive for any particular director to try to increase enrollment, even though student attendance was one element in the overall Peruvian education budget.

As an extreme example of Peru's politicized decisionmaking, in 1986 Garcia created 26 USEs (education service units) in Lima, thus devolving further the decisions about hiring, and provided funds to contract 100,000 new teachers. By nearly every account, these were largely political appointments and not linked with enrollments. In practice, parents' associations (AFAFAS), parishes, and community groups built Peru's classrooms. Theoretically, at the end of student matriculation, by March 31, information from teachers was sent from each school to be processed by the ministry. But, in reality, information seldom reached Lima because the teachers never knew why it was necessary or what it was to be used for. The disconnection of budget and planning created little incentive even to collect information. Prior to 1980, Peru made three annual censuses of the student population. Beginning with the first Belaunde Ministry, in 1980, there was only a single census each June. Under Belaunde and continuing for the first four years of the APRA administration, in June the ministry would deliver forms to each Peruvian school center, and these were to be completed by the administrator of each administrative unit (the USE in Lima and Callao, or the Regional Department outside of these areas). However, after 1989 the ministry was given no funds to develop, print, or even to deliver these materials. Instead, the ministry was forced to rely on haphazard, nonstandardized, and usually incomplete communications from each unit regarding its number of teachers, students, and even buildings. For several years, no one in Peru's Ministry of Education could do better than roughly estimate the number of children who were enrolled in state schools.

In sum, during the entire period of our Peruvian case study, and by sharp contrast with Chile, budgets were overtly political products, with no linkage and thus no incentive for student attendance. Teachers and school principals understand that resources at both the school and USE level are unrelated to numbers of local children who enroll and remain students. As education advisor Luis Carlos Gorriti commented, "Education spending is decided by the Ministry of Economy and Finance, not by using technical criteria or any study of demand, enrollment, or of regional or national development. Simply, they take account of the precedents from prior years and apply a factor related to demographic growth." Nevertheless, the Ministry of Economy and Finance does request an official wish list from the USE and from the ministry. Under the APRA government, the education ministry would send technical representatives to negotiate over budgets with the Ministry of Economy and Finance.

Mercedes Cabanillas, a minister of education under the Garcia government, recalled that she "was a minister who confronted her colleagues in Economy and Finance and would arrive with or without an appointment to make my own claims because every month or every three months I always readjusted the salaries of the teachers." In part, Cabanillas tried to create her own subsidies, independent of union demands, including hardship bonuses for those teaching in high altitudes, unsafe regions, or in a zone under a state of military emergency during the campaign against Sendero Luminoso. The result was a concentration of power, and a circumvention of the teacher's union. Cabanillas also found opposition from the government's Ministry of Economy and Finance.

Under Fujimori, the Ministry of Economy and Finance simply requested reports directly from each USE, bypassing the Ministry of Education. There is widespread disbelief that these reports have any impact on the size of budgets allocated by the Ministry of Economy and Finance. Forcing the education minister out of the communication loop, this pattern undercuts that institution as well as the authority of the teachers' union. After 1993, local units were ignored as channels of demands despite the initial Fujimori plan to decentralize education. In 1995, the president of Fujimori's own Council of Ministers, and his minister of education, made a historic address to the Peruvian congress. Dante Córdova (Peru 1995) admitted that growth of the "bureaucratic apparatus of the Ministry of Education has ended up expropriating all management capacity from the directors of schools." Consequently, "directors have no capacity for decision nor instruments of management that permit them to assume real control." He promised a reform of the system, apparently assured of Fujimori's confidence. But he was soon forced from office, and in later years he recalled bitterly the shortcomings of the system. In his view, the role of the USE is "basically to administer spending. They present a list of necessities . . . but the decision to assign resources is made as a function of the tendencies of spending and not much on the needs or projects or modernization. In the end, the budgets end up subject to what is given out by the Ministry of Economy and Finance, with little or no consideration of the needs." At the school level, the effect of this top-down style is evident. One principal's comments are typical: "We've been informed that there going to be a distribution of breakfasts; we have to form a commission to receive and administer this program and we've been told there will be benefits from a distribution of shoes through the Ministry of the Presidency but we're still waiting for this."

The administrative centralism of Peruvian public education stands in sharp contrast with Chilean decentralization. Asked whether budgets of their schools tended to increase with student numbers, one Peruvian primary-school principal replied: "We get paid a salary and period. What incentives could there be according to the law? According to law there are incentives but this is not followed; there are congratulations, resolutions but in terms of tangible incentives, we have to say no. They don't exist. What the government does is to donate materials, but not using any ranking of schools by attendance or performance, for example." In later years, funding for school repairs and cleaning has been most often provided by schools' parent groups (APAFA, the Associations of Parents and Family Members). These typically solicit parents and relatives for a membership fee each year. The decisionmaking authority of these school associations provides an indirect form of community involvement, as well as much-needed basic maintenance in Peru's schools. But these bases of support were undercut by the education ministry, despite the fact that there are no national resources allocated through the service units. A principal told us, "For enrollments they pay not a cent in the state schools. Where they pay is through the APAFA, and the APAFA is controlled by a ministerial resolution that authorizes parents to meet and they themselves fix a membership fee. . . . But

The Norms and Institutions of Education   125

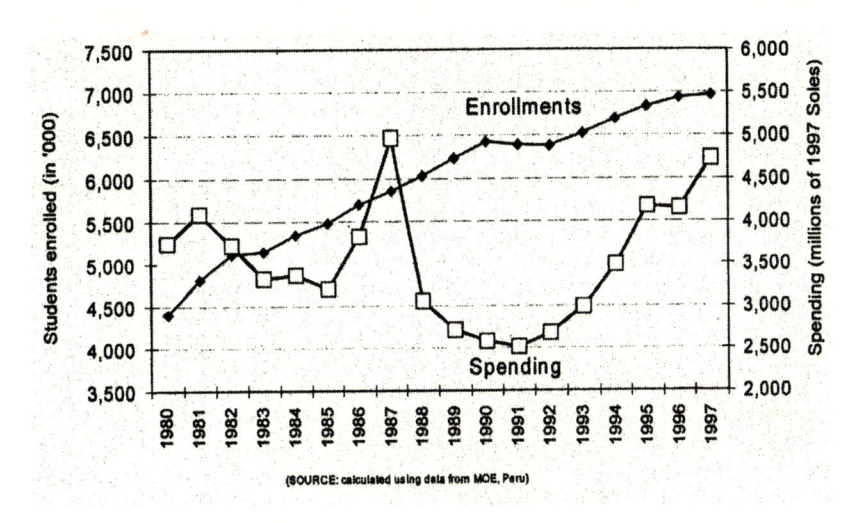

FIGURE 3.4 Constant Recurrent Spending and Total Enrollments in Peru (all levels)

now what happens? The minister of education has been going to all the schools to say that, no, attendance is free, that they shouldn't pay. Here come all the parents, and they don't even pay for the APAFA. The say they're short of cash and the state says that it's free. And this is pure politics and demagoguery."

Historical trends in public education spending are available for total education spending, but not for each level. Figure 3.4 illustrates the value of recurrent spending (nearly all of which pays for teachers and, thus, indicates the supply of classroom spaces). Over a long period, there was a steady decline in spending until the early 1990s. By 1991, remunerations for teachers were less than one tenth what they had been in 1976 (Saavedra et al. 1997). There was a short-lived period of renewed spending during the Garcia government in 1986 and 1987, after which time budgets reverted to the same downward spending pattern as before Alan Garcia's election. Enrollment increases, meanwhile, though they briefly paused in 1991 and 1992, continued at a faster rate than the growth in the population as a whole. This meant that, at an individual level, the odds of attending school increased, as will be seen in the next chapters. Finally, as economic growth returned to Peru, the government again increased its appropriations for teachers.

One commonality of Peru's spending with Chile and, as we will see, Mexico, is that rapid increases were made starting in the early 1990s. But, as we have discussed earlier in this chapter, differences outweigh similarities. First, during the early 1990s the number of students and the school-age population increased more rapidly in Peru than in Mexico or, especially, Chile (where it actually had declined). As a result, the overall spending per pupil was not very much different in 1997 (when it was about US$227 / student) than it had been in 1985, at the beginning of our study period. Second, in terms of its public commitment, Peru's increase reflected mostly increased spending by the state generally, and only very slight rises in the prioritization of education within the national budget.

But why *should* Peru further incentivize children to attend school, given its already very high school-participation rates and the fact that child labor is officially "protected" rather than prohibited? As we have already seen from household survey data presented in Chapter 1, most Peruvian working children also attend school (unlike in Mexico). The miracle of Peruvian education is that popular faith is so widespread for an institution in which Peru's governments have invested so little.

Apart from the longstanding esteem that Peruvians have felt for education, there are administrative clues for persistently high rates of attendance. The 1992 Code for Children and Adolescents embodies a belief that we found also among principals of secondary schools. As one Lima principal reported:

> There are dropouts here in this school—more or less 3 percent—and that is low in comparison with other schools. There is also a group of students who work, and this affects their performance and their attendance. It's something that can't be controlled; all that we can do is to help them continue, give them their exams, their grades, and give them some extra help so they can continue because it's so painful. These are boys who disappear for a week and come and say "Sir, I've been working"; "I work in a gas sta-

tion;" "I work in such and such, selling papers;" "I help out my parents." And what do you want me to say to them? No? That I can't help them? I have to help the boy to get ahead!

This principal's rock-solid faith that education is the way ahead appears to continue the historical faith in schooling that was first noticed by Capelo (cited earlier). Peruvians continue to associate education with upward mobility, a finding that emerges in surveys of parents (Ansión et al. 1998) as well as students (Post 1994). Respondents invariably place education above "personal effort" or "contacts" as the way to attain their dreams.

Mexico: Federalism and Decentralization

Similar to the Peruvian experience, during the years of this study in Mexico the opportunities and legal norms were extended upward in 1993. Similar to Chile, over this period Mexico moved (slowly) toward a decentralized provision and control of its school system. In common with both Peru and Chile, Mexico's economy has faltered in the recent past. At the century's end there was a substantial proportion of Mexican families who had seen no improvement in their income or living standards for a generation. In terms of cultural diversity, Mexico matches Peru (and far surpasses Chile) in its number of indigenous language groups and distinctive communities. But, while there are clear parallels in the context and intentions of Mexico and those of Peru and Chile, we must be clear that there are great differences between Mexico and the two Andean countries of this study. These must be kept in mind when comparing children's activities and the policy responses to them.

As already discussed in the first chapter, sheer size is one important difference: Since the mid–1980s, Mexico has been responsible for the schooling of five times as many children as has Peru, and ten times as many children as has Chile. The National Indigenous Institute estimated that there were ten million indigenous Mexicans at the start of the 1990s, who comprised the majority population in almost one-third of Mexico's approximately 2,500 municipalities. But, unlike Peru, there is no single majority indigenous language group, and this partly accounts for the fact that bilingual education was never an official goal of Mexico's education system (Quechua, the language of the Inca empire, was declared an official language during Peru's nationalist military government). Mexicans frequently point out another dubious distinction in Latin America: They are "so far from God and so close to the United States." Mexico's northern border bears on almost every aspect of social life and public policy, including those which are the subject of this study. The remittances sent home to Mexico by family members who work seasonally in the United States constitute a resource for children, while at the same time the prolonged absence of parents can also negatively affect school continuation (Kandel and Kao 2000, Kandel and Kao 2001). By reason of its political constitution as a federation, Mexico differs from the Andean republics in the assignment of responsibilities for education. Unlike the 1980 reform in the Republic of Chile, devolution under the charter of the Mexican federation had different meanings and was not the radical break from the past that it was in Chile. Mexico's constitution long envisioned "free and sovereign states with respect to all that concerns their internal governance." However, the Mexican constitution also stipulated certain "concurrent" faculties, responsibilities that would be shared between the federal and state governments. The General Law of Education is one such concurrent power.

Historians and political analysts have argued that, since 1910, Mexico has been a federation in name only. Beginning in the late 1970s, a deconcentration of decisionmaking was initiated (Prawda 1987), and a first step toward organizational decentralization was taken under President Miguel de la Madrid in 1982. Later, with the administration of Carlos Salinas de Gortari, an education reform known as the "modernization" of basic education, included a formal social "agreement" (*El Acuerdo Nacional*) establishing that decisionmaking should rest in the hands of Mexico's states, counties, and parents. This reform also pledged that the education system, while remaining flexible and adaptive to the needs of the states, should improve in several areas and extend compulsory schooling to the secondary level.

Under the terms of this agreement, which were subsequently codified through the General Law of Education in 1993 and through a constitutional amendment, the federal government transferred to state governments all administrative responsibility for schools. This included management of the budget and—critically—labor relations and negotiations. The transference was immediately seen by leaders of the national teachers unions as an attempt to diffuse their power and deflect conflict to state capitals. Teachers constitute one of the largest and best-organized groups in Mexico, and frequently exercise their power to paralyze Mexico City during periods of contract negotiation. Thus, decentralizing the negotiations would have the effect of fragmenting union mobilization into thirty-two weaker units. These units would lack the capacity to seize national attention during contract negotiations, much as has been the case in the United States and other decentralized school systems.

To counter the arguments by teachers, the Zedillo administration invoked market-based and quality control language to justify decentralization, claiming that "decentralization permits the federated entities to recognize their needs more rapidly, to design more effective and realistic policies, to improve the assignment of resources and to improve both the quality and access to the services contributing to regional development" (Poder Ejecutivo 1996). However, by comparison with many other decentralization reforms attempted in Latin America, the Mexican reform maintains far greater control by the central government. To date, resource generation and allocation has remained largely a federal responsibility. The federal government further retains other key responsibilities, including: setting the program of study nationally; establishing the school calendar; publishing free textbooks; authorizing all texts used in primary and secondary schools; and regulating the training of teachers. The Acuerdo included a provision for committees of social participation (CPS) at the regional and municipal level (the CEM). Like Peru's education reform of 1972, this was an attempt to create stakeholders beyond the parent associations of each school and to provide an institution for input into decisionmaking. However, at the conclusion of the period we study, and four years after their establishment, Gershberg (1999) could find no successful examples of either type of committee operating as it was intended.

Mexico's reforms in the 1990s had a more ambitious goal than merely to extend obligatory schooling for three more years to the secondary level. Rather, the modernization and constitutional reforms aimed to create a new system of basic education, like that of Chile, including the curricula and infrastructures of both the primary and secondary education establishments. But the responsibility for the development of a unified system was given to state governments. Consequently, at the conclusion of the Mexican case study, there were still many unaddressed and unsettled issues. These included whether there should be a uniform purpose and a common curriculum for all obligatory schooling and the linkages between the primary and secondary school sites (de Ibarrola 1996). In the absence of this link, there are excellent reasons to worry—as did Mexico's own undersecretary for basic education—that expanding comprehensive secondary school in rural areas will "cream off" the top students and encourage their out-migration to urban areas. Will children graduating from rural secondary schools find any reason to remain in remote communities, where there are no employment options? The undersecretary, Olac Fuentes (1996, p. 56) urged the development of linkages between multiple, diversified types of secondary school experiences with the multiple needs of Mexico's rural communities.

While decentralization has been only partially institutionalized, as a political process it allows local actors legitimately to claim responsibility and credit for the nation's most important public services and spending areas. Decentralization, in cases where opposition parties control a state government, works to concede and share power, thereby legitimizing the openness of the PRI. At the same time, decentralization also consolidates the authority of local political leaders and administration. Other actors include the national and local leaders of the teachers unions. The former see decentralization as an unmitigated disaster, arguing that insufficient resources are being transferred to states to resolve their educational problems. Local leaders have argued for a distribution of union dues to strengthen state affiliates of the organization.

Thus far, most debate and political action has been focused on the motives of the federal government leaders in promulgating decentralization. Does it serve to fragment collective bargaining? Will decentralized education accede to opposition demands? Does the process reserve ultimate fiscal authority for the federal government while appearing conciliatory? (McGinn and Street 1986). Ornelas (1995) judges the decentralization to be incomplete and highly misleading, given that most decisions about curriculum and finance are centralized. Other discussions have examined the means to achieve efficiency through institutionalizing channels for public input in local school governance.

Surprisingly little attention has been given in Mexico to what was considered one of the major shortcomings of decentralization in Chile: maintaining a national education system in the face of uneven development and resources between and within regions. Few commentators have acknowledged the perils of a process of decentralization in the context of extreme regional differences in development and wealth. At least during the early years of the decentralization reform, which are covered by our study, there was no consistent policy by the federal government about whether its allocation of resources to states should attempt to eliminate interstate inequality or, rather, should reward states that attempt to improve schools by raising their own revenues. Rather than to conceive of resource equalization as a corollary to school decentralization, Mexican policy relies on compensatory, targeted social assistance, which, as was discussed in Chapter 2, did not originally focus on education at the time inaugurated. And the impact of these programs on national inequalities of school participation has only begun to be assessed.

During the period of this study, Mexican primary and secondary education became more heterogeneous even while the schools became more formally integrated and expanded in their coverage. In part, the diversification of tracks and modules is precisely what allowed greater coverage. Separate programs for indigenous peoples and rural communities were developed over the period of the study. Were it not for these expansions, Mexico's SEP estimates that the absolute numbers of student in primary schools would have fallen (SEP 1999). To understand the trends in contemporary Mexican enrollments, we must disaggregate the sources of these changes. As seen in the left-hand panel of Figure 3.5, after the decentralizing reforms of 1993 and after three years of secondary schooling were made compulsory, all enrollments at schools that previously had been owned and operated by the federal S.E.P. were amalgamated with the schools that previously had been operated by each of Mexico's states. Following 1993, secondary enrollments began a gradual rise, and we can observe from Figure 3.5 that this was due exclusively to increases in public—not private—education. What the figure does not show—but what is also true—is that the increase in the enrollments at the lower secondary level can be attributed entirely to increases in students attending secondary schools that used televisions rather than teachers. As we will see in Chapter 5, Secundaria enrollments rose largely because the number of graduates from primary school were rising, and not because of an increasing proportion of primary graduates continuing to the secondary level. Unfortunately, because of the decentralized funding mechanisms for public state and federal secondary education, there are no reliable estimates of total secondary spending over the time period of our 1984—1996 study.

In the right-hand panel of Figure 3.5, we can observe comparable figures for Educación Media Superior, control for which continued to be divided between federal and state governments, private schools, and universities. Media superior also comprised a professional education level. The second panel of Figure 3.5 is intended to emphasize two important points about the media superior level. Notice that the overall numbers are far lower than at the prior secondary level. In part this is because secondary graduates are not obliged and most often did not continue to the next level. However, it also reflects the extremely high dropout rates within the media superior level. Terminal efficiency rates are officially very high over the course of the three years of media superior, and this results in low average enrollments, as compared to

The Norms and Institutions of Education   133

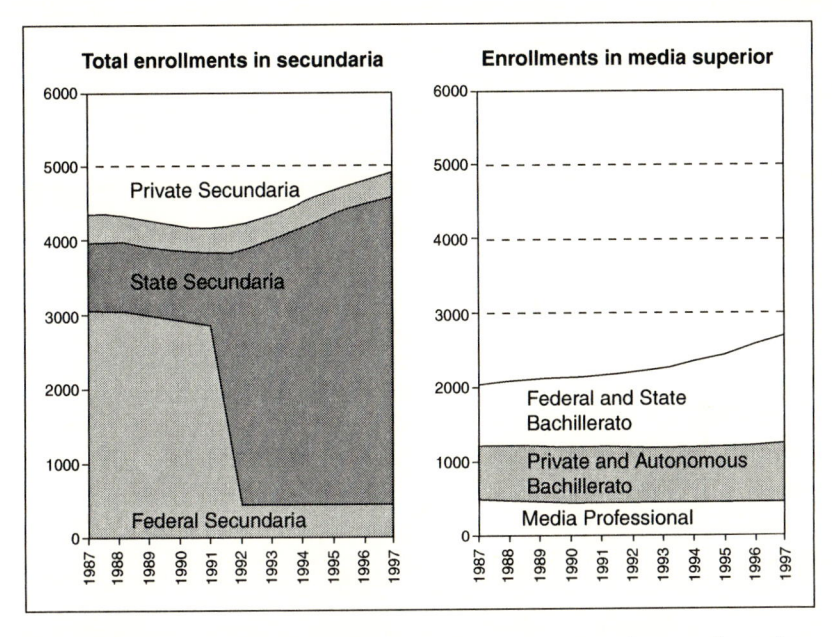

FIGURE 3.5 Enrollment Trends in Mexican Secundaria and Media Superior

secundaria. The other point to note in this figure is that, as with increases in secundaria, growth occurred exclusively in public schools offered by the federal or state governments.

Did this growth occur for the same reasons suggested earlier for the growth of media enrollments in Chile, that is, because of massive infusions of public spending? Probably not. Unlike the difficulty of spending data for the public secundaria level, in Mexico there are is a reliable series of information about total public (state and federal) spending at the media superior level. These official estimates are presented in Figure 3.6, which is comparable to Figure 3.3 (for Chilean Media) and very roughly similar to Figure 3.4 (for total Peruvian enrollments and spending). In Figure 3.6 note that, as was true for social spending generally during Mexico's economic recession, constant spending on public media superior fell at the start of the period under study (no reliable estimates are available for the 1984–86 years). Unlike Chile, enrollments continued to rise in Mexico even after Mexico's population of children had stopped growing, as more children completed primaria. For this reason,

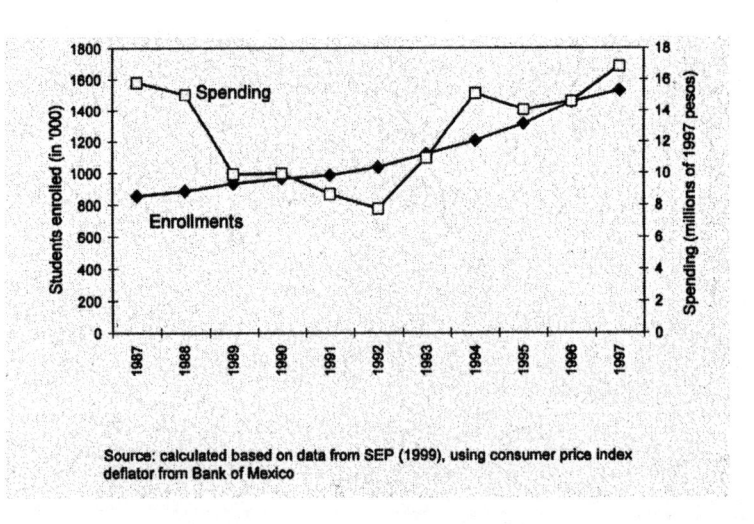

FIGURE 3.6 Constant Spending and Total Public Enrollments in Mexico's Educación Media Superior

Mexico shares with Peru the problem of playing catch up in its spending: Although the overall public spending on media superior students regained the levels of the early years of the study, by the end of our time-period, spending per pupil was still below that of the mid–1980s. And it would appear that education spending, at least for this level, was more likely a response to changes in children's activities than it was a cause of those changes.

THE IMPACT OF SCHOOL AND EDUCATION IDEALS FOR CHILDREN'S ACTIVITY

Officially sanctioned ideals of what activities are good for children are institutionalized within school systems, as well as in the labor laws and welfare programs discussed in the previous chapter. Changes in ideals at an institutional level may also be reflected in changing family awareness of their responsibilities to support children. It is probably not possible to disentangle the communication of these ideals, at either the institutional or the family level, from a much more concrete role that is played by the

Chilean, Peruvian, and Mexican state: their sponsorship and supply of education opportunity, along with these states' loose control over its quality. However, our understanding of administrative reform in each nation's school system does give us some basis to expect change in family allocations of children's time.

In studies of financing, a widely used approach to international comparisons of education effort can be gleaned from analysis of yearly school budgets. Two conventional indicators of this effort are useful: changes in amounts spent by each central government as percentages of a) the gross domestic product and, b) the total central government spending. For each country of this study, these percentages are presented in Figure 3.7. The indicators are not directly comparable between countries because, as previously explained, Mexico's states raise revenues and partially fund school systems in that federation. And Peru's spending figures include funding for its higher education system, and they thus overestimate what is spent for compulsory schooling because per-pupil spending tends to be greater for higher education than for primary and secondary schools. But what we *can* compare in this figure are differences in the Chilean, Peruvian, and Mexican tendencies over time, since within each country there are comparable spending definitions over the time period that is indicated.

When making these comparisons, there are similarities as well as differences. Most clearly, the effort by Mexico's federal government was fairly stable in the earlier period of our study, but its effort has grown impressively since the late 1980s. Recall from the discussion in Chapter 1 that these years correspond to the leveling off of Mexico's school age population. Thus, it is all the more impressive that Mexico nevertheless gave education increasing priority. For similar reasons, Chile's prioritization of education is noteworthy after the return to democracy under Aylwin and Frei, and continuing with Ricardo Lagos. As compared with Mexico and Peru, children are a much smaller proportion of the Chilean population, and their absolute numbers even declined in some years. But Chile invested larger percentages of its total economic product in the school system and larger percentages of its total government budget. By contrast with Chile and Mexico,

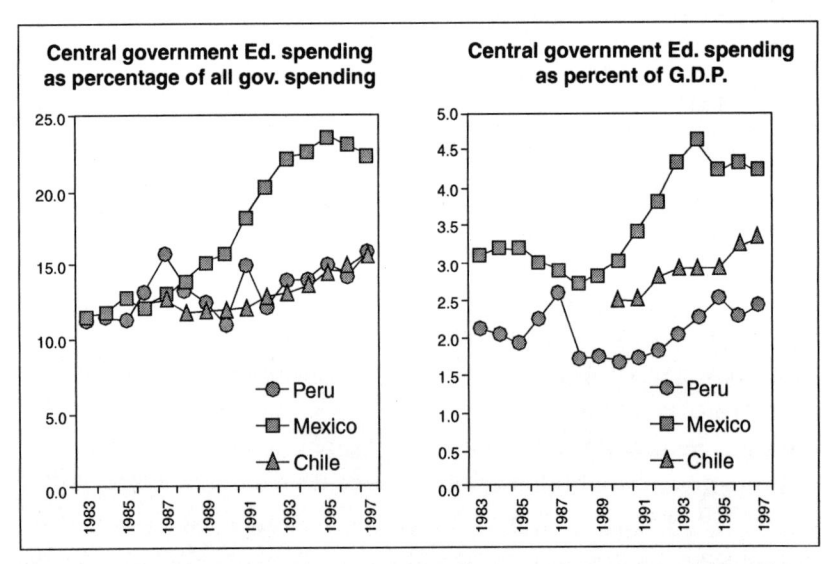

FIGURE 3.7 Expenditures on Public Education in Chile, Peru, and Mexico

Source: Chile, Garcia-Huidobro and Cox (1999) and provided by Ministry of Education: Peru, data provided by Ministry of Education; Mexico, Poder Ejecutivo (1999)

Peru's populations of school-aged children rose steadily over the entire period of this study (and are expected to continue to rise until the end of the first decade of the twenty-first century). But the government's public commitment is inconsistent, as seen by an attempt under Garcia to increase education spending and another proportional increase during the first years of the 1990s. In the most recent years, spending rose again, but even at the end of the period, Peru's effort did not approach Chile's (where figures did not include spending on higher education). Reimers (1994, p. 56) reports that during the 1980s the percentages of government spending on education were comparable in Latin America to other regions of the world. However, as a percent of GDP education spending was lower because national governments were themselves underfinanced. "There is a point where attempting to improve starving education systems becomes like trying to squeeze water out of stones," Reimers writes.

What is the overall implication of changing education policies for changes in the activities pursued by children in each country?

In Chile, the incentives represented by school meals was expanded beyond the poorest families, who had been targeted under the Pinochet regime. The finance of schooling was increased for rural students over the period of this study: The subvention eventually came to three times that provided to municipalities for students in more densely-populated areas. Increased preschool education meant fewer childcare responsibilities for elder siblings. General improvements in the quality of education and in the incentives to enroll students (by across-the-board increases in subvention values) would be expected to promote participation by young people in the school system and, indirectly, reduce further the likelihood of alternative activities. In a universal language, actions speak louder than words. Prioritization of education by the coalition government was far from hidden from public view after 1990. On the contrary, due to the "bidding" for public support that characterizes multi-party competition in Chile and other democracies, continuous attention was drawn to the infusion of money for education to address what President Aylwin called Chile's "social deficit" from the military period. Public support was all the more needed, as the revenues for education increases came from an 18 percent value added tax, never popular with Chile's electorate. The attention to public education policies through coalition government action could well have raised the consciousness of Chile's parents for the need for children to complete their schooling before entering the workforce.

In Peru, none of these administrative factors changed the interface of families and schools. Attendance continued to rise and fall in response to student demand but without any concomitant financial support for schools based on their enrollments. Parents had very little input into where schools were built or which schools their children attended. These decisions were determined based on political expediency rather than planning. During the period of the Peruvian study, control over school meal programs was removed from the Ministry of Education and, like school construction, brought closer to direct presidential authority. Teachers lost voice and teachers' morale—already low—fell even further.

Against these extremely negative factors in the subjective orientation of Peruvian families toward the educational alternatives, we can note only one positive influence, albeit an important one: the 1993 constitutional extension of compulsory schooling to include the entire five years of the secondary level. Yet information about the constitution is not widespread in Peru, there are many constitutional provisions which are obviously ignored, and the document itself does not enjoy the same legitimacy as do current constitutions of Mexico and Chile. Even the Fujimori government made little effort to promulgate the education reforms that it originally sought, moving on to other priorities and plans (including one to shorten secondary schooling to four years). The discontinuities in Peruvian education present the public with a confused picture of the commitment by the government to education. In Latin America generally, education ministers typically have a far shorter tenure in office then do ministers of economy and finance, because reform of education is such a long term project without any immediate political reward. Nonetheless, the average term for education ministers under both Garcia and Fujimori—less than one year—is far less even than the two-and-a-half-year average for Latin America nations generally (Corrales 2000).

Mexico's reforms could be expected to alter the needs and opportunities of families as they allocated their children's time. Most importantly, a system of basic education was instituted, as secondary school became compulsory. Much more ambiguously, with respect to incentives to families, the responsibility to govern education passed from Mexico City to the state governments. Governors attempted to increase the number of stakeholders in the success of quality, compulsory schooling, but by the end point of our study there was still no evidence that new channels of input had been expanded. Regional and ethnic disadvantages were addressed through integral family welfare programs, which aimed explicitly to incentivize families. The real funding per pupil increased for all levels, and teacher salaries recouped some of the ground they lost during the 1980s. In Mexico, we have reason to

4

A Multivariate Model Of Child Labor and School Attendance

LEIF JENSEN, DAVID ABLER, HÉCTOR ROBLES-VÁSQUEZ, PATRICIA MUÑOZ-SALAZAR, AND DAVID POST

As described in Chapter 1, for the investigation of Mexico we draw on the 1992 and 1996 rounds of the *Encuesta Nacional de Ingresos y Gastos de los Hogares (ENIGH)*, a household survey on socioeconomic characteristics, incomes, and expenditures. For Peru we draw on data from the 1985 and 1997 applications of the *Encuesta Nacional de Niveles de Vida (ENNIV)*, a household survey on time allocation, education, incomes, and expenditures. The *LSMS* (Living Standards Measurement Survey), as the *ENNIV* is known in English, was developed as a questionnaire "template" that was subsequently adapted and enlarged according to the precise needs of each country implementing the survey (Grosh and Glewwe 1995). Finally, for Chile we use data from the 1990 and 1996 applications of the *Encuesta de Caracterización Socio-Económica Nacional (CASEN)*, a comprehensive household survey on socioeconomic conditions, education, employment, and incomes.

This chapter investigates the activities of Chileans, Peruvians, and Mexicans who are ages twelve to seventeen, with a special focus on the determinants of their school participation. Because we have either no information, or very ambiguous information, about the family resources of children who are not members of the household (for example, domestic servants, children of domestic servants, tenants, guests), these children are excluded from our analyses. In the case of the 1992 and 1996 Mexican *ENIGH*s, and in the case of the 1985 Peruvian *ENNIV*, we also exclude households surveyed during the summer, when children were not attending school. Fortunately for our purposes, the sampling designs of the *ENIGH* and the *ENNIV* are not time-dependent. And the other surveys were all fielded entirely during the school year.

CHILDREN'S ACTIVITIES IN MEXICO, PERU, AND CHILE

The previous chapters of this book discuss theory and evidence about children's labor and schooling, focusing especially on the debate in Mexico, Peru, and Chile, and documenting the public regulation of children's alternatives. This chapter provides a detailed examination of factors leading children to labor force participation, either as an alternative to education or in conjunction with school attendance. Drawing on the national household survey data previously described in Chapter 1, multivariate models are estimated here in order to test possible reasons why some children attend school on a full-time basis, why others combine school with work, and why still others drop out of school and elect to work full-time. We compare our results across the three countries in order to ascertain whether factors determining child labor and school attendance differ internationally. We further compare our results over time to see how the determinants of child labor and school attendance have changed since the 1980s and early 1990s.

While Chapter 1 summarized the broad categories of children's activities, for our purposes here we must provide more detailed information about the alternatives and our methods of analysis. Appendix 4.1 presents the numbers of children engaged in each category of activity. We report these distributions for all of those aged twelve to seventeen as a whole, and broken down by two age groups (ages twelve to fourteen and fifteen to seventeen). Appendix 4.1 provides further detail by gender, residence (rural, urban), and income status (households divided into quintiles based on the reported income per capita). Based on their reported activities, we divide activities into four mutually exclusive and exhaustive categories. One category contains children who are neither attending school nor in the labor force (most likely who are performing unpaid domestic work). Another category contains children who participate in the labor force but do not attend school (whom we label as "full-time workers"). One category includes children who attend school but who also participate in the labor force. A fourth and final category is our reference group and forms the basis of the missing category in our mulitnomial logistic regression analysis (explained below). This category consists of children who are attending school but are not in the labor force (a group we sometimes refer to as "full-time students"). Although we have no direct information about the activities of the "neither school nor employment" group, we sometimes refer to these children as "home workers." This label is only a shorthand convenience, since the group includes not only children who are caring for siblings and doing household chores but also those who for one reason or another are unable (or unwilling) to attend school or work outside the home.

Of the three countries we study, Mexico has by far the highest incidence of children who are reported by their household heads neither to be working nor in school. About one-eighth (13 percent) of Mexicans aged twelve to seventeen were "home workers" in 1996, compared to only 3 percent in Peru in 1997 and 6 percent in Chile in 1996. Gender comparisons reveal that in Mexico girls are far more likely to be home workers (22 percent) than are boys (only 4 percent). Mexico is also characterized by the highest percentage of full-time workers. Nearly one-fifth (19 percent) of Mexican children were full-time workers in 1996, compared to 12 percent in Peru in 1997 and only about 5 percent in Chile in 1996. Consistent with traditional gender roles, the sex differences for full-time employment work in the opposite direction. Approximately 27 percent of Mexican boys were full-time workers in 1996, compared with 12 percent of girls.

The remaining two categories of children's activities involve school attendance, whether part- or full-time. Relative to Mexico and Chile, Peru has by far the highest prevalence of part-time students. Well more than a quarter (29 percent) of Peruvian children aged twelve to seventeen were part-time workers in 1997, compared to only 6 percent of Mexican and 1 percent of Chilean children in 1996. Chile, on the other hand, stands out for its remarkably high prevalence of full-time school attendance. Nearly nine out of ten (87 percent) children aged twelve to seventeen in Chile were attending school and were not in the labor force in 1996, compared with 62 percent of Mexican children and 56 percent of Peruvian children. Chile also ranks highest among the three countries if we calculate the percentage of children attending school on either a part-time or a full-time basis. About 89 percent of Chilean children were attending school on a part- or full-time basis in 1996, compared with 85 percent of Peruvian children in 1997 and 68 percent of Mexican children in 1996.

What changes in activities are most obvious over time? Both Peru and Chile showed statistically significant improvements in the percentages of children who were full-time students, while in Mexico there was little change in this regard. Peru and Chile also showed a corresponding decline in the percentage of children who were full-time workers. In Mexico, however, the percentage of children who were full-time workers was about the same in 1996 as in 1992 (19 percent). All three countries saw statistically significant declines over time in the percentage of children who were neither working nor in school (and who, hence, were likely to be "home workers"). However, whereas the decline in the prevalence of home workers in Peru and Chile was accompanied by a rise in the percentage of full-time students, in Mexico it was accompanied by a rise in the percentage of part-time students.

Age group differences in children's activities are as one might expect from the evidence seen previously in Chapter 1. In each country, the percentage of children who are full-time students is lower among fifteen to seventeen year olds than among those aged twelve to fourteen. Conversely, the prevalence of full-time work increases sharply with age, as does the likelihood of working at home. Interestingly, combining school and work (that is, the prevalence of part-time students) is not strongly related to age in these three countries.

When broken down by place of residence, the surveys reveal that child labor is concentrated in rural areas. This is unsurprising, because children often work on family-owned farms. To be sure, many urban children work in family-owned small businesses in these three countries, but this is less common than agricultural work among rural children. In Chile, gains in school attendance and decreases in child labor occurred in both rural and urban areas. In Peru, gains in school attendance also occurred in both areas. In Mexico, on the other hand, the percentage of children who were full-time students stayed the same in urban areas, but decreased in rural areas. Similarly, the percentage of children who were full-time workers declined slightly between 1992 and 1996 in urban areas but rose in rural areas. Robles Vásquez (2000) argues that these changes in children's activities in rural areas of Mexico stemmed from changes in Mexican agricultural price and trade policies. In 1989, the Mexican government began to phase out its system of agricultural price supports ("*precios de garantía*"). In addition, the implementation of NAFTA in the 1990s began a process of liberalizing agricultural trade that has put significant downward pressure on corn prices received by Mexican farmers, a staple crop for large numbers of poor farmers. Impoverished farmers responded to these economic shocks by diversifying their income sources and switching to more labor-intensive production technologies (De Janvry et al. 1997). In this context, it is likely that small farmers increased their use of family labor, including child labor.

To facilitate comparisons of the role of income over time, we attempted to standardize the relative wealth and poverty of each household. We tested the impact on children's activities of a child's economic status as measured by their position in the national distribution of per capita household income, divided into quintiles. In both Mexico and Peru, the percentage of children who were full-time workers was substantially larger in the poorest quintile than the richest quintile. The middle three quintiles in each country fall between the bottom and top quintiles in terms of child labor force participation. Appendix 4.1 provides the survey sample cell number of cases in each group, for each age, for each year, and in each country. For Peru, the percentage of children who were part-time students was significantly larger in the poorer quintiles than in the richer quintiles. For all three countries, the percentage of children who were full-time students was substantially smaller within the bottom quintile as compared to the top quintile. For example, in the case of Mexico, only about one-half of children in the bottom quintile were full-time students, while over four-fifths of children in the top quintile were full-time students. For Peru, the proportion of children who were full-time students was a little more than one-fourth in the bottom quintile versus more than three-fourths in the top quintile. In Chile, the prevalence of full-time students increased over time in all five quintiles, with a corresponding decline in the prevalence of children who were full-time workers. Peru also showed improvements across quintiles, but not to as uniform a degree as Chile. In Mexico, the percentage of children who were full-time students increased between 1992 and 1996 in the second and fourth quintiles but showed no statistically significant change in the other quintiles.

A MULTINOMIAL MODEL OF CHILDREN'S ACTIVITIES

In this section we describe a statistical model commonly used to investigate reasons why some children attend school on a full-time basis, why others combine school with work, and why still others drop out of school and work full-time. The model we have used is a multinomial logistic regression model. Under the simplifying assumptions of a multinomial logistic regression model, a decision agent (either an individual or a household) faces the problem of a choice between discrete options, for example about which activity to pursue, where to live, or which candidate to vote for. The individual or household is assumed to make a choice that maximizes their utility and satisfaction. The level of utility associated with each option is assumed to depend, in a manner specified by the multinomial logistic model, on the characteristics of that individual and possibly also the characteristics of the individual's household and community. Multinomial logistic models have been used extensively by social scientists for modeling choices among occupations and activities. The properties, advantages, and limitations of the multinomial logistic model are discussed by Maddala (1983) and Liao (1994).

In our investigation, households are assumed to choose among four mutually exclusive and exhaustive activities for each of their children: neither attend school nor participate in the labor force (home worker); drop out of school and participate in the labor force (full-time worker); attend school without participating in the labor force (full-time student); and attend school while also participating in the labor force (part-time student). The so-called "reference" category in our model is that of full-time students. This means that the estimates produced by our model indicate the influence of the model's explanatory variables on the probability that a household selects one of the alternative options, relative to the probability that the child is a full-time student without any reported economic activity.

We estimate separate models for each year in order to permit us to see how the determinants of child labor and school attendance may have changed over time in each country. For each country and year, we estimate separate models for rural and urban areas because of significant rural-urban differences in labor force participation rates, the types of work performed by children, and socioeconomic conditions (Muñoz-Salazar 2000). In the case of Peru, the number of rural children in the 1997 sample who were home workers was too small to permit the inclusion of home workers as a separate category. Therefore, in order to preserve comparability among results for rural and urban areas, we combine home workers and full-time workers into a single category in all the estimations for Peru.

The multinomial logistic models are estimated using weighted maximum likelihood as described by Maddala (1983). The weight for each observation is the household's population weight. The weights are employed to account for the non-proportional sampling scheme used in each household survey; in other words, some regions of each country were oversampled relative to their populations while others were undersampled. The weights are scaled so that the average weight in each sample is one, yielding weighted N's approximately equal to sample size.

The dependent and explanatory variables used in the analysis can be found in Appendix 4.2. In order to maximize comparability in results among the three countries, the variables are defined in the same way for all three countries, with the exception of the geographic dummy variables. The geographic dummies are defined in a way appropriate to each country. We now provide the justification for the explanatory variables included in the model.

A dummy variable for whether the child's age falls within the fifteen to seventeen range versus the twelve to fourteen range (*Age15–17*) is included because older children are more likely to work than younger ones. Labor market opportunities increase with age, and it is normatively more acceptable and less objectionable for children to work as they grow older (Basu 1999; Grootaert and Kanbur 1995). The number of years of education completed by the child at the time of the survey (*Education*) is included because it indicates parents' previous commitments to schooling prior to the time of the survey, as well as the child's ability to succeed in school (Barnes 1999; Powell and Steelman 1993). We include a dummy variable for the child's gender (*Gender*) because of the abundant research showing that boys tend to have greater educational opportunities than do girls (for reviews see Post 2001; King and Hill 1993; Salazar 1991). A dummy variable for whether the child is the son or daughter of the household head (*HeadKid*) is included because heads may favor their own children over other children in the household when it comes to investments in education. In urban areas, families sometimes have an arrangement with rural relatives whereby a child from the rural family lives with the urban family in exchange for work in household enterprises or "rent" financed by working as a wage earner (Robles Vásquez 2000).

Four variables measuring the sibship structure of the household are included: the number of siblings within one year of age of the child (*sibship density*); the number of siblings ages five or younger (*Num5*); the number of males in the household ages eighteen or older, not counting the head and spouse (*Num18M*); and the number of females in the household aged eighteen or older, excluding the head and spouse (*Num18F*). Research indicates that not only is the number of brothers and sisters important in terms of household investments in education but so, too, is the order among siblings (Butcher and Case 1994; King and Hill 1993; Patrinos and Psacharopoulos 1997; Powell and Steelman 1990, 1993; Shavit and Pierce 1991). Children in households where many children are close in age face greater competition for scarce family resources for books, clothes, and other school supplies. This close proximity may represent a barrier to discourage schooling. Children with more siblings aged five or younger may be pressed into work as wage earners or in household enterprises in order to help cover the expenses of these younger siblings. Girls may also be expected to drop out of school to help care for younger siblings and do household chores. Children in households with more adult males or females may be more likely to attend school because these adults can do some of the work that children would otherwise do as wage earners, in household enterprises, or in the home itself.

The number of years of education completed by the household head (*HeadEducation*) is included in the model because of widespread evidence that parents' education has a strong positive influence on the education of their children (Kuo and Hauser 1996; Strauss and Thomas 1995). The household head's age (*HeadAge*) is included because older heads tend to have greater income-earning potential (due to their greater work experience) and more assets, which would encourage them to leave their children in school rather than pull them out to work. For very old household heads, the advantages of being older may diminish or even turn into disadvantages, but the majority of household heads in our samples are relatively young (fifty-five or younger). The head's gender (*HeadGender*) is included because females tend to have less income-earning potential than males due to labor market discrimination and lower levels of labor market experience (Desai 1992; ECLAC 1999; Lloyd and Desai 1992). This may force female-headed households to put their children to work to help cover household expenses. On the other hand, female-headed households may allocate a larger percentage of their resources to education (and less to alcohol and tobacco) than male-headed households (Lloyd and Blanc 1996).

The head's occupational status is represented by three dummy variables: whether or not the head is working (*HeadNotWork*); if the head is working, whether he/she is an entrepreneur or self-employed (*HeadSelfEmp*); and if the head is working, whether he/she is a wage earner (*HeadWageEmp*). The reference category, which is excluded from the analysis to prevent perfect multi-collinearity with the model's intercept, is *HeadWageEmp*. There is some evidence that parents who work in self-employed activities such as agriculture are less likely to invest in their children's education (Knaul and Parker 1998; Salazar 1991). This could be due to the fact that agriculture and family-owned enterprises provide ready opportunities for parents to put children to work.

With respect to the head's spouse, we include a dummy variable (*NoSpouse*) to indicate whether or not there is a spouse in the household. Single-headed households are more likely to have a lower income-earning potential, particularly if the head is female (Desai 1992; ECLAC 1999; Lloyd and Desai 1992). This may encourage such households to put their children to work. In addition, the head in a single-headed household must do both the work and household chores that would otherwise be divided in some way between the head and spouse. Children in such households, particularly girls, may be kept out of school to help with household chores.

The spouse's occupational status is represented by three dummy variables: whether or not the spouse is working (*SpouseNotWork*); if the spouse is working, whether he/she is an entrepreneur or self-employed (*SpouseSelfEmp*); and if the spouse is working, whether he/she is a wage earner (*SpouseWageEmp*). Each of these three dummy variables is set equal to zero in the case where there is no spouse in the household. The reference category, which is excluded from the analysis, is *SpouseNotWork*.

Household income is represented by five dummy variables for household per capita income (*Quintile1, Quintile2, Quintile3, Quintile4, Quintile5*). The dummy variable *Quintile1* is equal to one if the household falls within the first (or poorest) quintile in terms of per capita income, and equal to zero otherwise. The other four household income variables are defined in a similar manner. The reference category, which is excluded from the analysis, is *Quintile5*. We use per capita income rather than total income in order to account for the fact that larger households must spread their income across a larger number of members. Poverty or low household income is generally considered one of the main causes of child labor in developing countries (Basu 1999; Grootaert and Kanbur 1995; Salazar 1991). Nonetheless, there are a few studies finding little relation between household income and school attendance or child labor, holding constant other factors that influence child time allocation (Patrinos and Psacharopoulos 1997; Psacharopoulos 1997; Rodríguez and Abler 1998).

We also include geographic dummy variables appropriate to each country. The geographic dummies are meant to capture differences between national regions in the determinants of children's activities that are not captured by the other explanatory variables in the model.

FINDINGS FOR MEXICO

The estimates of the multinomial logistic regression model for Mexico are presented in Tables 4.1–4.4. Table 4.1 presents results for rural Mexico, 1992; Table 4.2 for urban Mexico, 1992; Table 4.3 for rural Mexico, 1996; and Table 4.4 for urban Mexico, 1996. Values for McFadden's R^2, a commonly used pseudo-R^2 to measure explained variation in nonlinear statistical models, range from 0.25 to 0.31. These values are relatively good considering the micro-level nature of the data, which tends to depress R^2 measures because it is often difficult to capture the wide range of unique factors that can influence an individual's choices. An asterisk in Tables 4.1–4.4 indicates a coefficient that is statistically significant. For these variables, the null hypothesis that the coefficient is equal to zero can be rejected at a 5 percent significance level. Our discussion here centers on the statistically significant coefficients.

In addition to reporting the parameter estimates and their standard errors, Tables 4.1–4.4 also report relative risk ratios for each variable in the model and their respective standard errors. The "relative risk ratio" (RRR) expresses the effect of a one-unit increase in an explanatory variable on the probability ratio, where [insertsymbol] is the probability that a child is engaged in activity ([insertsymbol] = 1 for home workers, 2 for full-time workers, and 4 for part-time students) and [insertsymbol] is the probability that a child is a full-time student (the reference category). A value of RRR greater than one indicates that an increase in an explanatory variable leads to an *increase* in the probability ratio , so that there is a increase in the probability of a child being engaged in activity relative to the probability of the child being a full-time student. By contrast, a value of RRR less than one indicates that an increase in an explanatory variable leads to a *decrease* in the probability ratio, so that there is a decrease in the probability of a child being engaged in activity relative to the probability of the child being a full-time student.

The multivariate results in Tables 4.1–4.4 reinforce several of the descriptive findings noted above. The results indicate that fifteen- to seventeen-year-old children are substantially less likely than are twelve- to fourteen- year-olds to be full-time students and substantially more likely to be engaged in other activities (home worker, full-time worker, part-time student). This is evidenced by the estimated RRR's for the *Age15–17* variable, which are all substantially greater than one. The results also indicate that girls are significantly more likely than boys to be home workers and significantly less likely to be full-time workers or part-time students. This is reflected in the estimated RRR's for the

Table 4.1: Multinomial Logistic Regression Model Estimates and Relative Risk Ratio, Rural Mexico, 1992

Estimates (Reference Category is Full-Time Students)

Variable	No work or study Coefficient	Std. Error	Full-Time Workers Coefficient	Std. Error	Works and studies Coefficient	Std. Error
Age15-17	1.895*	0.171	3.407*	0.195	0.744*	0.379
Gender	2.318*	0.187	-1.550*	0.175	-0.667*	0.340
Education	-0.185*	0.035	-0.325*	0.036	-0.092	0.076
Num5	0.120	0.077	0.023	0.084	0.232	0.181
Num18M	0.171	0.096	-0.211*	0.107	-0.889*	0.337
Num18F	-0.138	0.105	-0.072	0.102	-0.795*	0.311
HeadEducation	-0.127*	0.037	-0.108*	0.038	0.038	0.074
HeadAge	-0.028*	0.009	-0.017*	0.009	0.057*	0.017
HeadGender	-2.048*	0.564	-0.902	0.676	0.798	1.816
Quintile1	-0.384	0.642	0.278	0.603	-1.023	0.862
Quintile2	-0.667	0.642	0.781	0.601	-0.544	0.842
Quintile3	-0.653	0.653	1.168	0.607	-0.427	0.852
Quintile4	-1.557*	0.718	1.046	0.636	-0.455	0.913
Density	-0.156	0.185	0.092	0.185	0.030	0.406
HeadKid	-0.749*	0.296	0.383	0.330	0.387	0.707
North	0.339	0.234	-0.068	0.230	1.204*	0.464
NorthPacific	-0.713	0.393	-0.608	0.343	0.606	0.680
Gulf	-0.442*	0.202	-1.594*	0.233	0.229	0.481
SouthPacific	-0.512*	0.213	-1.254*	0.222	0.325	0.508
HeadNotWork	0.426	0.310	-0.078	0.328	-0.845	0.851
HeadSelfEmp	-0.116	0.160	0.654*	0.176	-0.061	0.361
NoSpouse	1.340*	0.517	1.466*	0.634	0.343	1.745
SpouseWageEmp	-1.271*	0.518	-0.792	0.438	-0.047	1.045
SpouseSelfEmp	-0.537*	0.233	-0.433	0.242	0.554	0.388
Intercept	0.895	0.885	0.246	0.893	-5.039*	1.668

Relative Risk Ratio (RRR)

Variable	No work or study RRR	Std. Error	Full-Time Workers RRR	Std. Error	Works and studies RRR	Std. Error
Age15-17	6.651*	1.137	30.186*	5.885	2.105*	0.799
Gender	10.156*	1.898	0.212*	0.037	0.513*	0.175
Education	0.831*	0.029	0.723*	0.026	0.912	0.069
Num5	1.128	0.087	1.024	0.086	1.261	0.228
Num18M	1.187	0.114	0.809*	0.086	0.411*	0.138
Num18F	0.871	0.091	0.931	0.095	0.451*	0.140
HeadEducation	0.881*	0.032	0.898*	0.034	1.039	0.077
HeadAge	0.972*	0.008	0.983*	0.009	1.058*	0.018
HeadGender	0.129*	0.073	0.406	0.274	2.222	4.034
Quintile1	0.681	0.437	1.321	0.797	0.360	0.310
Quintile2	0.513	0.330	2.183	1.312	0.580	0.489
Quintile3	0.520	0.340	3.217	1.954	0.652	0.556
Quintile4	0.211*	0.151	2.848	1.812	0.634	0.579
Density	0.855	0.158	1.096	0.203	1.031	0.418
HeadKid	0.473*	0.140	1.467	0.484	1.473	1.042
North	1.403	0.329	0.934	0.215	3.334*	1.546
NorthPacific	0.490	0.192	0.544	0.186	1.833	1.246
Gulf	0.643*	0.130	0.203*	0.047	1.258	0.605
SouthPacific	0.599*	0.128	0.285*	0.063	1.384	0.703
HeadNotWork	1.531	0.475	0.925	0.303	0.430	0.366
HeadSelfEmp	0.890	0.142	1.924*	0.338	0.940	0.339
NoSpouse	3.818*	1.973	4.331*	2.747	1.410	2.459
SpouseWageEmp	0.281*	0.145	0.453	0.199	0.954	0.997
SpouseSelfEmp	0.584*	0.136	0.648	0.157	1.740	0.675

Note: $N = 1,850$. McFadden's $R^2 = 0.31$. An * denotes statistical significance at the 5% level.

Table 4.2: Multinomial Logistic Regression Model Estimates and Relative Risk Ratio, Urban Mexico, 1992

	Estimates (Reference Category is Full-Time Students)						Relative Risk Ratio (RRR)					
	No work or study		Full-Time Workers		Works and studies		No work or study		Full-Time Workers		Works and studies	
Variable	Coefficient	Standard Error	Coefficient	Standard Error	Coefficient	Standard Error	RRR	Standard Error	RRR	Standard Error	RRR	Standard Error
Age 15-17	2.521*	0.212	3.677*	0.213	1.299*	0.341	12.437*	2.641	39.535*	8.426	3.665*	1.251
Gender	1.807*	0.192	-0.728*	0.153	-0.233	0.248	6.091*	1.171	0.483*	0.074	0.792	0.197
Education	-0.449*	0.042	-0.390*	0.038	0.105	0.076	0.638*	0.027	0.677*	0.026	1.111	0.084
Num5	0.136	0.096	0.290*	0.091	0.257	0.169	1.146	0.109	1.337*	0.122	1.294	0.218
Num18M	0.319*	0.100	-0.312*	0.100	-0.551*	0.187	1.376*	0.138	0.732*	0.073	0.576*	0.108
Num18F	0.119	0.092	0.005	0.089	0.106	0.147	1.127	0.103	1.005	0.089	1.112	0.164
HeadEducation	-0.242*	0.034	-0.220*	0.028	-0.111*	0.042	0.785*	0.027	0.802*	0.022	0.895*	0.037
HeadAge	-0.030*	0.011	-0.033*	0.009	-0.001	0.015	0.970*	0.010	0.968*	0.009	0.999	0.015
HeadGender	0.201	0.545	-0.099	0.440	0.167	0.694	1.222	0.667	0.906	0.399	1.181	0.820
Quintile1	1.687*	0.458	1.390*	0.404	1.087	0.610	5.405*	2.474	4.014*	1.621	2.966	1.810
Quintile2	0.507	0.423	0.954*	0.351	-0.258	0.542	1.661	0.703	2.596*	0.911	0.773	0.419
Quintile3	0.626	0.413	0.876*	0.343	0.600	0.467	1.870	0.772	2.401*	0.824	1.821	0.850
Quintile4	0.611	0.412	1.024*	0.338	0.785	0.445	1.841	0.758	2.785*	0.942	2.192	0.975
Density	0.126	0.197	0.533*	0.160	0.650*	0.269	1.134	0.223	1.704*	0.273	1.915*	0.515
HeadKid	-0.662*	0.294	-0.767*	0.249	-0.130	0.445	0.516*	0.151	0.465*	0.116	0.878	0.391
North	-0.124	0.251	0.336	0.199	0.911*	0.338	0.883	0.222	1.400	0.279	2.486*	0.841
NorthPacific	0.126	0.348	0.083	0.294	0.742	0.447	1.134	0.395	1.087	0.320	2.100	0.939
Gulf	-0.527	0.288	-0.399	0.256	0.395	0.477	0.590	0.170	0.671	0.172	1.485	0.709
SouthPacific	-1.265*	0.286	-0.831*	0.256	1.573*	0.360	0.282*	0.081	0.435*	0.111	4.822*	1.738
HeadNotWork	-0.725*	0.298	-0.356	0.260	0.164	0.450	0.484*	0.144	0.701	0.182	1.179	0.531
HeadSelfEmp	-0.207	0.203	0.075	0.175	0.727*	0.286	0.813	0.165	1.078	0.188	2.070*	0.592
NoSpouse	-0.051	0.522	0.380	0.427	0.509	0.703	0.950	0.497	1.463	0.624	1.663	1.169
SpouseWageEmp	-0.151	0.309	-0.171	0.242	-0.190	0.482	0.859	0.266	0.843	0.204	0.827	0.399
SpouseSelfEmp	0.123	0.245	0.089	0.229	0.795*	0.315	1.131	0.277	1.093	0.250	2.214*	0.697
Intercept	0.789	0.837	1.363	0.704	-5.260*	1.259						

Note: $N = 2,333$. McFadden's $R^2 = 0.31$. An * denotes statistical significance at the 5% level.

Table 4.3: Multinomial Logistic Regression Model Estimates and Relative Risk Ratio, Rural Mexico, 1996

	Estimates (Reference Category is Full-Time Students)						Relative Risk Ratio (RRR)					
	No work or study		Full-Time Workers		Works and studies		No work or study		Full-Time Workers		Works and studies	
Variable	Coefficient	Standard Error	Coefficient	Standard Error	Coefficient	Standard Error	RRR	Standard Error	RRR	Standard Error	RRR	Standard Error
Age15-17	1.847*	0.168	2.749*	0.154	0.505*	0.200	6.342*	1.064	15.633*	2.403	1.657*	0.332
Gender	2.395*	0.210	-1.092*	0.140	-1.161*	0.179	10.968*	2.300	0.336*	0.047	0.313*	0.056
Education	-0.210*	0.034	-0.267*	0.030	0.006	0.040	0.811*	0.028	0.765*	0.023	1.006	0.041
Num5	0.140	0.084	0.098	0.073	-0.035	0.096	1.150	0.097	1.103	0.080	0.965	0.093
Num18M	0.195	0.105	0.047	0.092	0.165	0.120	1.215	0.127	1.048	0.096	1.179	0.142
Num18F	-0.569*	0.118	-0.040	0.096	0.120	0.128	0.566*	0.067	0.961	0.092	1.127	0.145
HeadEducation	-0.139*	0.040	-0.083*	0.033	0.102*	0.038	0.870*	0.035	0.920*	0.030	1.107	0.042
HeadAge	0.014	0.009	0.010	0.008	-0.003	0.010	1.014	0.009	1.010	0.008	0.997	0.010
HeadGender	-0.891	0.516	-0.794	0.440	-0.741	0.563	0.410	0.212	0.452	0.199	0.477	0.268
Quintile1	1.169	0.650	0.379	0.418	1.565*	0.698	3.218	2.090	1.461	0.611	4.782*	3.337
Quintile2	1.140	0.647	0.517	0.417	1.591*	0.700	3.125	2.023	1.677	0.699	4.911*	3.438
Quintile3	1.201	0.659	0.293	0.435	2.070*	0.699	3.322	2.190	1.341	0.583	7.928*	5.539
Quintile4	0.622	0.724	-0.333	0.483	1.123	0.774	1.863	1.349	0.717	0.346	3.075	2.380
Density	0.017	0.167	0.051	0.150	-0.032	0.200	1.017	0.170	1.052	0.158	0.969	0.194
HeadKid	-0.831*	0.255	0.284	0.249	0.971*	0.385	0.436*	0.111	1.328	0.331	2.640*	1.015
North	0.117	0.257	0.401	0.209	-0.841*	0.337	1.124	0.289	1.494	0.313	0.431*	0.145
NorthPacific	-0.059	0.342	-0.790*	0.321	-1.212*	0.491	0.943	0.323	0.454*	0.146	0.298*	0.146
Gulf	0.205	0.226	-0.589*	0.199	-0.542*	0.257	1.227	0.277	0.555*	0.111	0.581*	0.149
SouthPacific	0.198	0.207	0.008	0.172	0.323	0.204	1.219	0.253	1.008	0.174	1.382	0.282
HeadNotWork	-0.141	0.265	-0.574*	0.252	0.978*	0.310	0.868	0.230	0.564*	0.142	2.660*	0.824
HeadSelfEmp	-0.258	0.177	-0.096	0.147	0.601*	0.197	0.773	0.137	0.908	0.134	1.824*	0.359
NoSpouse	-0.068	0.459	1.066*	0.413	1.233*	0.523	0.934	0.429	2.904*	1.198	3.433*	1.794
SpouseWageEmp	-0.531	0.274	-0.158	0.258	0.566	0.314	0.588	0.161	0.853	0.220	1.761	0.553
SpouseSelfEmp	-0.546*	0.187	0.504*	0.155	1.062*	0.190	0.579*	0.108	1.655*	0.257	2.893*	0.550
Intercept	-2.683*	0.904	-0.862	0.694	-4.813*	1.073						

Note: N = 2,030. McFadden's R^2 = 0.24. An * denotes statistical significance at the 5% level.

Table 4.4: Multinomial Logistic Regression Model Estimates and Relative Risk Ratio, Urban Mexico, 1996

Estimates (Reference Category is Full-Time Students)

Variable	No work or study Coefficient	No work or study Standard Error	Full-Time Workers Coefficient	Full-Time Workers Standard Error	Works and studies Coefficient	Works and studies Standard Error
Age15-17	2.559*	0.198	3.247*	0.187	1.021*	0.234
Gender	1.555*	0.176	-0.469*	0.135	-0.649*	0.189
Education	-0.395*	0.037	-0.439*	0.033	-0.098*	0.049
Num5	0.339*	0.086	0.134	0.086	0.349*	0.119
Num18M	0.211*	0.089	-0.199*	0.090	-0.161	0.140
Num18F	-0.284*	0.096	-0.066	0.080	0.108	0.114
HeadEducation	-0.097*	0.024	-0.149*	0.022	-0.078*	0.027
HeadAge	0.011	0.009	0.011	0.008	-0.009	0.012
HeadGender	0.143	0.451	0.896*	0.417	1.364*	0.690
Quintile1	1.102*	0.359	1.364*	0.337	0.381	0.422
Quintile2	0.716*	0.323	1.134*	0.305	0.563	0.357
Quintile3	0.622*	0.309	0.963*	0.297	0.106	0.366
Quintile4	0.069	0.320	0.954*	0.297	0.631	0.333
Density	-0.079	0.192	0.558*	0.155	0.298	0.234
HeadKid	-0.797*	0.235	0.075*	0.239	0.180	0.372
North	-0.054	0.199	0.019	0.175	-0.038	0.287
NorthPacific	-0.333	0.313	0.254	0.251	0.212	0.373
Gulf	-0.515	0.276	-0.466	0.249	0.904*	0.259
SouthPacific	-0.835*	0.314	-0.487*	0.241	0.922*	0.265
HeadNotWork	-1.035*	0.261	-0.309	0.205	-0.342	0.322
HeadSelfEmp	-0.245	0.187	0.397*	0.157	0.939*	0.201
NoSpouse	0.124	0.437	-0.457	0.408	-0.772	0.687
SpouseWageEmp	0.329	0.228	0.225	0.216	0.129	0.309
SpouseSelfEmp	0.247	0.232	0.422*	0.198	0.949*	0.232
Intercept	-1.465*	0.692	-1.374*	0.624	-2.982*	0.874

Relative Risk Ratio (RRR)

Variable	No work or study RRR	No work or study Standard Error	Full-Time Workers RRR	Full-Time Workers Standard Error	Works and studies RRR	Works and studies Standard Error
Age15-17	12.923*	2.555	5.725*	4.815	2.777*	0.651
Gender	4.736*	0.835	0.626*	0.084	0.522*	0.098
Education	0.674*	0.025	0.645*	0.021	0.907*	0.044
Num5	1.404*	0.120	1.143	0.098	1.417*	0.168
Num18M	1.235*	0.110	0.820*	0.074	0.851	0.119
Num18F	0.753*	0.072	0.936	0.075	1.114	0.127
HeadEducation	0.908*	0.022	0.862*	0.019	0.925*	0.025
HeadAge	1.011	0.009	1.011	0.008	0.991	0.012
HeadGender	1.154	0.521	2.449*	1.022	3.910*	2.699
Quintile1	3.010*	1.080	3.910*	1.319	1.463	0.618
Quintile2	2.045*	0.661	3.107*	0.946	1.757	0.627
Quintile3	1.862*	0.576	2.621*	0.780	1.112	0.407
Quintile4	1.071	0.343	2.597*	0.771	1.879	0.626
Density	0.924	0.177	1.748*	0.272	1.347	0.315
HeadKid	0.451*	0.106	1.078	0.257	1.185	0.441
North	0.948	0.188	1.020	0.179	0.963	0.276
NorthPacific	0.717	0.224	1.289	0.324	1.236	0.462
Gulf	0.597	0.165	0.627	0.156	2.470*	0.641
SouthPacific	0.434*	0.136	0.614*	0.148	2.514*	0.666
HeadNotWork	0.355*	0.093	0.734	0.150	0.711	0.229
HeadSelfEmp	0.782	0.147	1.487*	0.233	2.558*	0.514
NoSpouse	1.132	0.495	0.633	0.258	0.462	0.317
SpouseWageEmp	1.390	0.317	1.253	0.270	1.137	0.352
SpouseSelfEmp	1.280	0.298	1.525*	0.302	2.584*	0.599

Note: $N = 3,007$. McFadden's $R^2 = 0.25$. An * denotes statistical significance at the 5% level.

Gender variable, which are significantly greater than one for the home worker category and less than one for the full-time worker and part-time student categories.

Next we consider the effects of educational attainment, both of children themselves and of their household head. The estimated RRR's for the *Education* variable are generally in the 0.6–0.8 range and are statistically significant. This means that a one-year increase in a child's education is associated with a reduction by 20–40 percent in the likelihood that child is a home worker, a full-time worker, or combines work with school, as opposed to the child being a full-time student. As noted above, the number of years of education completed by a child is an indicator of parents' previous commitments to education before the survey, and the child's prior demonstrated ability to succeed in school based on personal and family resources. The estimated RRR's for the *HeadEducation* variable for the home-worker and full-time worker categories are all in the neighborhood of 0.8–0.9 and statistically significant. This means that a one-year increase in the household head's education reduces the likelihood that the child is a home worker or full-time worker (as opposed to a full-time student) by 10–20 percent.

The estimates of the *HeadKid* variable in the neither school nor work category suggest that daughters and sons of household heads (when compared to stepchildren living in the household) are only about half as likely to be a home worker rather than a full-time student. Quite possibly heads favor their biological children over other children in the household when it comes to investing in education. The estimated coefficients for the *HeadGender* variable are generally not statistically significant. However, some of the estimated coefficients for the *NoSpouse* variable, which is another indicator in our model of female-headed households, are statistically significant. They suggest that, at least in rural areas, children in households without a spouse are significantly more likely to be full-time workers (and possibly also home workers) as opposed to being full-time students.

The variables for the head's occupation and spouse's occupation are also statistically significant in some cases, but not in others, with few clear tendencies across survey years. Perhaps the most important finding is that children in households in which the head or spouse are self-employed are generally more likely to be part-time students rather than full-time students. It appears that children in households where either the head or spouse is self-employed are approximately two to three times more likely than other children to be part-time students rather than full-time students. Children in households in which both the head and spouse are self-employed are approximately four to five times more likely to be part-time students rather than full-time students. This may be explained by the fact that agriculture and family-owned enterprises provide ready opportunities for parents to put children to work.

The sibship size and structure variables are statistically significant in some cases but not others, again with few clear tendencies across survey years. For urban Mexico, the estimates for the *Num18M* variable for the full-time worker category suggest that children in households with more adult males are 20–30 percent less likely to be full-time workers as opposed to full-time students. This also means that children in such households are 20–40 percent more likely to be home workers rather than full-time students. Finally, the *Density* variable for the full-time worker category indicate that children who have more siblings present who are close in age have a greater likelihood of being full-time workers as opposed to full-time students.

Household economic resources, measured as membership in one of five income per capita quintiles, have some effect on children's activities. In urban Mexico children in the first four per capita income quintiles are 2.4 to 4 times more likely than children in the top quintile to be full-time workers as opposed to full-time students. Similarly, in rural Mexico, the results for 1996 indicate that children in the first three quintiles are 4.8–7.9 times more likely than children in the top quintile of being part-time students as opposed to full-time students.

In sum, the most important factors determining the activities of Mexican children are the age of the child, the child's gender, the household's per capita income, the years of education completed by the child, the years of education completed by the household head, whether the head and/or spouse are self-employed and, in rural areas, the presence or absence of a spouse.

On the whole, the results for 1992 and 1996 are reasonably similar, which one might expect given that only four years separate the two surveys. However, there are two major differences worth noting. The estimated RRR for the *Age15–17* variable for the full-time workers category in rural areas is approximately 30 in 1992, but was approximately 16 in 1996. Similarly, the estimated RRR for the *Age15–17* variable for the full-time workers category in urban areas is approximately 40 in 1992, but was approximately 26 in 1996. This means that while fifteen- to seventeen-year-olds were substantially more likely than twelve- to fourteen-year-olds to be full-time workers in both survey years, the impact of being older was not as great in 1996 as in 1992. However, this does not appear to be due to any decline between 1992 and 1996 in the probability of fifteen- to seventeen-year-olds being full-time workers. Instead, as already suggested by the figures in Chapter 1 and in Appendix 4.1, twelve- to fourteen-year-olds were more likely to work full-time in 1996 than in 1992.

FINDINGS FOR PERU

The Peruvian estimates of the multinomial logistic regression model are shown in Tables 4.5–4.8. Table 4.5 presents results for rural Peru, 1985; Table 4.6 for urban Peru, 1985; Table 4.7 for rural Peru, 1997; and Table 4.8 for urban Peru, 1997. Values for McFadden's R^2 range from 0.12 to 0.20. These are not as high as the McFadden's R^2's for Mexico, indicating that the model fits the Peruvian data less well than the Mexican data. As before, an asterisk indicates that a coefficient is statistically significant at the 5 percent level, and our discussion centers on significant coefficients. Because of smaller sample sizes, we had to combine the "no work or schooling" and the full-time workers into a single category in all the estimations for Peru. Our multivariate results for Peru suggest that fifteen- to seventeen-year-old children are substantially less likely than twelve- to fourteen-year-olds to be full-time students, while they are substantially more likely to home workers or full-time workers. The coefficients for the *Age15–17* variable for the part-time student category, on the other hand, are generally insignificant or weak. This means that older (as compared to younger) children are only somewhat more likely to be part-time students as opposed to full-time students. The results for *Gender* indicate that females are generally less likely than boys to be part-time students as opposed to full-time students. With the exception of rural Peru in 1985, gender does not have a statistically significant impact on whether a child is in the home worker/full-time worker category, as opposed to the full-time student category. This surprising finding probably reflects the fact that we combined the home worker and full-time worker categories for Peru in order to obtain the necessary larger cell sizes for the analysis.

The results of children's educational attainment (*Education*) for the home worker/full-time worker category suggest that increasing a child's education by one year reduces the likelihood of the child being a home worker or full-time worker as opposed to a full-time student by 10–30 percent. On the other hand, children with more education are neither more nor less likely to be part-time students than full-time students. The coefficients for the *HeadEducation* variable indicate, as was the case in Mexico, that children with better-educated household heads are less likely to be a home worker, full-time worker, or part-time student as opposed to a full-time student.

The estimated RRR's for the *HeadKid* variable for the work while study category are 1.9 for rural Peru in 1985 and 2.3 for rural Peru in 1997. This means that daughters and sons of household heads in rural areas are about twice as likely as other children in the household to combine work with schooling, as opposed to being solely a full-time student. This seems puzzling, since we expect household heads to favor their own children in terms of investments in education free from employment. Having other children in the household might indicate living in an extended household, with multiple families, a situation in which the

Table 4.5: Multinomial Logistic Regression Model Estimates and Relative Risk Ratio, Rural Peru, 1985

	Estimates (Reference Category is Full-Time Students)								Relative Risk Ratio (RRR)			
	No work or study & Full-Time Workers		Works and studies				No work or study & Full-Time Workers				Works and studies	
Variable	Coefficient	Standard Error	Coefficient	Standard Error			Coefficient	Standard Error			RRR	Standard Error
Age15-17	2.219*	0.206	0.439*	0.192			9.199*	1.891			1.551*	0.298
Gender	0.608*	0.172	-0.304	0.156			1.836*	0.316			0.738	0.115
Education	-0.255*	0.044	-0.023	0.041			0.775*	0.034			0.977	0.040
Num5	0.128	0.086	0.008	0.082			1.137	0.098			1.008	0.083
Num18M	-0.069	0.114	0.046	0.097			0.933	0.106			1.047	0.102
Num18F	-0.617*	0.144	-0.239*	0.117			0.539*	0.078			0.788*	0.092
HeadEducation	-0.088*	0.036	-0.073*	0.032			0.916*	0.033			0.930*	0.030
HeadAge	-0.017	0.010	-0.003	0.009			0.983	0.009			0.997	0.009
HeadGender	-0.308	0.459	-0.359	0.424			0.735	0.337			0.698	0.296
Quintile1	0.870	0.466	0.049	0.392			2.386	1.111			1.050	0.412
Quintile2	0.450	0.472	-0.350	0.399			1.569	0.741			0.705	0.281
Quintile3	-0.226	0.491	-0.369	0.407			0.798	0.392			0.692	0.282
Quintile4	-0.034	0.515	-0.596	0.426			0.967	0.498			0.551	0.235
Density	0.266	0.238	0.489*	0.214			1.304	0.311			1.630*	0.349
HeadKid	0.295	0.310	0.654*	0.289			1.343	0.416			1.923*	0.556
Coast	-0.421	0.254	-0.472*	0.217			0.657	0.167			0.624*	0.135
Selva	-0.260	0.220	-0.667*	0.211			0.771	0.169			0.513*	0.108
HeadNotWork	0.606	0.394	0.490	0.363			1.833	0.722			1.632	0.592
HeadSelfEmp	0.839*	0.239	0.651*	0.208			2.315*	0.554			1.918*	0.399
NoSpouse	0.078	0.464	1.023*	0.455			1.082	0.502			2.782*	1.265
SpouseWageEmp	0.024	0.716	1.027	0.647			1.024	0.733			2.794	1.806
SpouseSelfEmp	-0.113	0.250	1.235*	0.278			0.893	0.224			3.437*	0.955
Intercept	0.297	0.874	-0.780	0.813								

Note: $N = 1,199$. McFadden's $R^2 = 0.15$. An * denotes statistical significance at the 5% level.

Table 4.6: Multinomial Logistic Regression Model Estimates and Relative Risk Ratio, Urban Peru, 1985

	Estimates (Reference Category is Full-Time Students)				Relative Risk Ratio (RRR)			
	No work or study & Full-Time Workers		Works and studies		No work or study & Full-Time Workers		Works and studies	
Variable	Coefficient	Standard Error	Coefficient	Standard Error	Coefficient	Standard Error	RRR	Standard Error
Age15-17	1.612*	0.206	0.527*	0.169	5.012*	1.032	1.693*	0.286
Gender	0.016	0.171	-0.489*	0.139	1.016	0.173	0.613*	0.085
Education	-0.177*	0.046	0.002	0.042	0.838*	0.039	1.002	0.042
Num5	0.062	0.098	0.109	0.080	1.064	0.104	1.115	0.089
Num18M	-0.223*	0.107	-0.064	0.080	0.800*	0.116	0.949	0.079
HeadEducation	-0.105*	0.026	-0.057*	0.021	0.900*	0.024	0.944*	0.020
HeadAge	-0.008	0.010	-0.006	0.008	0.992	0.010	0.994	0.008
HeadGender	-0.007	0.403	-0.185	0.337	0.993	0.400	0.831	0.280
Quintile1	0.273	0.331	0.381	0.306	1.314	0.435	1.464	0.448
Quintile2	0.306	0.285	0.744*	0.242	1.358	0.387	2.105*	0.510
Quintile3	0.191	0.276	.688*	0.231	1.210	0.334	1.989*	0.459
Quintile4	-0.236	0.284	0.649*	0.217	0.790	0.224	1.914*	0.415
Density	0.355	0.198	-0.033	0.171	1.426	0.283	0.967	0.165
HeadKid	-0.181	0.238	-0.110	0.208	0.835	0.198	0.895	0.186
Coast	0.589*	0.209	-0.328	0.170	1.801*	0.377	0.720	0.123
Sierra	0.847*	0.246	0.170	0.192	2.332*	0.573	1.186	0.228
Selva	-0.047	0.400	0.096	0.268	0.954	0.381	1.100	0.294
HeadNotWork	-0.076	0.269	-0.024	0.247	0.927	0.249	0.976	0.242
HeadSelfEmp	-0.104	0.194	0.694*	0.156	0.902	0.175	2.002*	0.312
NoSpouse	0.569	0.407	1.566*	0.368	1.766	0.719	4.788*	1.762
SpouseWageEmp	0.106	0.355	0.673*	0.327	1.112	0.395	1.960*	0.641
SpouseSelfEmp	0.348	0.230	1.579*	0.228	1.416	0.326	4.848*	1.105
Intercept	-0.920	0.739	-2.390*	0.642				

Note: $N = 1,556$. McFadden's $R^2 = 0.12$. An * denotes statistical significance at the 5% level.

Table 4.7: Multinomial Logistic Regression Model Estimates and Relative Risk Ratio, Rural Peru, 1997

	Estimates (Reference Category is Full-Time Students)								Relative Risk Ratio (RRR)			
	No work or study & Full-Time Workers		Works and studies				No work or study & Full-Time Workers				Works and studies	
Variable	Coefficient	Standard Error	Coefficient	Standard Error			Coefficient	Standard Error			RRR	Standard Error
Age15-17	2.551*	0.263	0.361	0.211			12.826*	3.369			1.435	0.303
Gender	-0.366	0.208	-0.54*	0.166			0.693	0.144			0.579*	0.096
Education	-0.346*	0.060	0.006	0.052			0.707*	0.042			1.006	0.052
Num5	0.209	0.120	-0.008	0.099			1.232	0.148			0.992	0.098
Num18M	0.127	0.127	-0.151	0.133			1.149	0.109			1.149	0.153
HeadEducation	-0.110*	0.038	-0.040	0.029			0.896*	0.034			0.960	0.027
HeadAge	0.001	0.012	-0.009	0.010			1.001	0.012			0.991	0.010
HeadGender	-0.739	0.593	0.467	0.544			4.747	3.793			1.562	0.883
Quintile2	0.604	0.795	-0.337	0.558			1.829	1.453			0.714	0.399
Quintile3	0.424	0.828	-0.502	0.574			1.528	1.265			0.605	0.347
Quintile4	1.090	0.865	-0.408	0.614			2.975	2.573			0.665	0.408
Density	0.139	0.279	-0.351	0.241			1.149	0.321			0.704	0.170
HeadKid	-0.026	0.381	0.825*	0.354			0.975	0.371			2.281*	0.809
Coast	-0.250	0.287	-1.069*	0.237			0.778	0.224			0.343*	0.082
Selva	-0.540*	0.269	-0.775*	0.215			0.583*	0.157			0.461*	0.099
HeadNotWork	-0.391	0.451	0.060	0.353			0.676	0.305			1.062	0.375
HeadSelfEmp	0.624*	0.250	0.763*	0.193			1.866*	0.466			2.145*	0.413
NoSpouse	1.936*	0.546	0.945	0.513			6.933*	3.786			2.572	1.320
SpouseWageEmp	-0.468	0.621	0.436	0.430			0.626	0.389			1.546	0.664
SpouseSelfEmp	0.780*	0.254	1.414*	0.209			2.182*	0.554			4.112*	0.860
Intercept	-0.818	1.167	-0.719	0.950								

Note: N = 1,018. McFadden's R^2 = 0.20. An * denotes statistical significance at the 5% level.

Table 4.8: Multinomial Logistic Regression Model Estimates and Relative Risk Ratio, Urban Peru, 1997

	Estimates (Reference Category is Full-Time Students)				Relative Risk Ratio (RRR)			
	No work or study & Full-Time Workers		Works and studies		No work or study & Full-Time Workers		Works and studies	
Variable	Coefficient	Standard Error	Coefficient	Standard Error	Coefficient	Standard Error	RRR	Standard Error
Age15-17	2.665*	0.273	0.806*	0.186	14.367*	3.923	2.238*	0.416
Gender	0.088	0.192	-0.499*	0.152	1.092	0.209	0.607*	0.092
Education	-0.117*	0.047	0.011	0.045	0.889*	0.042	1.011	0.045
Num5	0.243	0.131	0.255*	0.105	1.275	0.167	1.291*	0.135
Num18M	0.071	0.098	-0.212*	0.096	1.073	0.105	0.809*	0.078
Num18F	-0.018	0.118	-0.160	0.101	0.982	0.116	0.852	0.086
HeadEducation	-0.116*	0.028	-0.049*	0.022	0.891*	0.025	0.953*	0.021
HeadAge	-0.013	0.012	0.002	0.009	0.988	0.012	1.002	0.009
HeadGender	0.692	0.434	0.701	0.366	1.998	0.867	2.016*	0.738
Quintile1	0.513	0.424	0.486	0.359	1.670	0.707	1.626	0.583
Quintile2	-0.008	0.345	0.668*	0.273	0.992	0.342	1.950*	0.532
Quintile3	-0.128	0.308	0.276	0.250	0.880	0.271	1.318	0.329
Quintile4	-0.175	0.295	0.253	0.239	0.840	0.248	1.288	0.308
Density	0.418	0.233	-0.191	0.224	1.519	0.354	0.826	0.185
HeadKid	0.022	0.293	0.039	0.251	1.022	0.299	1.040	0.261
Coast	-0.047	0.235	0.374	0.199	0.954	0.224	1.453	0.289
Sierra	-0.373	0.307	0.682*	0.209	0.689	0.211	1.978*	0.413
Selva	0.059	0.321	0.855*	0.239	1.061	0.341	2.351*	0.561
HeadNotWork	0.649*	0.299	0.156	0.263	1.914*	0.572	1.169	0.308
HeadSelfEmp	0.615*	0.224	0.696*	0.171	1.849*	0.413	2.007	0.343
NoSpouse	0.045	0.430	0.639	0.368	1.046	0.449	1.894	0.697
SpouseWageEmp	0.618	0.331	0.770*	0.295	1.854	0.614	2.161*	0.638
SpouseSelfEmp	0.509*	0.237	1.499*	0.192	1.663*	0.395	4.479*	0.861
Intercept	-2.188*	0.889	-3.176*	0.721				

Note: $N = 1,018$. McFadden's $R^2 = 0.20$. An * denotes statistical significance at the 5% level.

head would have little control over the activities of other families' children. The estimates for the *HeadKid* variable are not statistically significant in the urban models. As was the case in Mexico, children in households in which the head's spouse is not present (*NoSpouse*) are disadvantaged. They are generally more likely to be home workers, full-time workers, or to combine work with school as opposed to studying full-time.

The most important finding with respect to the variables for the head's occupation and spouse's occupation is that children in households where the head or spouse are self-employed are generally more likely to combine work with schooling, as opposed to being full-time students. The RRR's for the *HeadSelfEmp* and *SpouseSelfEmp* variables for the part-time student category are for the most part statistically significant, being in the range of 1.9–4.8. This means that children in households where either the head or the spouse is self-employed are two to five times more likely to be part-time students rather than full-time students. Children living in households where *both* the head and the spouse are self-employed are five to seven times more likely to be part-time students, as opposed to being full-time students. For 1997, there is also evidence that children in households where the head or spouse are self-employed are more likely to work at home or in the labor force, as opposed to being full-time students.

The estimated coefficients for sibship size and structure, and for the household per capita income variables, are generally not statistically significant. The most important exception is urban Peru, 1985, where the estimates suggest that children in the second, third, and fourth quintiles were about twice as likely as children in the top quintile to be part-time students rather than full-time students.

In sum, the most important factors determining the activities of Peruvian children are the age of the child, the child's gender, the years of education completed by the child, whether the head and/or spouse are self-employed, and the presence or absence of a spouse.

Some important differences emerge when comparing the 1985 and the 1997 results. In rural Peru, during 1985, the absence of a spouse (*NoSpouse*) had no statistically significant impact on the probability of a child being a home worker or full-time worker as opposed to a full-time student. In rural Peru during 1997, however, the RRR for the *NoSpouse* variable for the home worker/full-time worker category was approximately 6.9. This means that, in 1985, children in rural households without a spouse were no more or less likely than children in households with a spouse to be home workers or full-time workers as opposed to full-time students. By 1997, however, not having a spouse in the household meant that children were nearly seven times more likely to be home workers or full-time workers rather than full-time students. Another important difference concerns the *Age15–17* variable. The estimated RRR for the *Age15–17* variable for the home worker/full-time worker category in urban areas was approximately 5 in 1985 versus approximately 14 in 1997. This means that, while fifteen- to seventeen-year-olds were substantially more likely than twelve- to fourteen-year-olds to be home workers or full-time workers in both survey years, the impact of being older was larger in urban areas in 1997 than in 1985. The figures in Appendix 4.1 suggest this may be due to the fact that a larger percentage of twelve- to fourteen-year-olds were full-time students in 1997 than in 1985.

FINDINGS FOR CHILE

The estimates of the multinomial logistic regression model for Chile are given in Tables 4.9–4.12. Table 4.9 shows the results for rural Chile in 1990; Table 4.10 for urban Chile in 1990; Table 4.11 for rural Chile in 1996; and Table 4.12 for urban Chile, 1996. Values for McFadden's R^2 for these models range from .26 to .33, suggesting the model fit is on par with that estimated above using the Mexican data, and superior to that based on the Peruvian data. The model appears to do a better job of estimating children's activities in rural than in urban Chile, especially in 1990. This may reflect the lower level of variation (and thus lower variation to be explained) in children's activities in urban

Table 4.9: Multinomial Logistic Regression Model Estimates and Relative Risk Ratio, Rural Chile, 1990

Estimates (Reference Category is Full-Time Students)

Variable	No work or study Coefficient	No work or study Standard Error	Full-Time Workers Coefficient	Full-Time Workers Standard Error	Works and studies Coefficient	Works and studies Standard Error
Age15-17	3.222*	0.160	3.995*	0.189	1.179*	0.519
Gender	1.309*	0.132	-1.204*	0.140	-1.269*	0.492
Education	-0.639*	0.035	-0.560*	0.035	0.036	0.120
Num5	0.225*	0.080	0.226*	0.088	0.167	0.343
Num18M	0.256*	0.064	0.043	0.070	0.350	0.194
Num18F	-0.238*	0.097	-0.286*	0.098	-1.553*	0.340
HeadEducation	-0.093*	0.020	-0.085*	0.020	-0.241*	0.073
HeadAge	-0.050	0.007	0.005	0.007	-1.004	0.024
HeadGender	0.701*	0.363	0.659	0.365	-0.385	1.228
Quintile1	0.272	0.354	-0.581*	0.300	-2.304*	0.950
Quintile2	0.207	0.356	-0.304	0.299	-1.480	0.791
Quintile3	0.372	0.362	0.311	.295	-0.403	0.723
Quintile4	0.811*	0.376	0.410	0.316	0.128	0.757
Density	-0.070	0.152	0.324*	0.147	0.075	0.557
HeadKid	0.017	0.196	0.791*	0.298	0.487	0.809
Central	0.231	0.280	0.154	0.246	-1.189	0.781
South	0.611*	0.273	0.032	0.242	-0.070	0.633
HeadNotWork	0.040	0.183	-0.677*	0.207	-1.914*	0.934
HeadSelfEmp	-0.169	0.156	-0.305*	0.160	-0.628	0.473
NoSpouse	-0.253	0.340	0.020	0.330	0.330	0.864
SpouseWageEmp	-0.712*	0.304	0.194	0.241	-1.562	1.506
SpouseSelfEmp	0.110	0.359	0.224	0.347	1.166	0.752
Intercept	0.183	0.631	0.648	0.616	-1.417	1.966

Relative Risk Ratio (RRR)

Variable	No work or study RRR	No work or study Standard Error	Full-Time Workers RRR	Full-Time Workers Standard Error	Works and studies RRR	Works and studies Standard Error
Age15-17	25.086*	4.012	54.343*	10.261	3.253*	1.687
Gender	3.704*	0.488	0.300*	0.042	0.281*	0.138
Education	9.528*	0.018	0.571*	0.020	1.037	0.125
Num5	1.252*	0.101	1.253*	0.110	1.182	0.405
Num18M	1.292*	0.083	1.044	0.073	1.419	0.275
Num18F	0.788*	0.076	0.751*	0.074	0.575	0.196
HeadEducation	0.911*	0.019	0.918*	0.018	0.786*	0.571
HeadAge	0.995	0.006	1.005	0.007	0.996	0.024
HeadGender	2.015*	0.731	1.934	0.705	0.681	0.836
Quintile1	1.312	0.465	0.559*	0.168	0.099*	0.095
Quintile2	1.231	0.438	0.737	0.220	0.228	0.180
Quintile3	1.451	0.526	1.365	0.403	0.669	0.483
Quintile4	2.250*	0.846	1.507	0.477	1.137	0.860
Density	0.932	0.142	1.382*	0.204	1.077	0.600
HeadKid	1.522	0.529	2.206*	0.658	1.628	1.316
Central	1.260	0.353	1.166	0.287	0.304	0.238
South	1.842*	0.503	1.032	0.250	0.933	0.590
HeadNotWork	1.041	0.190	0.508*	0.105	0.147*	0.138
HeadSelfEmp	0.845	0.132	0.737	0.118	0.535	0.252
NoSpouse	0.776	0.264	1.020	0.336	1.391	1.202
SpouseWageEmp	0.491*	0.149	1.214	0.293	0.210	0.316
SpouseSelfEmp	1.117	0.401	1.251	0.435	3.209	2.414

Note: $N = 3,230$. McFadden's $R^2 = 0.33$. An * denotes statistical significance at the 5% level.

Table 4.10: Multinomial Logistic Regression Model Estimates and Relative Risk Ratio, Urban Chile, 1990

	Estimates (Reference Category is Full-Time Students)						Relative Risk Ratio (RRR)					
	No work or study		Full-Time Workers		Works and studies		No work or study		Full-Time Workers		Works and studies	
Variable	Coefficient	Standard Error	Coefficient	Standard Error	Coefficient	Standard Error	RRR	Standard Error	RRR	Standard Error	RRR	Standard Error
Age15-17	3.089*	0.148	4.385*	0.248	2.186*	0.289	21.953*	3.258	80.205*	10.866	8.897*	2.573
Gender	0.453*	0.105	-0.975*	0.132	-0.940*	0.208	1.574*	0.166	0.377*	0.050	0.391*	00.081
Education	-0.519*	0.025	-0.493*	0.028	-0.164*	0.054	0.595*	0.015	0.611*	0.017	0.849*	0.456
Num5	0.453*	0.069	0.466*	0.085	0.521*	0.131	1.572*	0.109	1.593*	0.135	1.684*	0.220
Num18M	0.307*	0.058	0.193*	0.070	-0.022	0.129	1.359*	0.080	1.212*	0.085	0.978	0.126
Num18F	-0.254*	0.075	-0.240*	0.090	-0.251	0.148	0.775*	0.584	0.786*	0.071	0.778	0.115
HeadEducation	-0.084*	0.014	-0.117*	0.017	-0.141*	0.025	0.919*	0.013	0.889*	0.015	0.868*	0.022
HeadAge	-0.006	0.006	-0.031*	0.007	-0.033*	0.011	0.994	0.006	0.969*	0.007	0.968*	0.011
HeadGender	-0.386	0.243	0.499	0.318	-0.054	0.468	0.680	0.166	1.646	0.523	0.948	0.444
Quintile1	0.654*	0.257	-0.229	0.275	-0.589	0.384	1.923*	0.494	0.796	0.219	0.555	0.213
Quintile2	0.615*	0.250	0.024	0.263	-0.673	0.377	1.850*	0.462	1.025	0.269	0.510	0.192
Quintile3	0.481*	0.251	0.141	0.260	0.065	0.335	1.618	0.406	1.151	0.300	1.067	0.357
Quintile4	0.189	0.266	0.252	0.266	-0.108	0.352	1.207	0.321	1.287	0.342	0.897	0.316
Density	0.422*	0.125	0.418*	0.149	0.689*	0.217	1.526*	0.191	1.520*	0.227	1.992*	0.433
HeadKid	-0.371*	0.157	-0.653*	0.177	-0.854*	0.277	0.690*	0.108	0.521*	0.921	0.426*	0.118
North	-0.467*	0.180	-0.496*	0.226	0.505*	0.252	0.627*	0.113	0.609	0.138	1.657*	0.417
Central	-0.311*	0.141	0.005	0.161	-0.053	0.253	0.733*	0.104	1.009	0.162	0.948	0.240
South	-0.246	0.132	0.113	0.152	-0.611*	0.302	0.782	0.103	1.120	0.171	0.543*	0.164
HeadNotWork	-0.156	0.147	-0.087	0.176	-0.343	0.308	0.856	0.126	0.917	0.161	0.710	0.218
HeadSelfEmp	-0.061	0.138	0.220	0.154	0.197	0.228	0.940	0.130	1.246	0.192	1.217	0.277
NoSpouse	0.833*	0.238	0.249	0.315	0.765	0.465	2.300*	0.548	1.283	0.405	2.149	1.000
SpouseWageEmp	0.141	0.165	-0.138	0.197	-0.112	0.318	1.151	0.190	0.871	0.171	0.894	0.284
SpouseSelfEmp	0.068	0.220	-0.418	0.273	0.880*	0.292	1.070	0.235	0.658	0.179	2.410*	0.705
Intercept	-0.390	0.500	0.447	0.584	-0.777	0.862						

Note: N = 8,684. McFadden's R^2 = 0.26. An * denotes statistical significance at the 5% level.

167

Table 4.11: Multinomial Logistic Regression Model Estimates and Relative Risk Ratio, Rural Chile, 1996

Estimates (Reference Category is Full-Time Students)

Variable	No work or study Coefficient	No work or study Standard Error	Full-Time Workers Coefficient	Full-Time Workers Standard Error	Works and studies Coefficient	Works and studies Standard Error
Age15-17	3.127*	0.144	3.674*	0.171	-0.155	0.494
Gender	1.002*	0.116	-1.134*	0.132	-1.130*	0.421
Education	-0.666*	0.030	-0.558*	0.030	0.054	0.122
Num5	0.201*	0.079	0.154	0.089	0.979*	0.199
Num18M	-0.047	0.068	0.130	0.068	-0.938*	0.412
Num18F	0.002	0.088	-0.061	0.088	-1.497*	0.510
HeadEducation	-0.032	0.021	-0.124*	0.022	-0.004	0.057
HeadAge	-0.004	0.006	-0.006	0.006	0.036	0.023
HeadGender	-0.500*	0.239	-0.555*	0.264	0.441	1.541
Quintile1	5.219	2.853	-0.497	0.374	1.533	2.097
Quintile2	5.230	2.853	0.231	0.371	0.935	2.117
Quintile3	4.755	2.857	0.288	0.378	2.488	2.081
Quintile4	3.868	2.874	0.360	0.408	0.823	2.235
Density	-0.303	0.166	-0.229	0.174	0.897*	0.386
HeadKid	0.392*	0.166	0.020	0.166	-0.957	0.525
North	0.343	0.319	1.187*	0.379	-0.986	0.743
Central	0.176	0.274	1.341*	0.331	-0.527	0.522
South	0.422	0.269	1.231*	0.329	-1.197*	0.557
HeadNotWork	0.408*	0.178	0.342	0.193	-1.535	0.974
HeadSelfEmp	0.276*	0.139	0.199	0.143	0.084	0.452
NoSpouse	1.133*	0.219	0.587*	0.243	-0.809	1.540
SpouseWageEmp	0.088	0.213	0.105	0.200	1.513*	0.442
SpouseSelfEmp	-0.407	0.291	0.062	0.250	0.319	0.799
Intercept	-5.372	2.896	-0.600	0.623	-6.577*	2.686

Relative Risk Ratio (RRR)

Variable	No work or study RRR	No work or study Standard Error	Full-Time Workers RRR	Full-Time Workers Standard Error	Works and studies RRR	Works and studies Standard Error
Age15-17	22.797*	3.286	39.415*	6.733	0.856	0.423
Gender	2.724*	0.317	0.322*	0.042	0.323*	0.136
Education	0.514*	0.016	0.572*	0.017	1.056	0.129
Num5	1.222*	0.098	1.167	0.104	2.661*	0.530
Num18M	0.954	0.065	1.139	0.077	0.391*	0.161
Num18F	1.002	0.088	0.940	0.083	0.224*	0.114
HeadEducation	0.969	0.020	0.883*	0.019	0.996	0.057
HeadAge	0.996	0.006	0.994	0.006	1.037	0.023
HeadGender	0.607*	0.145	0.574*	0.152	1.554	2.395
Quintile1	184.839	527.422	0.609	0.228	4.630	9.707
Quintile2	186.755	532.894	1.260	0.468	2.548	5.393
Quintile3	116.198	331.937	1.333	0.505	12.035	25.039
Quintile4	47.568	137.568	1.434	0.585	2.277	5.088
Density	0.738	0.122	0.795	0.138	2.454*	0.947
HeadKid	1.480*	0.246	1.020	0.169	0.384	0.202
North	1.409	0.450	3.277*	1.241	0.373	0.277
Central	1.192	0.327	3.823*	1.264	0.590	0.308
South	1.524	0.409	3.426*	1.129	0.302*	0.168
HeadNotWork	1.503*	0.267	1.408	0.272	0.216	0.210
HeadSelfEmp	1.317*	0.183	1.221	0.174	1.088	0.492
NoSpouse	3.106*	0.678	1.799*	0.436	0.446	0.687
SpouseWageEmp	1.092	0.233	1.110	0.222	4.541*	2.006
SpouseSelfEmp	0.666	0.194	1.064	0.266	1.375	1.099

Note: N = 5,126. McFadden's R^2 = 0.31. An * denotes statistical significance at the 5% level.

Table 4.12: Multinomial Logistic Regression Model Estimates and Relative Risk Ratio, Urban Chile, 1996

Estimates (Reference Category is Full-Time Students)

Variable	No work or study Coefficient	No work or study Standard Error	Full-Time Workers Coefficient	Full-Time Workers Standard Error	Works and studies Coefficient	Works and studies Standard Error
Age15-17	3.160*	0.140	4.054*	0.213	0.703*	0.208
Gender	0.406*	0.103	-0.808*	0.124	-0.455*	0.141
Education	-0.579*	0.022	-0.510*	0.026	0.101	0.055
Num5	0.575*	0.070	0.590*	0.084	0.385*	0.124
Num18M	0.200*	0.062	0.252*	0.069	0.088	0.98
Num18F	-0.004	0.071	-0.347*	0.094	-0.373*	0.123
HeadEducation	-0.105*	0.014	-0.181*	0.016	-0.064*	0.018
HeadAge	-0.016*	0.006	-0.046*	0.006	-0.032*	0.008
HeadGender	0.194	0.193	-0.368	0.208	-0.602*	0.274
Quintile1	0.773*	0.238	0.597	0.307	-0.483	0.296
Quintile2	0.777*	0.225	0.513	0.299	-0.504	0.265
Quintile3	0.266	0.230	0.859*	0.249	0.320	0.208
Quintile4	-0.182	0.252	0.509	0.306	-0.208	0.215
Density	-0.224	0.155	0.286	0.150	0.038	0.216
HeadKid	-0.437*	0.140	-0.476*	0.157	-0.868*	0.201
North	-0.326	0.172	-0.674*	0.232	0.622*	0.217
Central	-0.077	0.132	0.091	0.155	0.611*	0.183
South	-0.455*	0.135	0.213	0.143	0.552*	0.181
HeadNotWork	-0.589*	0.158	0.217	0.166	-0.708*	0.289
HeadSelfEmp	0.139	0.129	0.312*	0.149	0.668*	0.155
NoSpouse	0.425*	0.199	0.959*	0.212	1.549*	0.287
SpouseWageEmp	0.017	0.164	0.544*	0.167	1.426*	0.181
SpouseSelfEmp	0.490*	0.188	-0.240	0.272	1.081*	0.235
Intercept	0.273	0.455	0.611	0.540	-3.482*	0.673

Relative Risk Ratio (RRR)

Variable	No work or study RRR	No work or study Standard Error	Full-Time Workers RRR	Full-Time Workers Standard Error	Works and studies RRR	Works and studies Standard Error
Age15-17	23.577*	3.294	57.653*	12.267	2.021*	0.420
Gender	1.502*	0.154	0.446*	0.055	0.634*	0.089
Education	0.560*	0.013	0.600*	0.015	1.107	0.061
Num5	1.777*	0.124	1.805*	0.152	1.469*	0.182
Num18M	1.222*	0.076	1.286*	0.088	1.092	0.107
Num18F	0.996	0.071	0.707*	0.067	0.689*	0.084
HeadEducation	0.900*	0.012	0.834*	0.014	0.938*	0.017
HeadAge	0.984*	0.006	0.955*	0.006	0.969*	0.008
HeadGender	1.215	0.235	0.692	0.144	0.548*	0.150
Quintile1	2.166*	0.515	1.816	0.558	0.617	0.183
Quintile2	2.177*	0.490	1.671	0.500	0.604	0.160
Quintile3	1.443	0.331	2.361*	0.694	1.378	0.287
Quintile4	0.834	0.210	1.663	0.509	0.812	0.174
Density	0.799	0.124	1.331	0.199	1.039	0.224
HeadKid	0.646*	0.091	0.621*	0.098	0.420*	0.084
North	0.722	0.124	0.510*	0.118	1.862*	0.403
Central	0.927	0.122	1.096	0.170	1.842*	0.337
South	0.634*	0.086	1.238	0.177	1.737*	0.314
HeadNotWork	0.555*	0.088	1.242	0.207	0.492*	0.142
HeadSelfEmp	1.149	0.148	1.367*	0.0.203	1.950*	0.302
NoSpouse	1.529*	0.304	2.611*	0.554	4.707*	1.349
SpouseWageEmp	1.017	0.167	1.724*	0.288	4.163*	0.755
SpouseSelfEmp	1.632*	0.306	0.787	0.214	2.947*	0.692

Note: N = 13,583. McFadden's R^2 = 0.29. An * denotes statistical significance at the 5% level.

Chile, where the vast majority of children are going to school full-time. Asterisks are used to denote statistical significance of coefficients at the 5 percent level, and we focus only on significant effects. Again, the estimates are presented both in metric form (with standard errors) and as relative risk ratios (RRR's).

The results confirm that, as in Mexico and Peru, older Chilean children (those aged fifteen to seventeen) are significantly less likely to be full-time students than are twelve- to fourteen-year-olds, and they are correspondingly more likely to be working in the home or working full-time. With the exception of rural Chile in 1996, older teens are also somewhat more likely to be combining school and work. With respect to gender, Chapter 1 and Appendix 4.1 have already showed that boys and girls in Chile enjoy roughly equivalent levels of full-time school attendance. However, the multivariate results confirm that, when they are not attending school full-time, girls are far more likely than boys to be in the "neither work nor school" category. Girls are much less likely than boys to be working full-time or combining work and school.

The effects of the child's previous education confirm that children with more years of education completed are, other things equal, significantly less likely to be working at home or working full-time as compared to going to school full-time. However, completed years of education do not strongly differentiate students who are combining school and work versus going to school only. Children with better educated heads of family are likewise less likely to be doing things other than going to school full-time, as evidenced by the RRR's that are consistently less than one for the *HeadEducation* variable.

The estimates for the *Headkid* variable suggest that children who are the sons or daughters of the household head are less likely (than those with other relationships to the head) to be doing things other than attending school full-time. This is consistent with the idea that parents emphasize the well-being of their own children first. Interestingly, this effect is seen only in urban Chile. It should be emphasized that the overwhelming majority of Chilean children analyzed here are the natural offspring of their household heads. As compared with Peru and Mexico, in Chile it is less common for children to live in a female-headed family (Muñoz Salazar 2000). Perhaps for this reason, the coefficients for this variable do not tell a consistent story. It does not appear that female-headship in and of itself has uniformly detrimental consequences in terms of children's activities. The variable *NoSpouse*, which indicates that the head has no spouse present, does increase the likelihood that a child will work in the home or work full-time, especially in 1996.

Once controlling for other factors, as our model does here, head's and spouse's employment circumstances do not affect children's activities in consistent ways, either across years or between rural and urban areas. For example, being in a household in which the head is *not* working *reduces* the likelihood of a child working full-time, but only in rural areas in 1990. The lack of a clear pattern for this variable could reflect the fact that it captures countervailing forces. A non-working head might increase children's propensity to work as a way to help families survive. On the other hand, if heads are not working because of limited opportunities in the local labor market, then children's opportunities might be similarly constrained. Similarly, the effects of head's self-employment and spouse's wage employment and self-employment are usually insignificant. When they *are* significant, their effects usually suggest that wage- or self-employment reduce the likelihood of full-time schooling for children. Finally, while the effects of household income are generally insignificant, they do suggest that for both years in urban Chile, poor children are significantly more likely than those in the richest income quintile to be working at home rather than going to school. Poverty has no such effect in rural Chile, at least after controlling for the child's previously attained years of schooling.

With respect to presence of younger siblings, the results in Tables 4.9–4.12 suggest that the presence of siblings under five years old (*Num5*) increases the likelihood of engaging in domestic or market work, as opposed to going to school full-time. It is likely that having younger siblings means either increased need for childcare, supplemental income, or both. Estimates for the variable *Density* are not uniformly significant. When the *Density* coefficients are significant (as in urban areas in 1990) they suggest that having additional siblings close in age increases the likelihood of working at home or in the labor market. The presence of older males (*Num18M*) and older females (*Num18F*) in the household (other than the head or spouse) seems to affect children's activities differentially. That is, especially in urban Chile, having older males in the household increases the likelihood that a child will work at home or work full-time. By contrast, the presence of older females reduces the likelihood that a child will engage in these alternatives to full-time schooling.

In sum, the activities of Chilean children are shaped by a variety of individual and household characteristics. Consistently across time and place of residence, older children are less likely to attend school full-time, while they are more likely to be engaged in domestic or market work. Gender also consistently sorts girls into domestic work and boys into the paid labor force. Children with greater previous educational attainment and with better-educated parents are also more likely to continue to attend school full-time. With respect to changes over time, the sets and signs of significant coefficients differ somewhat between 1990 and 1996 (especially for rural Chile). Noteworthy among the inter-temporal differences is the apparently weakening effect of having additional adults in the household. For example, in rural Chile the number of additional male and female adults became insignificant as predictors of working at home versus going to school full-time. Another general observation is that several of the household employment status variables become significant as predictors of children's activities. For example, in both rural and urban Chile, wage employment by the spouse (*SpouseWageEmp*) became significant as a predictor of children's part-time work.

CONCLUSIONS

The multivariate analysis in this chapter provides insight into ways in which the characteristics of children and those of their parents, households, and places of residence combine to influence the likelihood of children's schooling and work in Latin America. Given the complexity of the social and economic processes giving rise to variations in children's activities, it is hardly surprising that our results differ when based on different data sets at different points in time. But there are meaningful consistencies. Indeed, many of the most important determinants of children's activities are the same across countries and over time. Not surprisingly, children's age has strong and consistent effects. Older children are less likely to attend school and more likely to either combine school and work or to forsake school altogether for either domestic or market work. With respect to gender, among children engaged in work activities outside school, girls are generally more likely to work in home production, while boys are more likely to work for wages outside the home. Also, in all three countries the same educational selectivity processes seem to be at play. Those with more years of formal education—who presumably are more successful as students—are generally more likely to be going to school only, rather than working (whether at home or in the market).

Much of the research and policy interest in children's schooling and work is motivated by the assumption that poverty is tightly bound up with decisions to leave school and either work at home (in the case of girls), or work outside the home at a regular job. Our results suggest that while household income matters, its effect is more cumulative than instantaneous. After controlling for other household characteristics and for the child's previous educational attainment, as we do in this chapter, the effect of being in a particular income quintile is sometimes insignificant. It seems plausible that even poor parents seek to keep their children in school on a full-time basis. But of course poverty manifests itself in other ways than merely through low incomes. Living in poverty often means that there is no secondary school in the community, that if there is a secondary school it may be a very poor one, that transportation is limited, health care is limited so children are often sick, and so forth. And poverty, as we will see in the next chapter, also means that a child of any given age had probably attained fewer school years at the time of the survey on which we based our estimates in this chapter. Thus, our control for completed education may also capture indirectly the effect of income, and low educational attainment would mediate the cumulative effect of poverty. Our results for sibship size and structure indicate that these variables matter, but again not as much as one might have expected.

While many of the coefficients in our estimations are significant, they often are weak in magnitude. One implication is that these variables would make a difference only in very large families. For the most part, sibship size and structure have little meaningful bearing on children's school attendance and work. Similarly, the characteristics of children's household heads often matter. In particular, a finding that cuts across time and space is that children with better educated parents are, other things equal, more likely to be exclusively attending school rather than working. Finally, we must acknowledge the limitations of any cross-sectional, comparative statistical modeling. While our approach can be useful in explaining differences among children within a country, we must exercise considerable humility in our interpretation of cross-country differences in school attendance and child labor. Ours is a comparative case study of three countries chosen for their differences and commonalities. The activity patterns we explore in Chile, Peru, and Mexico are not representative of the experiences of children in any other region, just as the countries in our study do not constitute a sample of any population of countries. In a different approach, we might have developed a model taking into account not only the variables available in our survey data, but also cross-country differences in the economic incentives to attend school; the availability and quality of schooling; social and cultural factors affecting schooling; and the degree of enforcement of school attendance legislation.

5
Region And Gender Differences In Children's Work And Schooling

The roles of children in Latin America's family economies need to be understood not only for effective education, labor, and welfare policies in the countries of this study. Understanding the social causes of children's work and school activities also is important in its own right, as part of a broader, worldwide investigation. Social researchers ask not only how societies are constructed, but also whether societies can be reconstructed in future generations, using alternative architectures. In the last chapter, we analyzed the individual and family factors that have led children to work and to school. In this chapter, I widen the focus to investigate the effects of two additional factors that influence children's work and school activity and the changing roles these play in assigning children to different futures. In this chapter, I also scrutinize the interaction of poverty with gender and region. I look at changes in the direct effect of poverty, and I gauge the impact poverty has had, particularly on girls.

Our consideration in this chapter—on the effects of region and gender—has a rich heritage. In the early twentieth century, the great Russian émigré sociologist, Pitirm Sorokin (1927), coined the term "stratification" to describe the universal transmission of opportunities from parents to children through identifiable channels and along the separate dimensions of power, wealth, and knowledge. Although social stratification was constant throughout history, Sorokin argued that the relative importance of different stratifying dimensions could change over time. Education was already seen by Sorokin as one of the most important channels of upward mobility for individuals and for groups. Since Sorokin, one of the most widely accepted conclusions from the comparative study of education is that this institution became even more important over the twentieth century as other channels of status attainment became less important (for example, apprenticeships, the military, or the church). Schooling increased in its significance for adult status as other means of transmitting power and wealth lost their legitimacy (for example, land tenancy, race, or political party affiliation).

The most obvious way that governments affect educational mobility, and possibly reconfigure their opportunity structures, is by universalizing family access to education. When a minimal level of schooling for status attainment is guaranteed for all, then the sources of inequality that were transmitted through unequal opportunity for basic educational attainment will wane in their importance. Thus, a core question from the social sciences is applicable to the case studies described in this book: Can governments, through universalizing minimum levels of education, create more egalitarian societies as a consequence? While that possibility remains open, there are several reasons to doubt that a leveling of opportunities will inevitably follow universal education. First, with decreased transmission of inequality in access to basic education (as when Mexico extended compulsory schooling to nine years in 1993) there may be an *exacerbated* transmission of inequality when students transit to higher education (Post 2000). Second, unequal quality of basic education may emerge, although this is beyond our ability to investigate using household survey data. Third, and most importantly, increases in school attendance could be accompanied by greater tendencies to work while in school, as we have already seen has occurred in Peru and Mexico.

Sorokin's concept of vertically stratified societies was adapted to nonindustrialized settings by one of his closest readers, Philip Foster. Based on Foster's own experiences and research in Ghana, social "differentiation" rather than "stratification" was seen as a more relevant concept in societies where there are "multiple bases of social differentiation including race, ethnicity, occupation, regional origin, lineage, and sex" (Foster 1977, p. 215). Spatial distributions are of paramount importance, for Foster observed there were huge disparities in the propensity for school enrollment within countries, irrespective of any other single indicator of status as had been conceived by U.S.-based researchers who followed in the wake of Sorokin. Foster's attention to the systematic but non-vertical variations in life chances are applicable to two sources of differentiation in Mexico, Peru, and Chile that are found in our survey data: region and gender.

Regional inequality in children's access to schooling and economic activity reflects differences both in family demand for children's time and differences in school provision by central governments to each area. When it is possible to "net out" the factors that determine families' demand for education and need for children's work—to hold these factors constant—then the remaining differences in regional activities will reflect the supply of opportunities for work (for example, in agriculture) and the opportunities for education (the availability of schools, especially of high quality schools). National governments, in fulfilling their public responsibility to educate their entire nations, influence both of these supply-side factors. As discussed in Chapter 2, legislation, and the accompanying social norms, now sanction child labor, even labor in family employment. And, as discussed in Chapter 3, public education systems that are well-financed, with schools closely situated even near rural families, work as incentives for children to attend school. When governments target rural zones of their nations, as Chile did by prioritizing the 900 worst-performing schools and then increasing the subsidy provided for each rural student, governments act to expand the alternatives to child labor. More importantly, such targeting reduces spatial differentiation, in Foster's sense. When nations provide stipends to children in poorer regions–as Mexico did through its PARE and PROGRESA initiatives—they hope to effect the same ends. Thus, one goal of this chapter is to document the evolution of regional differentiation in children's activity during the 1990s, net of differences in family resources. In so doing, we can evaluate government efforts to equalize school opportunities in each nation.

Aside from region, gender is a second element that has strongly differentiated children's activities in many areas of the world, including two of the countries of this study. In recent years, governments have attempted to eliminate gender inequality, under pressure from national and international women's movements. In opposition to the gender-neutral ideas of Sorokin and stratification theorists, Firestone (1970), Tinker (1976), Hartmann (1981, 1994) and many feminists argued that the division of power along gender lines will persist, independent of other changes in the social stratification system that were accompanied by educational expansion. The prospect of an interaction between gender-based and other forms of stratification was foreseen by Boserup (1990, p. 19), who recognized that the universalization of education—a public ideal in nearly all nations today—posed an inherent threat to the continuation of male hegemony and should not be expected ever completely to succeed, any more than other social strata could be expected to vanish completely of their own accord. Concretely, girls' access to education plays a mediating role in the creation of gender inequality among adults and gender inequalities in earnings.

Will increasing the access to schooling for all children bring special benefits to girls? One reason for the gender focus in programs like Mexico's PROGRESA is to make this outcome more likely. Some scholars and advocates of girls schooling view persisting disparities following reforms such as Mexico's in a sanguine light, arguing that lessons from many nations reveal that promoting girls' educations can be accomplished via policies aimed at lowering the direct costs and opportunity costs, increasing the relative returns for women's education (Bellew and King 1993; Herz et al. 1991). The general social benefits from increased access by girls to schooling are so great, in this view (Hill and King 1993), that societies must and will eventually take steps to overcome barriers to girls' full participation. In so doing, they will ultimately erode the gender-based dimension of educational stratification. Several such strategies are currently being attempted in Mexico, as has already been discussed. The hope is that, as barriers to girls fall and gender becomes less integral to educational stratification, the place of gender in social stratification generally also will diminish.

A contrasting perspective to this view suggests that access to schooling will continue to be determined partly by gender in the foreseeable future. Two reasons for this pessimism are often given. First, gender inequality is felt to be so basic to the formation of the state apparatus governing most education opportunities that few thorough-going reforms ever will be implemented, regardless of how thoughtfully they are formulated (Stromquist 1989; Stromquist 1995). Second, and more fundamentally, the domestic economy and the division of labor it replicates are distant from the domain of even the most activist policy intervention strategies. Women's traditional work and domestic roles create pressures on girls to leave school earlier than boys in order to assume unpaid household responsibilities for their parents and siblings and—eventually—for their husbands and their own children. With this future in mind, parents may perceive fewer benefits to schooling for daughters than for sons. Even when the benefits of schooling to the *individual* recipient are large, parents may view the returns to their own family as small because girls ultimately assist others in patrilocal societies. Girls remain disadvantaged (Massiah 1990; Heward 1998). These disadvantages are exacerbated with increased poverty, during downturns in the economy, or with retrenchment in redistributive welfare commitments from structural adjustment. At these times, girls' access to education can take large steps backward (Buchman 1996; Stromquist 1998).

The empirical study of girls' access to schooling during social development and the expansion of the public supply of education has been guided by several useful perspectives on the domestic sphere constraining girls' options. One particularly important approach uses inferences from household surveys to observe the internal power and resource allocation dynamics of the household, which is the most immediate institution for the replication of gender stratification. Building on the research by Blake (1989), investigations worldwide have turned to the impact of sibship size and composition for girls' educations and alternative activity. Work by anthropologists (Greenhalgh 1985), economists (Berhman and Wolfe 1987; Butcher and Case 1994), psychologists (Marjoribanks 1991) and sociologists (Powell and Steelman 1990, 1993) has now illuminated the nature and the consequence of the birth order and sex composition of children within their sibships. Historical studies in the United States (e.g., Sassler 1995) suggest what others have confirmed in developing economies (Post and Pong 1998). Girls' competition for home resources can be inferred from the dependence of girls' domestic versus school activity on their sibling size or sibling composition. When sibling size and sibling composition matter for girls' school participation, inferences are possible about the allocation of material and nonmaterial resources within the household unit.

Few investigators have probed sources of the intra-national dispersion of education sex differentials in school attendance. Bowman and Anderson (1980, p. S25) urged attention to pronounced intra-national differences in attendance rates in Morocco, Sierra Leone, and other areas. "Considering the mosaic of inducements and resistances, the stricter social selection among girls in relation to distance from school is not surprising." The patterned acceptance of education for girls reflects diffusion of norms and opportunities throughout national systems.

REGIONAL DIFFERENTIATION IN CHILDREN'S SCHOOL ATTAINMENTS

In each of the country case studies, household survey data make it possible to identify children's school attainments and school/work activities by geographic region (in Peru) or by administrative zone (in Chile and Mexico). The major focus of this investigation is with the evolution of children's activities, but at this juncture we also should consider regional changes in the number of years that children have remained in school. For this purpose, it is useful to investigate how many years of school were completed by children at the age of seventeen, the upper end of our age grouping. As a first approximation at the changing effects of region, it is possible to use each country's survey designation of "rural" versus "urban" or "non-rural" (these two terms are simply called "urban," for simplicity). One question for this chapter is how the effects of rural residence have changed over the time periods of each country case study. Tobit regression analysis is useful to address that question. To proceed, the later and earlier survey data were merged together as unified data files, and dichotomous "dummy" variables were created to identify membership in the latter survey year (that is, 1996 in Chile, 1997 in Peru, and 1996 in Mexico). In each country, the "omitted" comparison group referred to the earlier year (1990 in Chile, 1985 in Peru, and 1992 in Mexico). In each country, interaction terms were created for the effect of rural residence with belonging to the later year.

The results of the tobit regressions are presented in Table 5.1. Each coefficient can be interpreted as the change in the number of school years that a child would be likely to have completed by the age of seventeen, given a unit change in the corresponding independent variables. Notice that in all three countries, rural children completed less schooling than non-rural and urban children. Although rural children were poorer than non-rural children, their school disadvantage persists even after controlling for the effects of family income. What is most striking from Table 5.1 is the significant interaction effect between rurality and the time-period: There was an attenuation in the effect of rural residence over the years of this study in all three countries. The substantive importance of this change can be appreciated in Figure 5.1, which presents the conditional means of completed education, calculated from Table 5.1. These mean years of schooling are presented for each family income quintile, in each year, and for both rural and urban children. For every fifth of the income distribu-

Table 5.1 Determinants of School Years Attained by Age 17 in Chile, Peru, and Mexico: Direct and Time-Period Interaction Effects of Income Quintile and Rural Residence

(Tobit Regression Coefficients)

	Chile	Peru	Mexico
Time-period Effect (dummy var. for later time)	-0.907***	-1.590***	1.549***
Child is female	0.237***	-0.345*	0.840***
Child's age	0.802***	0.494***	0.731***
Number of children in home	-0.161***	-0.009	-0.268***
In 2nd Quintile of family income (rather than 1st)	0.018	0.115	0.493**
In 3rd Quintile of family income (rather than 1st)	0.188	0.427	0.778***
In 4th Quintile of family income (rather than 1st)	0.344**	0.783**	1.274***
In 5th Quintile of family income (rather than 1st)	0.755***	0.821**	1.860***
Lives in rural area (rather than urban)	-0.978***	-3.562***	-1.309***
Interaction of time-period effect with:			
2nd Quintile	0.151*	0.143	-0.081
3rd Quintile	0.137*	0.049	-0.015
4th Quintile	0.159*	-0.020	-0.036
5th Quintile	0.069	0.145	-0.318**
Being female	-0.011	0.201*	-0.442***
Child's age	0.027*	0.132***	-0.088***
Living in rural area	0.296***	1.440***	0.179**
Number of children in home	-0.004	-0.087***	0.055**
Constant	-3.124***	-0.328	-4.200***
Number of cases	22505	4715	15921
Chi-2 Statistic	13876***	3069***	6534***

Note: Time period effects for Chile measure the change from 1990 to 1996; for Peru, change from 1985 to 1997; for Mexico, from 1992 to 1996. * sig at < .05 level; ** sig at < .01 level; *** <.001 level. The omitted reference category for the income quintiles is the poorest fifth of family income. Source: Analysis of CASEN, ENNIV, and ENIGH.

tion in every country, the overall disadvantage suffered by rural children began to wane. Rural improvement was most prominent in Peru, where the gap had been greatest in 1985. However, keep in mind that the time-period for the Peruvian case study (1985–97) is twice as long as the time period for Chile (1990–96) and three times as long as the case of Mexico (1992–1996).

REGION AND CHILDREN'S ACTIVITIES

For two countries of this study, we can use the CASEN and ENIGH to estimate the provincial (Chile) or state (Mexico) proportions of children who are reported to be engaged in one of the four major activity categories described in Chapter 1. In Peru,

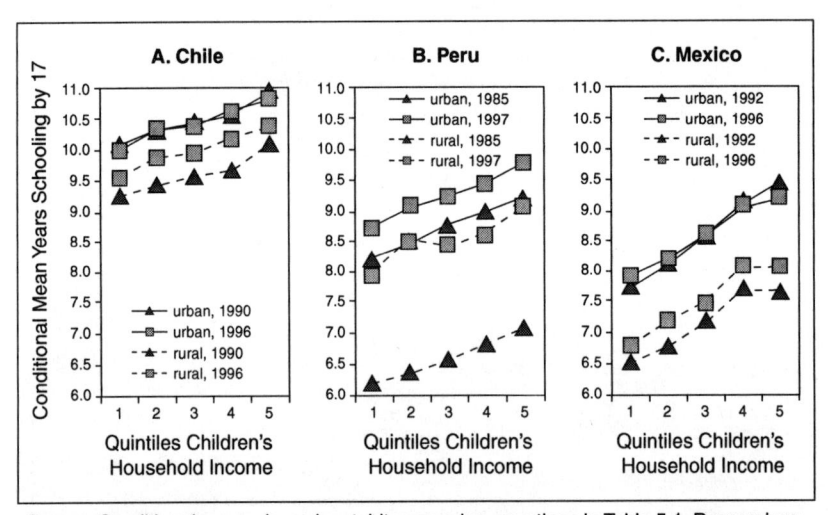

Source: Conditional means based on tobit regression equations in Table 5.1. Regressions control for direction and time-period interaction effects of: quintile, rural residence, number of children in home, gender.

FIGURE 5.1 Trends in the Effects of Income and Rural Residence on Educational Attainment at Age 17

there are insufficient cases for generalizing survey findings to each of that country's administrative departments. This is less worrisome than it might first appear, because Peru's education system was highly centralized during the twelve-year period studied in this book, and student attendance in Peru's education zones or nucleos was not likely to reflect differences in local finance or governance. Peruvian survey data can still be used to describe regional tendencies, because there are enough cases to estimate the activities of children in seven different regions of the country. Using the ENNIV, it is possible to estimate the changing activities of children who lived along Peru's rural and urban coast, its rural and urban highlands ("sierra"), and the rural and urban rainforest ("selva"). Separately, we also can observe the activities of children living in metropolitan Lima in 1985 and 1997.

Figure 5.2 reports the percentages of children who attended school, either exclusively (darker colored bars at bottom) or in combination with some type of economic activity (lighter bars above the "only school" areas). Based on the 1985 and 1997 EN-

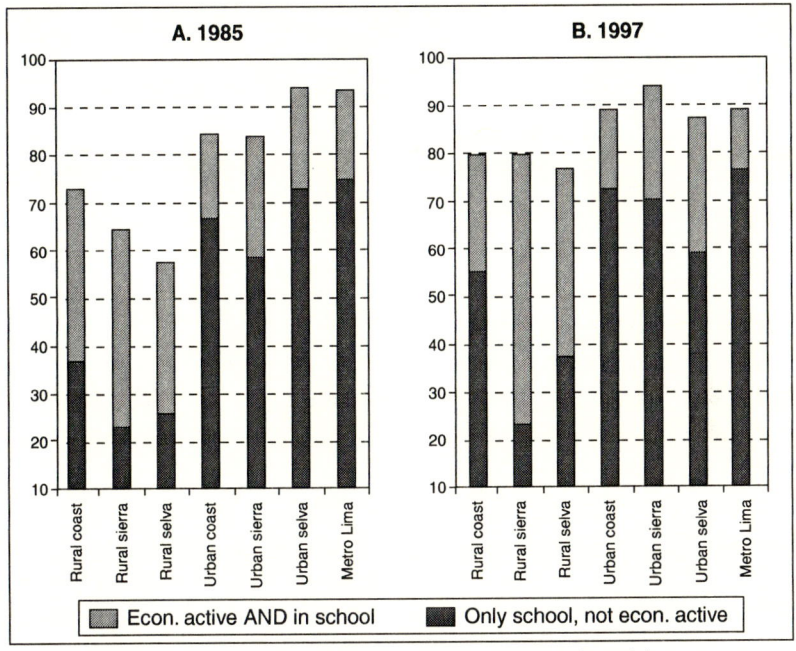

Region And Gender Differences In Children's Work And Schooling   183

A. 1985 / **B. 1997**

Econ. active AND in school | Only school, not econ. active

Source: Analysis of 1985 and 1997 ENNIV (non-summer months only)

FIGURE 5.2 Peruvian Trends in School Attendance and Economic Activity, 1985-1997, by Region

NIV data, Figure 5.2 illustrates the regional differentiation of children's activities for each year. It further illustrates how these activities and regional differences changed over the 1985–1997 period. As was already seen in Figure 1.5, in Chapter 1, there was an overall increase in school participation during this twelve-year period. Here, Figure 5.2 shows where these increases occurred: in Peru's rural selva, its rural sierra, and in its urban sierra. In these three regions, substantially greater percentages of children attended school at the end of the Peruvian case-study (1997) as compared to the beginning (1985). In the rural highlands of Peru, the "sierra," only 62 percent of persons aged twelve to seventeen attended school in 1985. By contrast, in the capital, 92 percent of these children were attending. Over the next twelve years—perhaps as a result of school construction but, more likely, as a reflection of social demand—school participation rates soared in the rural sierra. The result was that the gap with Lima diminished by half: regional inequality between the capital and the rural sierra declined, at least if we focus simply on school participation.

On closer scrutiny, however, we can see that regional inequality did not change nearly so much if we focus on differences in the percentages of students who only attended school. Of those who attended school in Lima, smaller percentages were economically active in 1997, as compared with 1985. But in the rural sierra, there was no change in the percentage of children attending school without working. The great majority of those who were students in the rural sierra were simultaneously working. Thus, by one measure, Peru's regional inequalities diminished; by another measure, they did not.

In the other two countries of this investigation we are able to make more detailed descriptions of spatial differences in educational opportunities. Our surveys are nationally comprehensive of every Mexican state and every Chilean province. To illustrate the changing regional distribution of activities in Mexico, it is useful to focus on children's activities in Chiapas and Oaxaca, two of Mexico's most agrarian, illiterate, and poorest states (as well as those with the greatest concentrations of persons speaking indigenous languages). Since at least the late nineteenth century, children living in Chiapas and Oaxaca have attained less formal education than children living in the more developed northern areas of Mexico. The school and school/work activities reported in the ENIGH confirm there were wide differences in the experiences of children in Chiapas and Oaxaca, on the one hand, and children in the rest of Mexico. However, as can be appreciated in Figure 5.3, during 1992 this gap reflected the fact that far more children lived in rural areas in Oaxaca and Chiapas than in the rest of Mexico. Figure 5.3 shows that, if we compare the experiences of rural children in those states only with other rural children in the rest of Mexico, and if we similarly compare only the activities of urban children in either area, then there was no obvious regional inequality in 1992. By 1996 regional differences had become more pronounced, however. Similar percentages of city children in each area attended

Region And Gender Differences In Children's Work And Schooling 185

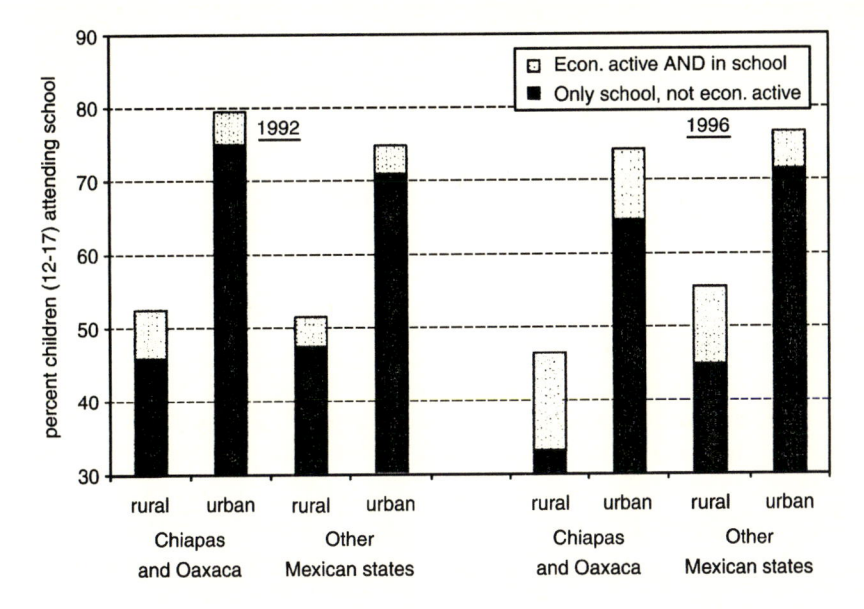

FIGURE 5.3 Regional Inequality in Economic and School Activities for Mexican Children (12-17), 1992 and 1996

school, but more urban students in Oaxaca and Chiapas were economically active at the same time that they were also in school. Comparing rural children, even greater contrasts emerged over the 1992–1996 period. By 1996, smaller percentages of rural children from Oaxaca or Chiapas attended school, both in absolute terms compared and compared with rural children in other Mexican states.

Overall, there were modest declines in school participation rates among both rural and urban children of Chiapas and Oaxaca. At the same time, there was a modest increase outside of these two states, and the divergent tendencies are especially clear if we focus only on children living in rural Mexico. Moreover, the over-time trends become especially apparent when we compare the percentages of children who were privileged to attend school without engaging in any economic activity. Not only did the school participation rates of southern Mexico decline during the 1992–1996 period, but the proportion of students who had to combine their studies with work actually increased. Outside of

Chiapas and Oaxaca, more students also worked; but more of these young people were attending school. By one measure—school participation—regional inequality did not change between the rest of Mexico, on the one hand, and Chiapas and Oaxaca, on the other. However, just as in the case of Peru, regional inequality widened if we consider changes in the percentages of children who attended school without working.

A similar analysis can be made of provinces in Chile. Unlike Mexico, where Chiapas and Oaxaca have a long histories of low educational attainment, Chile has no conspicuously illiterate, poor, or indigenous provinces. In Chile it is therefore more useful to focus on provinces where there were high percentages of children living in rural areas and to compare the school participation of urban and rural children in these provinces with urban and rural children in the rest of Chile. Figure 5.4 reports the results of this exercise. Between provinces of greater and lower concentrations of rural children, there was greater inequality in 1990 than in 1996. Too few students were reported to be economically active while in school to make accurate regional estimates of this sub-population, and so we should focus only on those who are in school. Rural students living in more heavily rural (and agrarian) areas of Chile were much less likely to attend school in 1990 than in 1996. But this group of students increased its school attendance rate more than 10 percentage points over the 1990–96 period, closing half of the distance that separated it from the experience of urban children in their own province. The gap also narrowed between school attendance rates of these rural children and those who lived in less rural areas of Chile (especially, as we will see, those living in Santiago).

A more detailed investigation of inter-province and inter-state inequality is possible for Chile and Mexico by using the regional mean years of adult education as an overall indicator of the social resources necessary for school participation in the younger generation. As already seen in Chapter 1, Figure 1.4, school attendance rates had become near universal in 1987 for children ages twelve and thirteen. Therefore, to observe changes over time more

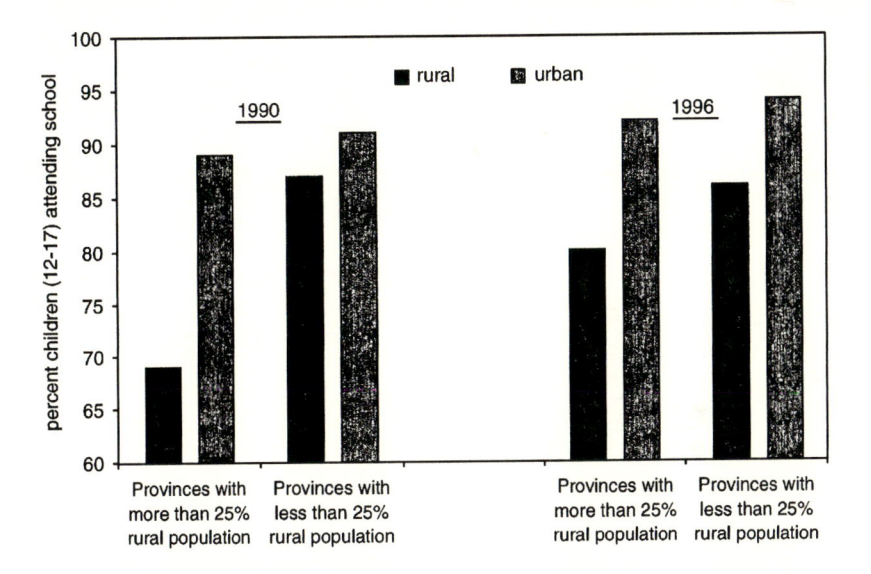

FIGURE 5.4 Percent of Chilean Children in School, by Child's Rural/Urban Residence and Provincial Concentration of Rural Children in Population

clearly, it is useful to focus on children of the Media years of age: fourteen to seventeen. For this age group, therefore, Figure 5.5 illustrates the differentiation of Chilean provinces in two dimensions. The X-axis shows the differences between provinces in the mean years of schooling that were completed by the household heads of the children in the CASEN samples of 1987 (Panel A) and 1996 (Panel B). The Y-axis shows provincial differences in the mean percentage of children who were in school full-time without economic activity.

In the 1987 CASEN, it is possible to observe a strong association between each of the provincial indicators: Children were less likely to attend school in provinces where parents had less education (just as was seen in Figure 5.4, in provinces that were heavily rural). The relationship between adult and children's education clusters tightly around a regression line with a goodness-of-fit statistic, the R-square, of 0.67. In other words, 67 percent of the variation in children's school participation rates in each province was explainable based on provincial differences in adult educa-

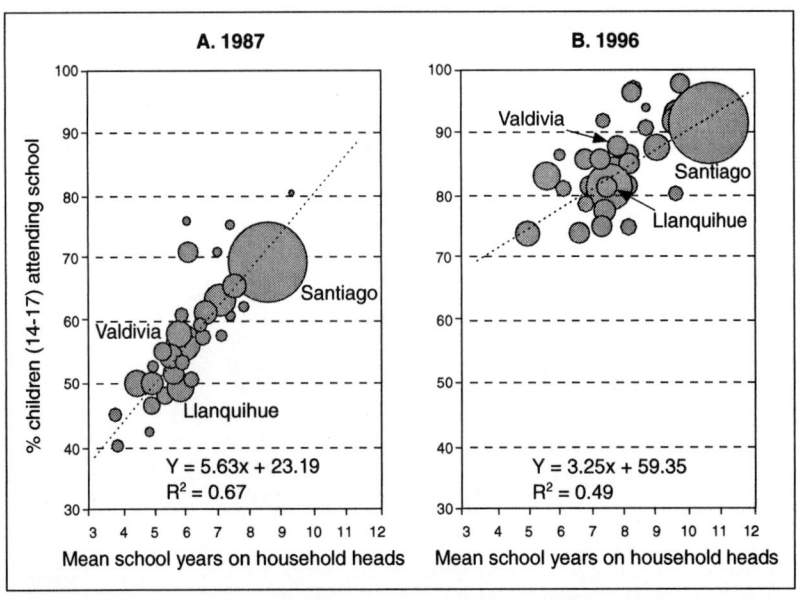

188 Region And Gender Differences In Children's Work And Schooling

A. 1987 / **B. 1996**

% children (14-17) attending school vs. Mean school years on household heads

Panel A: Y = 5.63x + 23.19, R² = 0.67 (labels: Santiago, Valdivia, Llanquihue)
Panel B: Y = 3.25x + 59.35, R² = 0.49 (labels: Valdivia, Santiago, Llanquihue)

Note: each circle represents an Chilean province. Their area is proportional to the number of children (14-17) living in the province. Regressions are weighted by populations of each province. Source: analysis of CASEN in 1987 and 1996.

FIGURE 5.5 Trends in Regional Education Inequality in Chile: Relations of Provincial Rates of Attendance and Mean Education of Household Heads

tion. The slope of the line is 5.63, meaning that, on average, provincial school participation rates increased 5.63 percentage points for every additional average year of completed adult education in the province.

The close 1987 relationship appears to have attenuated over the next nine years. In Panel B (based on the 1996 CASEN) there was a much looser fit of provinces around a regression line: The R-square statistic had been reduced to only 0.49. Moreover, the regression line slope was less steep. Provinces with more highly educated parents still had greater percentages of children in school, but the increase was only 3.23 percentage points for each additional year of adult education (rather than 5.63 points).

Results of similar analyses for Mexico suggest a very different historical tendency. In Mexico, Figure 5.6 illustrates the differentiation of Mexican states on the same two dimensions that were

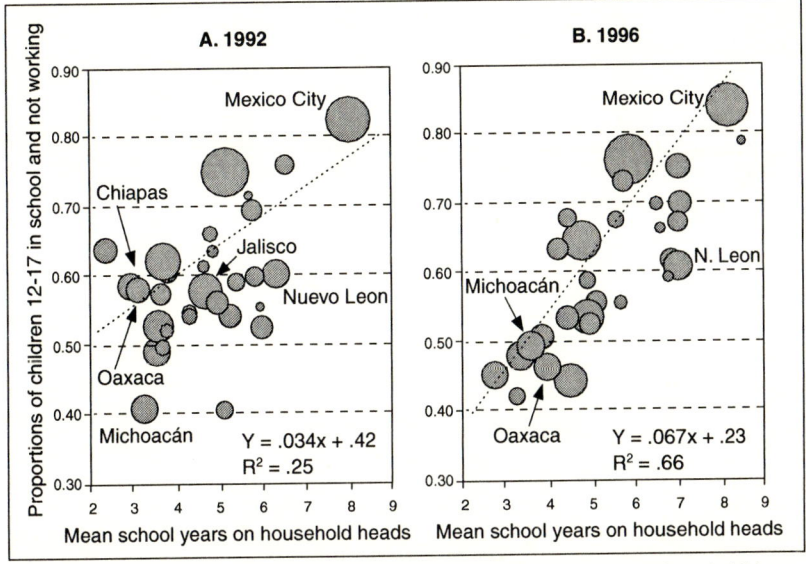

Region And Gender Differences In Children's Work And Schooling 189

FIGURE 5.6 Trends in Regional Educational Inequality in Mexico: Relations of State Rates of Full-time Enrollment and State Mean Parents' Education

Note: The position of each circle on the Y-axis represents the state's proportion of children who were in school without any reported economic activity. The position on the X-axis is each state's average years of schooling completed by the head's of these children's households (fathers in about 85 percent of the cases) The area of each circle is proportional to the 1990 population of the state. Regression equations and lines are weighted based on state population. Source: analysis of national income and expenditure surveys (ENIGH) for 1992 and 1996.

seen above for Chile. In Panel A (based on the ENIGH of 1992), we can observe a comparatively weak association between states' mean levels of parental education and state rates of full-time schooling. The goodness-of-fit statistic, the R-square, was only 0.24, while the slope was similar to that seen in Figure 5.5 for Chile in 1996: States had an average percentage-point increase in children's full-time schooling of 3.23 for each additional year of schooling by the household head. Notice that this relationship, initially not as strong as that in Chile, became much stronger over the next four years. By 1996, there was a tight association between state rates of children's full-time school attendance and states' average adult education. The R-square statistic increased, matching Chile's of 1987. Over the same four-year period, the slope of Mexico's regression line increased, until it was as steep as that of Chile in 1987. In Mexico, a simple inspection of state participation rates suggests that regional inequality became more pronounced over time and that, as compared with Chile, a very different type of regional development was occurring in which states became more differentiated.

The finding of widening regional inequality, based on Mexico's ENIGH, can be corroborated through a parallel investigation of changes in Mexico's secondary school enrollments. The investigation required several complementary sources of information on regions and on the school attendance of children in primary and secondary school and used municipio and state-level information provided by Mexico's secretary of public education (SEP). We also can use indicators of regional development or, as phrased in Mexican policy discussions, of regional "marginality." These indicators were created by the Consejo Nacional de Población (CONAPO), and derive from information in the 1990 census.

As a second source of information, we can use regional school enrollment figures, obtained from the Secretaria de Educación Publica. I used measures of student enrollment in the last year of primary school in 1984–85, 1989–90, and 1994–95. I similarly used measures of enrollment in the first year of secondary school for 1985–86, 1990–91, and 1995–96. In each year and for each level of schooling, I measured the numbers of new or first-time students (that is, not including the numbers of repeaters). For each state, I then created a net index of the rate of transition or continuation from primary to secondary school. These sums are provided in Appendix A5.1

A state's percentage of primary students who continue to the secondary level reflects, in an economic sense, the demand for and the supply of secondary schooling in that state. In its political sense, however, these continuation rates indicate regional differences in the capability of Mexico to carry out its 1993 constitutional reform, which aimed to make secondary education compulsory for children who have finished primary education, regardless of their place of residence. In 1985, the average rates of student continuation, from primary to secondary school, was

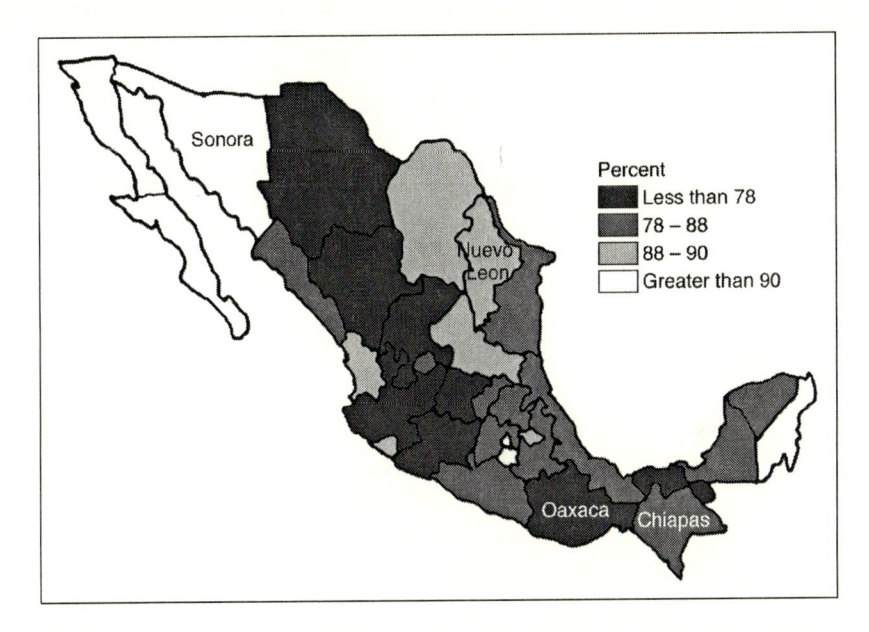

FIGURE 5.7a Percent of Primary Students Continuing to Secondary, 1985

geographically dispersed across Mexico (see Figure 5.7a). By 1995, however, there were large regional differences between the northern and southern states in the net continuations by students from primary to secondary school (see Figure 5.7b). A geographical clustering of school dropouts was occurring, just as Mexico decentralized its secondary school system and concomitantly with the legal mandate to universalize access to secondary schools.

Figure 5.7a illustrates transitions to secondary school a full two years following Mexico's declaration of universal and compulsory secondary school. It thus serves as a reminder of what historians of education frequently observe, that policy declarations are far from sufficient to ensure implementation. Figure 5.7a indicates the clustering of access to secondary schooling. Northern states, and the states around Mexico City, came closest to universal continuation to secondary school. Southern states were furthest from universal secondary continuation.

By law, Mexico's supply of secondary schooling—like Chile's—ought to be elastic. That is, school participation opportunities

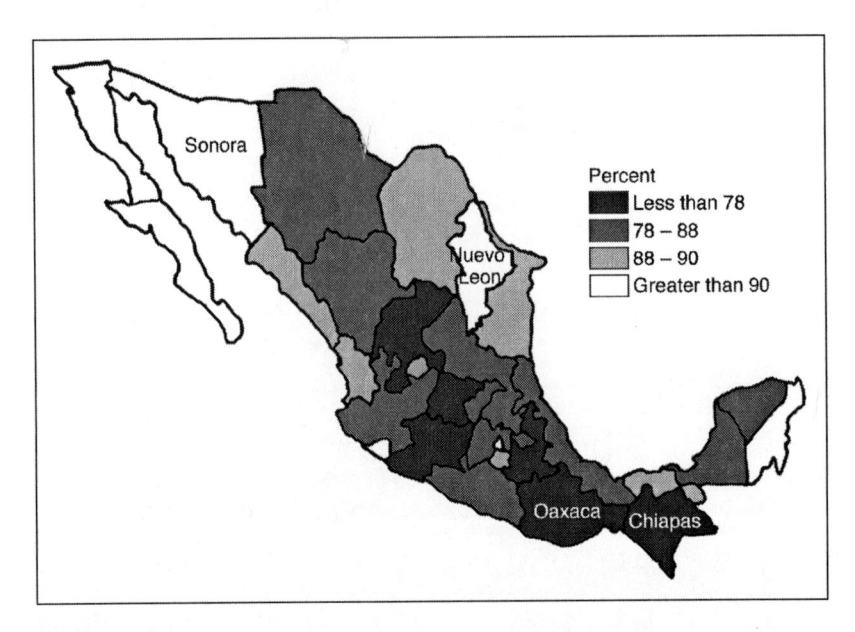

FIGURE 5.7b Percent of Primary Students Continuing to Secondary, 1995

should increase proportionately to increased demand for education. If the supply of free schooling is, in principle, available equally to all, then we must account for the fact that children in less developed regions of the country are in alternative activities. One explanation, though probably not very likely, is that regional North-South differences came to reflect cultural differences between the industrial North and heavily indigenous South. Perhaps different subcultures place different values on education as an end in itself. A second explanation, much more likely, is that Mexico's interstate inequality reflects differences in the ability of communities and parents to forgo their children's earnings or household assistance. Families and communities are unequally able to pay for the indirect costs of investing in children's education, that is, the costs associated with the value of children's time and labor. Even more importantly, from an education policy perspective, states have different abilities to supply free education, and these differences also may be reflected in the growing regional inequalities in continuation that are evident in Figure 5.7.

Note that a decline in the secondary school continuation rate does not necessarily indicate decreased demand for or supply of schooling. Primary education (the denominator of the continuation rate) may be expanding faster than the state can supply secondary schooling to the population of primary graduates. For example, Oaxaca increased the numbers of children in primary school during the 1985–95 decade, and this would necessarily increase the difficulty in meeting the obligation to provide free and compulsory secondary schooling in that state. The fact that Oaxaca was less able than northern states to enforce compulsory secondary attendance is a major cause for concern with decentralization policies.

The relation between state rates of primary-secondary transition and state levels of adult education suggested that in more marginalized Mexican states, fewer children continued past the primary level, and these correlations became more pronounced over time. That is, over time, there was an increased association between measures of regional development and rates of school continuation. A noticeable tightening in the relationship between continuation and this indicator of adult education can be appreciated in Figure 5.8.

Figure 5.8 plots the values for each Mexican state and Mexico City in 1985 and 1995. For each year, and for each state, these plots show the net rate of children's continuation to secondary school on the Y-axis (the net rate is defined in Appendix A5.1). The X-axis shows the percentage of adults in each state who had completed primary school in 1990. Regression slopes are estimated in each year in order to "fit" the relationship presented graphically.

I analyzed the relationship between secondary continuation and marginality over the years between 1985 and 1995. The findings are consistent with the trend seen in Figure 5.8: A closer association between marginality and continuation emerges over time. Several *alternative* indicators of marginality further confirm the pattern that is seen in this figure. I further tested the relationship between state transitions to secondary school and: the floor material of homes (percentage dirt), and percentages of low-in-

A. 1985

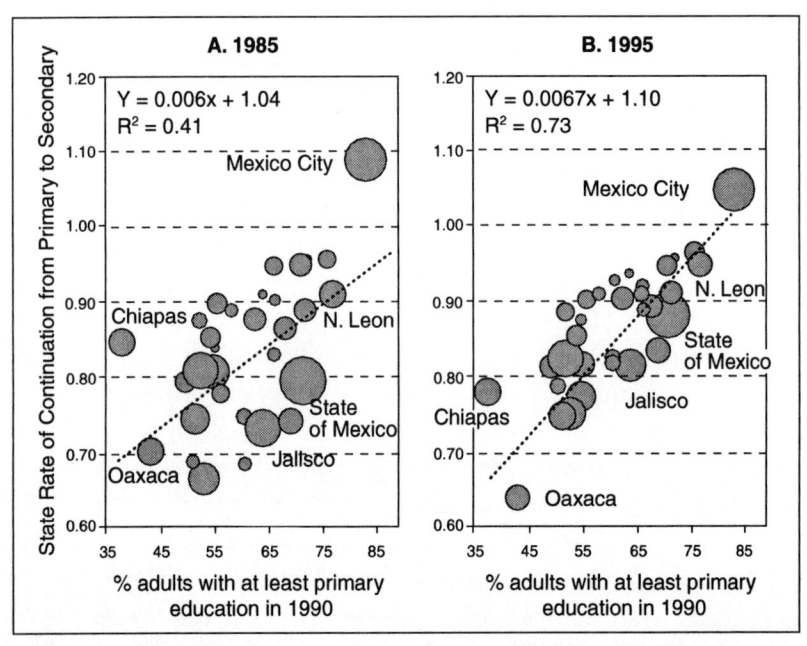

$Y = 0.006x + 1.04$
$R^2 = 0.41$

B. 1995

$Y = 0.0067x + 1.10$
$R^2 = 0.73$

Note: The position of each circle on the Y-axis represents the number of students each year who began the first grade of secondary school divided by the nubmer who began the last grade of primary school during the previous year. The area of each circle is proportional to the 1990 population of the state. Source: analysis of municipo enrollment data provided by Secretary of Public Education (SEP) and indicators of marginación provided by Consejo Nacional de Población. Regression equations and lines are weighted based on state population.

FIGURE 5.8 Trends in Regional Education Inequality in Mexico: Relation of State Rates of Transition From Primary to Secondary Level and State Levels of Adult Education

come workers (those receiving less than two minimum salaries). There is consistency in the findings, regardless of which indicator of community marginality is used. In each year, irrespective of how community inequality is measured—adult education, floor material, or low-income workers—I found that Mexico's disadvantaged or marginal areas send smaller proportions of children from primary to secondary school and that the relationship became more pronounced over time as Mexico's more affluent states gained ground and as its poorer and more marginalized states lost ground.

The pattern seen in Figure 5.8 (and for other indicators not presented) serves as a warning about decentralization. In 1985 there was already a significant correlation between each state's overall percentage of adults without secondary schooling and the continuation rate of children to secondary school. Regional inequality thus reflected educational stratification, that is, the association between the schooling attained by parents and their children. As can be seen in Figure 5.8 (just as in Figure 5.6), the correlation became greater over time. Ironically, the correlation increased over a decade when Mexico's federal government legislated universal attendance to secondary school. The statistic summarizing the tightness of fit of states around the regression slope, the R^2, increased from .41 in 1985 to .73 in 1995. Thus, at the end of this period, certain states could be seen as winners and certain states could be seen as losers in a complex economic and policy process. The winners included northern states, such as Nuevo Leon, where most adults had finished primary school. In these states, greater percentages of primary school students continued to secondary school. The losers included states like Oaxaca and Chiapas, where less than half the adults had finished primary school according to the 1990 census. These states lost not only when compared to the winners but in absolute terms: Smaller percentages of primary school students were continuing to secondary from the primary level (albeit, more children were finishing primary).

The relationships and over-time tendencies that are seen in Figure 5.8 also appear in similar analyses, not reported here, using alternative indicators of *county* (rather than state) indicators of marginalization. I also gauged the correlations between community-level resources and access to secondary school within particular states. I obtained Mexican enrollment data separately for each county (*"municipio"*). I then compared correlations between continuation rates and resources within Oaxaca and Chiapas, two of Mexico's most disadvantaged southern states. The same tendencies in the municipios of these southern states are evident as seen among states for the entire nation. That is, continuations to secondary school by primary students became *more* associated with a community's family resources in the latter period, despite the fact that federal legislation had been adopted to universalize secondary education.

REGIONAL DIFFERENTIATION, CONTEXTUAL POVERTY, AND CONTEXTUAL RURALITY

The opposing tendencies found in Chile and Mexico reflect changing inequality not only between provinces and states but also, simultaneously, intra-state inequality among families. Regional differences in children's likelihoods to work or attend school are partly a reflection of the regional differences in poverty or rural residence that are associated with regions. Thus, it is necessary to control for the effects of rural residence and poverty at the regional level, before concluding that regional differentiation has widened. I constructed similar indicators of regional poverty and rurality in Chile and Mexico. The ENIGH survey was designed for the purpose of measuring income, and it provides multiple measures of income. For each year I summed the value of income from all sources for the household head (the father of the child in 85 percent of cases). For each year, I then divided the sample of children into five equal parts based on the total income of the household head, similar to the procedure in Chapter 4, but this time using only the income of the head. I thus created income *quintiles* from this information, ranking households from the richest first quintile to the poorest fifth quintile of income. I used the same procedure to create income quintiles in Chile. Descriptions of Mexico's quintiles are presented in the appendix to Chapter 1.

PROGRESA and other poverty alleviation programs focus on the bottom fifth of Mexico's income distribution, and so I used this criteria to define "poverty." Then, I estimated logistic regression equations of full-time school attendance (without work), comparing in the analysis each of the upper four-fifths of the income distribution with the omitted reference category:

the poorest, bottom quintile of income. This approach allows us to gauge the impact of a child's own household head's income on the likelihood that she or he will attend school full-time. As control variables, I also estimated the effects of: the total number of siblings (sharing the household head's income); being female (rather than male); the child's age in years; the years of education attained by the household head; and whether the child's home was in an area classified by Mexico as rural (population less than 2,500) as opposed to non-rural (population greater than 2,500). I combined both the 1992 and 1996 survey data, and created interaction terms for the time period change in each of the control and income variables. This approach allows us to gauge changes in the role of income as a determinant of school participation. When both the direct and interaction effects of income quintile are measured, the direct effects inform us of the role of income in 1992. The interaction terms tell us whether and how much the 1992 effects increased or decreased in their importance over the following four years, the period when secondary school attendance was legally made universal and when states assumed responsibility for secondary school.

Children's poverty, and their reduced access to resources needed for school participation, are detrimental not only because of poverty within the child's own individual family. In addition, poorer children are increasingly concentrated in poorer regions, such as the states of Oaxaca and Chiapas. Similarly, rural residence affects children not only due to their individual difficulty in accessing schools or the dominance of agriculture opportunities for individual families. In addition, rural children live in sparsely populated regions, where urban children, and urban opportunities, are generally scarce. Figures 5.6 and 5.8, above, describing changes in school participation between Northern and Southern Mexico, each combine two associated but distinct changes over the period when decentralization occurred and compulsory education was extended. They reflect, first, changes in the role of individual family resources in determining access to school opportunities: Children in the South come from poorer families, especially rural southern children. And family poverty may have increased its impact on schooling after the 1994 recession and devaluation. Secondly, Figures 5.6 and 5.8 also reflect changes in the ability of poorer, more rural, and more marginalized *states* to enroll their populations in school and comply with the 1993 constitutional amendment. This second tendency, if borne out by evidence from the ENIGH, would have even greater policy relevance than the first.

To gauge the changing impact of regional context on the access to school in Mexico, I created two state-level indicators. As previously mentioned, a child's income quintile shows the relative position of the child in the national distribution of income in each year. But poorer and richer children are unevenly distributed across Mexican territory. I calculated the proportion of each state's population that was in the bottom quintile of the income distribution in each year. For example, in Chiapas in 1992 and in 1996, over 40 percent of children aged twelve to seventeen lived in families where the head's earnings were in the lowest fifth of Mexico's income distribution. By contrast, in Baja California, fewer than 3 percent of children were in this lowest income group. The net proportion of a state's poor children (defined as those living in the poorest quintile) gives a simple indicator of contextual poverty.

An alternative measure of context can be constructed similarly, based on the proportion of each state's population living in areas of low population density. The ability of children in Oaxaca or Chiapas to attend secondary school is determined by the availability of schooling to these children. In areas of very low population, states face special challenges in providing secondary schools to all students, even when television classes are offered. To create a contextual indicator of rural residence (separate from a child's individual place of residence), for each survey year I calculated the proportion of a state's twelve- to seventeen-year-old population living in localities of fewer than 2,500 persons. These proportions varied widely, from Chiapas (where, in 1996, three out of five children lived in rural localities) to Mexico City (where the homes of all children are considered "urban").

Region And Gender Differences In Children's Work And Schooling 199

Table 5.2: Determinants of Full-time Schooling for Chileans, Ages 12-17: Individual, Family, and Provincial-level Contextual Effects over 1990-96 Period

(Logistic Regression Coefficients)

	Model 1	Model 2	Model 3
Time period: survey year is 1996 (not 1990)	-0.358*	-0.411*	-0.630***
Household head's years of schooling	0.165***	0.166***	0.160***
Child is FEMALE (not male)	0.246***	0.246***	0.247***
Lives in RURAL area	-0.895***	-0.910***	-0.724***
Child's AGE	-0.607***	-0.606***	-0.609***
Number of SIBLINGS sharing household	-0.136***	-0.138***	-0.136***
Income Quintile Dummies (poorest ommited):			
Household head's income in 2nd quintile	0.001	0.004	-0.011
Household head's income is in 3rd quintile	0.010	0.017	-0.017
Household head's income is in 4th quintile	0.326**	0.335**	0.299**
Head's Income is in 5th quintile (wealthiest)	0.582***	0.590***	0.559**
Period interaction effects, individual level:			
period * 2nd income quintile	0.280*	0.291*	0.308*
period * 3rd income quintile	0.227	0.241	0.277
period * 4th income quintile	0.455**	0.478*	0.515*
period * 5th income quintile	-0.153	-0.132	-0.098
period * living in RURAL household	0.575***	0.550**	0.323*
period * being FEMALE	-0.081	-0.080	-0.082
period * head's years of schooling	0.014	0.015	0.022
Contextual effects and period interactions:			
Province's proportion of "poor" children	--------	0.248	--------
Period * proportion of "poor" children	--------	0.178	--------
Province's proportion rural children	--------	--------	-0.717*
period * proportion of rural children	--------	--------	1.111***
Constant	10.301***	10.250***	10.514***
Chi-square	3196***	2292***	229***
Numbers of children, both years	19631	18469	19631

Note: "Full-time" schooling means schooling without any after-school economic activity. Source: Analysis of CASEN-1990 and CASEN-1996. The omitted reference category for the income quintiles is the poorest fifth of family income, and "Poor" is defined as pertaining to the lowest quintile for the entire Chilean income distribution. * sig. at < .1 level; ** sig. at < .01 level; *** sig at .001 level. Significance levels are based on robust standard errors to account for non-variability of Provincial-level contextual effects.

Summary measures of a state's poverty and rural population are provided in Appendix A5.2. Just as I did with measures of individual family poverty and individual rural residence, I estimated the direct effects of contextual state poverty (proportion of poor children) and of contextual rural residence (proportion in rural areas). Since these contextual variables are highly correlated with one another, I estimated separate equations testing the effects of each one independently. Similarly, I estimated the effect of living in Oaxaca and Chiapas, as opposed to some other state.

Along with the direct effects of each contextual indicator, I also estimated their time-period interaction effects. The interaction effects of state context tell us whether—controlling for individual characteristics—there were any significant changes in the effect of state poverty, state rurality, or living in Oaxaca and Chiapas over the 1992–1996 period when decentralization occurred. The results of these models are presented in Table 5.2.

In each of the four models estimated and reported in Table 5.2, the effects of most control variables are significant statistically. The signs of the coefficients are in the direction that we would expect. Living in a rural locale decreased the likelihood that a child would be able to enroll in school full-time without working. A child's place in Mexico's distribution of income for each year was also a very important determinant of their activities: When compared with the category of "poor" children in the bottom quintile, children in each of the upper quintiles were all more likely to attend school full-time. The interaction effects of individual characteristics and the later time period are revealing. The experiences of children living in the second quintile of the income distribution came to resemble those of children in the poorest quintile. There was no change, however, in the experiences of children in the top 60 percent of the distribution, who remained as advantaged in 1996 as they had been in 1992. The advantage of having a household head with many years of education declined in importance, but the decline may reflect only the fact that more years of education were attained by parents in 1996 than in 1992.

Models 2, 3, and 4, shown in Table 5.2, present alternative tests for contextual effects of state poverty and rurality, as well as an explicit test of the hypothesis from Figure 5.6 and Figure 5.8 that living in Oaxaca or Chiapas in itself carried greater disadvantages for children in 1996 than in 1992. Controlling for the initial effects of family resources, and for their changes over the 1992—1996 period, Model 2 tests the *initial* 1992 effect of living in a state with a high concentration of poor children and also tests the *change* over time in this effect. Once controlling for family income, living in a "poor state" had no significant effect on the likelihood of full-time study in 1992. However, state poverty had become substantively detrimental by 1996. In the latter year, independent of a child's own poverty, living in a poor state meant that a child was less likely to attend school full-time. In Model 3 we observe that children in predominantly rural states were not, other things being equal, less likely to attend school full-time in 1992. However, by 1996 they *were* at a disadvantage. Model 3 reports the experience of children in Oaxaca and Chiapas. Controlling for parental education, income, number of siblings, and individual rural residence, children from Chiapas and Oaxaca were actually slightly *more* likely to attend school full-time than were similarly poor children from other states in 1992. By 1996, however, children from these states were significantly *less* likely to be in school full time.

The analysis presented in Table 5.2 confirms that children in the south, and in poor states generally, began to attend school less often after Mexico decentralized its school system and, perhaps not coincidentally, as greater work opportunities from farm exports were created in the wake of NAFTA. But analysis from Table 5.2 does not tell us what children did when they did not attend school exclusively. Nor do those analyses tell how much poor children (or affluent children) were affected by their state's level of poverty. To address these remaining questions, I used multinomial logistic regression analysis. This approach simultaneously estimates the effect of individual and contextual variables on the likelihood that a child will be engaged in one of the three alternatives to full-time schooling that are presented above in Chapter 1, Figure 1.5.

In the multinomial analysis, I estimated the effects of variables used in Model 2 from Table 5.2, testing in this way the individual and state-contextual effects of poverty. To probe the effects of contextual poverty among different income groups, I estimated the interaction effects of a state's proportion of "poor" with each of the upper-income quintiles (as before, the omitted quintile was the lowest, bottom quintile). The results (which are presented in Appendix A5.3) show that a state's proportion of poor children became more determinant over the 1992–96 period, causing children to be more likely to pursue one of the three alternatives to full-time schooling. That is, controlling for individual poverty, poorer states became more likely to send their children to some alternative to full-time education. The predicted probabilities for schooling in different states is presented in Appendix A5.3. Over time, children in the second quintile were more likely to work in economic activity rather than attend school. By contrast, children in the third and top fifth quintiles of income became relatively less likely to work and more likely to attend school full-time. The effect of relative income was greatest in poor states. Being from a household in the second or fourth income quintile caused children to be less likely to work—and more likely to attend school full-time—when they were in states where most other children were poor. Based on the multinomial logistic regression estimates and the predicted probabilities, I graphed the likelihood that a child would engage in work alone, work with school, and school alone. I separately calculated and graphed the predicted probabilities for children living in states with different proportions of poor children.

Figure 5.9 presents predicted probabilities of each activity, in each year, in each income quintile, and in two groups of states: states with low rates of child poverty and states with high rates of child poverty. Over the 1992–96 time period, children in states with low child poverty rates became more likely to be in school and less likely to work. The effect of income was substantially the same in each year for children in these states. By contrast, in poorer states, for all but the most affluent children in the top income quintile, full-time schooling free of work became less common over exactly the period when universal secondary schooling was made "compulsory."

The same analysis presented above in Table 5.2 for Mexico was conducted in the case of Chile. As in the Mexican case, poverty was defined as membership in a household at the bottom 20 percent of the income distribution. Provinces were ranked by their proportions of "poor" children as well as by their proportions of rural children. The results for the Chilean analysis are presented in Table 5.3. The findings are quite different from those seen for Mexico. Children living in poorer provinces of Chile were no less likely to attend school full-time in 1996, as compared with 1990. And children in more rural provinces—originally disadvantaged in terms of full-time schooling—became as likely to attend school full-time as children in more urban provinces of the country.

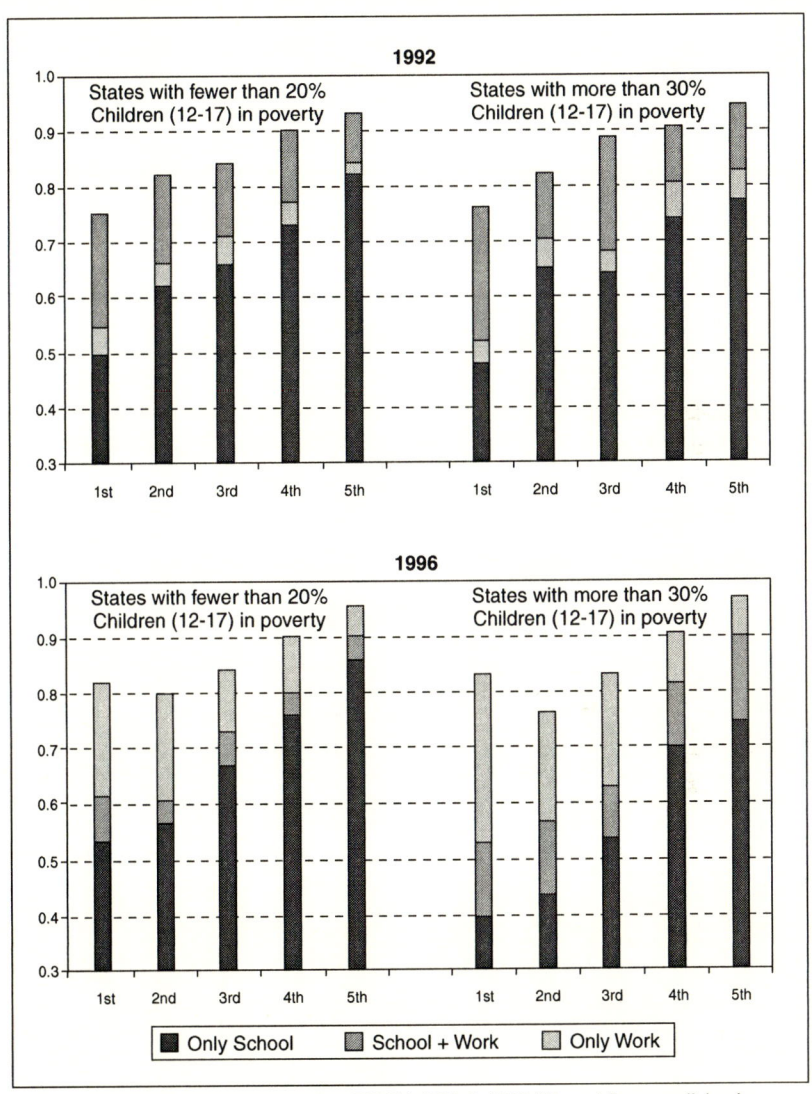

Source: Multinomial regressions using ENIGH 1992 & 1996. "Poverty" means living in a family in the lowest 20 percent of the overall national income distribution in each year. Regressions control for effects of parents' education, rural/urban residence, gender, number of siblings, and child's age. Differences in effects of household income and state poverty are significant at .01 level.

FIGURE 5.9 Predicted Probabilities of Work and Schooling in Mexico (Children 12-17) by Quintiles of Family Income and State Child Poverty Rate, 1992 and 1996

Table 5.3: Determinants of Full-time Schooling for Mexicans, Ages 12-17: Individual, Family, and State-level Contextual Effects over 1992-96 Period

(Logistic Regression Coefficients)

	Model 1	Model 2	Model 3	Model 4
Time period: survey year is 1996 (not 1992)	0.440**	0.954***	0.761**	0.483**
Household head's years of schooling	0.211***	0.216***	0.213***	0.212***
Child is FEMALE (not male)	0.071	0.073	0.071	0.071
Lives in RURAL area (pop. < 2,500)	-0.629***	-0.672***	-0.666***	-0.639***
Child's AGE	-0.569***	-0.572***	-0.571***	-0.566***
Number of SIBLINGS sharing household	-0.134***	-0.133***	-0.134***	-0.136***
Income Quintile Dummies (poorest ommited):				
Household head's income in 2nd quintile	0.292**	0.294**	0.286**	0.292**
Household head's income is in 3rd quintile	0.232*	0.274*	0.241*	0.261*
Household head's income is in 4th quintile	0.653***	0.703***	0.663***	0.686***
Head's Income is in 5th quintile (wealthiest)	0.668**	0.712***	0.667***	0.708***
Period interaction effects, individual level:				
Later time period * 2nd income quintile	-0.285*	-0.327*	-0.304*	-0.311**
Later time period * 3rd income quintile	0.114	0.010	0.070	0.048
Later time period * 4th income quintile	0.019	-0.118	-0.045	-0.104
Later time period * 5th income quintile	0.158	0.043	0.127	0.061
Later period * living in RURAL household	-0.284	-0.157	-0.158	-0.207
Later time period * being FEMALE	-0.106	-0.103	-0.103	-0.092
Later time period * head's years of schooling	-0.114***	-0.122***	-0.119***	-0.115***
Contextual effects and period interactions:				
State's proportion of "poor" children	-------	0.793	--------	--------
period * State's proportion of "poor" children	-------	-2.411**	--------	--------
State's proportion of rural children	-------	--------	0.278	--------
period * State's proportion of rural children	-------	--------	-1.008*	--------
Oaxaca or Chiapas (rather than other States)	-------	--------	--------	0.327*
Later time period * Oxaxaca/Chiapas	-------	--------	--------	-0.603***
Constant	8.314***	8.166***	8.250***	8.233***
Chi-square	7746***	12136 ***	9775***	7087***
Numbers of children, both years	15344	15344	15344	15344

Source: Analysis of ENIGH-1992 and ENIGH-1996. "Poor" is defined as pertaining to the lowest income quintile for the entire Mexican income distribution. * significant at .1 level; ** significant at .01 level; *** significan at .001 level. Significance levels are based on standard errors corrected to account for non-variability of state-level contextual effects.

GENDER AND CHILDREN'S ACTIVITIES SINCE THE 1980S

Survey data from each country of this study can be used to illuminate the changing role played by gender in determining children's activities. As we saw in Figure 1.4 and 1.5, in Chapter 1, gender inequalities in children's activities appear to have narrowed in Chile and Peru, but do not appear to have improved in Mexico.

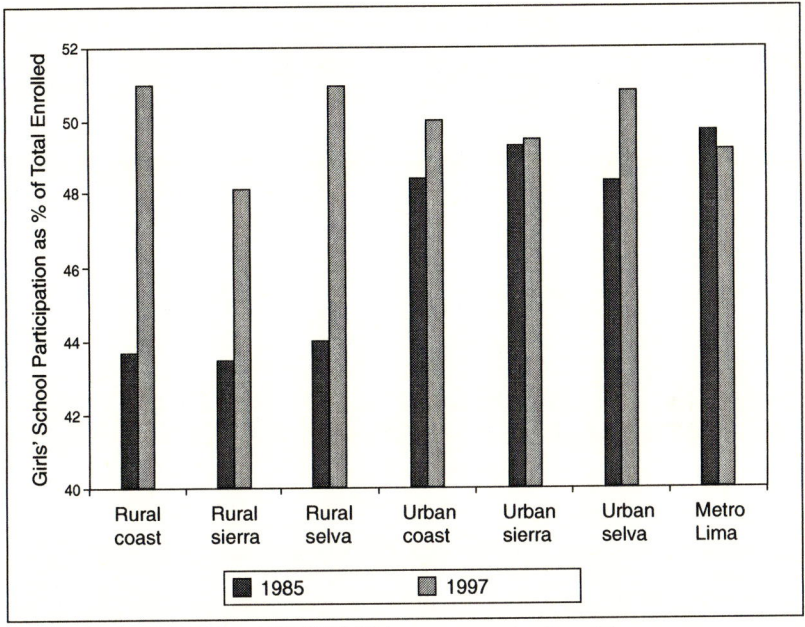

Region And Gender Differences In Children's Work And Schooling 205

FIGURE 5.10 Trends in Peruvian Girls' Relative School Participation

Source: Analysis of 1985 and 1997 ENNIV (non-summer months only)

In the case of Peru it is possible to confirm that, by 1997, girls were at parity with boys in every region of the country. Figure 5.10 illustrates the total school participation rates by Peruvian girls as percentages of total (boys' plus girls') participations. These relative shares of enrollment are further presented in each of seven areas of Peru, and in the earliest and latest years of available survey data. Figure 5.10 indicates that girls were at a greatest disadvantage in rural areas in 1985. By 1997, however, except in Peru's rural sierra, girls were as likely to attend school as boys: In each area, approximately half of the students were girls.

The case of Chile is unique in Latin America in terms of gender equity in education. In Chile, evidence from a 1970 longitudinal study of students finishing eight years of education found that girls had equaled or surpassed boys in terms of school attainment. Schiefelbein and Farrell (1980) place the comparative success of Chilean women in the historical context of the nation's early progressive policies in education and the fact that rigid colonial institutions played lesser roles in Chile than elsewhere in Latin America. By the beginning of the Chilean case study, the vast majority of girls had mothers with educations equal to those of their fathers. Consistent with this trend, there was no gender difference in the proportions of girls and boys who completed eight years of basic education.

The fact that no differences overall can be found by gender does not preclude gender effects in particular regions of Chile, just as was seen above for in the case of the Peruvian sierra. To investigate the relationship between regional development and gender equity, I replicated the regional analysis presented above in Figure 5.5. I first calculated the provincial rates at which girls and boys who had completed compulsory basic education continued on to the post-compulsory media level. Next, I estimated the percentage of the total students continuing who were girls. Assuming that there are approximately equal numbers of girls and boys in each province, there will be parity in the continuation to the media level when 50 percent of students who continue are female. Each province's continuation percentage is plotted on the Y-axis in Figure 5.11.

Two ways of viewing provincial education levels by parents are shown on the X-axis. The left panel shows the percentage of parents who completed fewer than eight years of formal schooling. The right panel simply shows the mean years completed by the household heads of children in the sample. As in earlier presentations, the size of each circle is determined by the populations of children living there. Each panel shows a significant "non-finding." Regardless of how parents' educations are measured, there appears to be no relationship between that dimension and the equality of girls. In the two largest provinces (Santiago and Concepción) equal percentages of girls and boys continued past basica to the media level of education. Other, smaller provinces, perhaps because their placements on the graph are based on fewer cases, show random variation about the mean line of 50 percent.

In terms of gender equity, as in terms of regional inequality, the case of Mexico appears quite different from that of Chile and

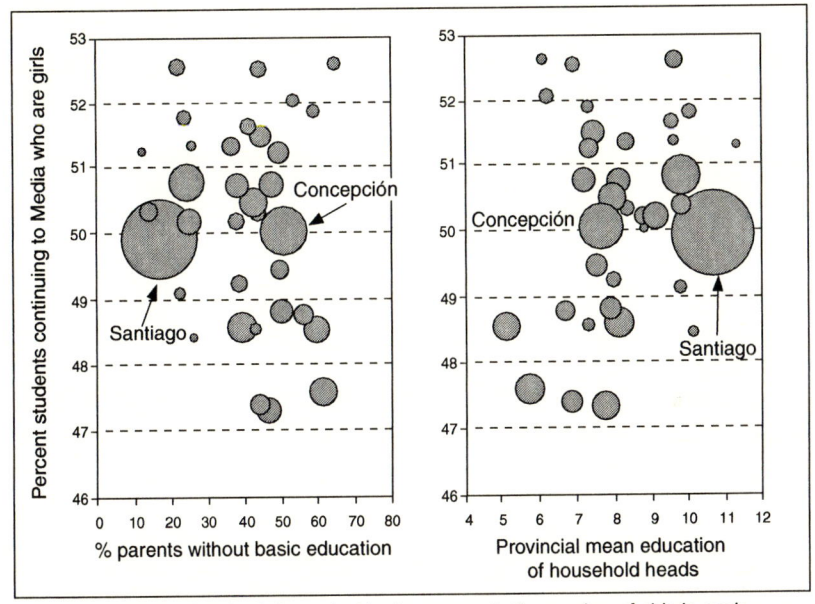

Region And Gender Differences In Children's Work And Schooling 207

Note: The position of each circle on the Y-axis represents the number of girls in each province who completed Chile's Basica level of education and continued to the Media level, divided by the total numbers of students (girls and boys) who continued secondary school in that province. The size of each circle is proportional to the population of children in 1996. Source: CASEN 1996.

FIGURE 5.11 Provincial Relation of Adult Education and Female Underrepresentation in Chilean Media-Level Schools, 1996

Peru. In Mexico we find substantial gender inequality in secondary school attendance, especially concentrated in poorer and more marginalized areas of the country. To eliminate this inequality was one key goal of PROGRESA, as discussed in Chapter 3. The need for such programmatic attention to poorer girls, and the benefit to their school participation, rests on the assumption that gender inequality interacts with both family income inequality and regional inequality in determining access to secondary school. That is, girls are suspected to be at greatest risk of discontinuing their educations after primary if they are living in poorer households and living in poorer regions. To investigate this hypothesis, I used enrollment data provided by the SEP (these enrollment data provide much more detailed national coverage, at the municipio level, than do the ENIGH data). Official enroll-

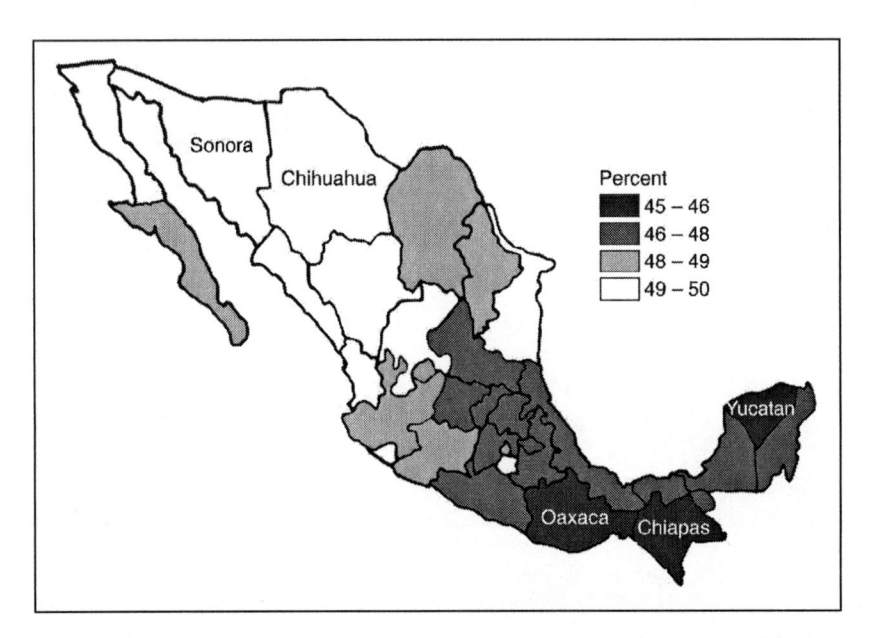

208   *Region And Gender Differences In Children's Work And Schooling*

FIGURE 5.12   Percentage of Students Beginning Secondary School Who Are Female, 1995

ment data reveal significant regional variations in the underrepresentation of girls who started secondary school, variations that are evident between states as well as between municipios. These inter-state disparities in female representation can be appreciated from the map in Figure 5.12 .

A striking finding from the map of gender inequality is its consistency with Mexico's concentration of poverty. Generally, girls are underrepresented in Mexico's poorer, less developed, and more indigenous southern states (especially Chiapas, Oaxaca, and Yucatán). What is the actual relationship between regional development and gender equity? To explore this question, I used one key indicator of regional "marginality," as it is measured by Mexico's National Council on Population (CONAPO). I used the state percentage of persons over fifteen years of age who had completed at least primary school, according to the 1990 census. As in the case of Chile, on the Y-axis I graphed each region's representation of girls as a percentage of total beginning secondary students. On the X-axis I graphed each region's percentage of

FIGURE 5.13 State and Municipio Relation of Adult Education and Female Underrepresentation in Mexican Secondary Schools, 1995

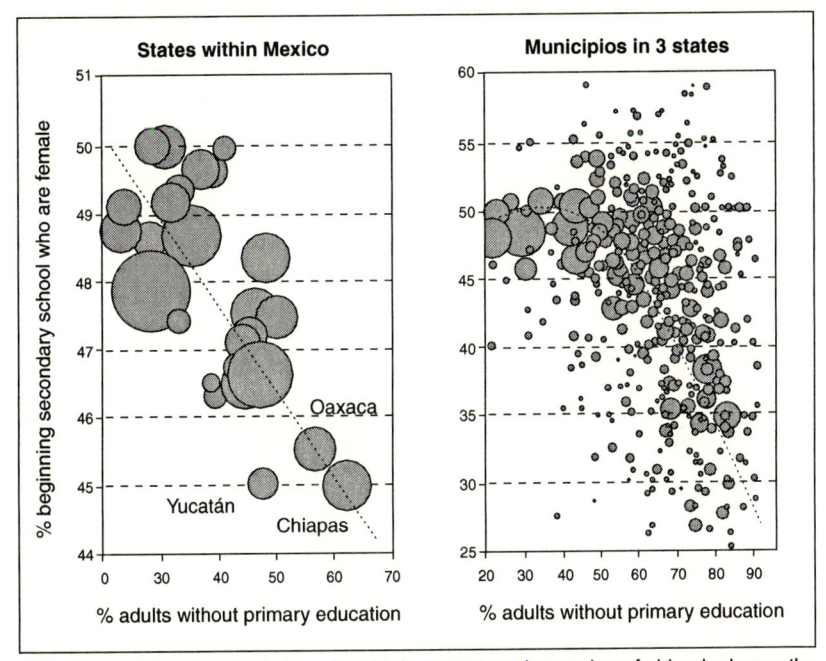

Note: The position of each circle on the Y-axis represents the number of girls who began the first grade of secondary school in (lerf panel) each state of Mexico in 1995 or (in right panel) each municipio of Yucatán, Chiapas, and Oaxaca, divided by the total students who began secondary in that state or in that municipio. The size of each circle is proportional to the population in 1990. Source: enrollments are from the SEP, state and municipio populations and adult education levels are from 1990 census.

adults who had completed primary schooling. In states where resources are generally scarcest, the fewest adults have finished primary school; in these states, also, girls are least represented in secondary school, and gender inequality is most acute. This relationship at the state level is illustrated in Figure 5.13.

In Figure 5.13, the Y-axis depicts the number of girls out of every one hundred students who begin secondary school. In a state where there is equity in girls' representation, such as Chihuahua, fifty out of one hundred students beginning secondary school were female. At the other extreme, there were three states in which only forty-five out of each one hundred students were girls: Chiapas, Oaxaca, and Yucatán. In the left-hand panel, a regression line closely "fits" the relationship between underrepresentation and representation, illustrating that state levels of adult education matter greatly for girls' equity.

Regional characteristics matter for girls *within* as well as *between* states. Those counties (*municipios*) that are least developed socially are also counties where girls are least represented as beginning secondary school students. Thus, if we examine the counties of Chiapas, Oaxaca, and Yucatán we find a similar pattern to that seen nationally between the states of Mexico. That is, girls are most underrepresented in those *municipios* where few adults have primary schooling. This can be appreciated in the right-hand panel of Figure 5.13, which graphs the relations *within* these three southern states between girls' representations and county marginality. At the level of each municipio, there is a close, curvilinear relationship between adult education and the underrepresentation of girls. In municipios where few adults had completed primary school girls were vastly underrepresented in the first year of secondary school, notwithstanding the fact that this level of education had been compulsory for two years at the time the data presented in Figure 5.13 were collected. Further investigations (not presented to conserve space) showed that there had been no significant change in the relationship since the mid–1980s.

At an individual level, as well as at the regional level, there is an interaction between the effect of poverty (and poor region) and the effect of being female. To appreciate the differential impact of poverty in determining the activities performed by girls, I used multinomial logistic regression analysis for both the 1992 and 1996 survey years. As control variables I entered: child's age; place of residence (rural versus urban); number of other siblings in the household; and the years of education attained by their household head (their father in about 85 percent of cases) The variables of interest were: gender (whether female), poverty, and the interaction of poverty with. To define poverty I again followed the general classification scheme of PROGRESA and considered as poor children those living in households in the lowest fifth (or the "first quintile") of the distribution of income. As in previous analyses, I first measured poverty at an individual level based upon the household head's income quintile in 1992 and 1996 (defining as "poor" those children whose household head's incomes were in the bottom 20 percent). As in Table 5.3, above, I also measured poverty at the state contextual level. Independently of whether an individual child was poor, I calculated the proportion of children living in each state who were poor. I estimated the separate effects of living in a poor household and living in a state with a high proportion of poor children. To understand the differential effect of poverty on girls, I created interaction terms of being female with living in a poor household and being female living in a poorer state. Appendix A5.5 reports the regression estimates and their significance level, and Figure 5.14 presents the predicted probabilities of each of four activities. These probabilities are presented separately for boys and girls, in non-poor and in poor households, based on estimates from the equations reported in Appendix A5.5.

Figure 5.14 illustrates that, in non-poor households, the activities of boys and girls differ, but school participation is not affected by the difference. Roughly equal proportions of girls and boys were not attending school during the 1992–96 period. Boys who did not attend school tended to be economically active, while girls who were out of school were more likely to perform domestic or other non-economic activity. By contrast with "non-poor" children (those in the upper 80 percent of the income distribution), the activities by boys and girls in the poorest 20 percent of families differ in ways that work to the disadvantage of girls' schooling. Compared with boys who are not "poor", poorer boys were much more likely to be economically active. But poorer boys were no more likely than non-poor boys to perform domestic or non-economic activity. Poorer girls were both more likely to be in economic activity and—especially—to be engaged in domestic or non-economic activity. The net result: Mexican girls in poorer families are less likely to attend school than poorer boys, primarily because girls in poorer families are called upon to undertake domestic responsibilities.

Put differently, girls living in the upper 80 percent of income households were no less likely than boys to attend school. While

Chart

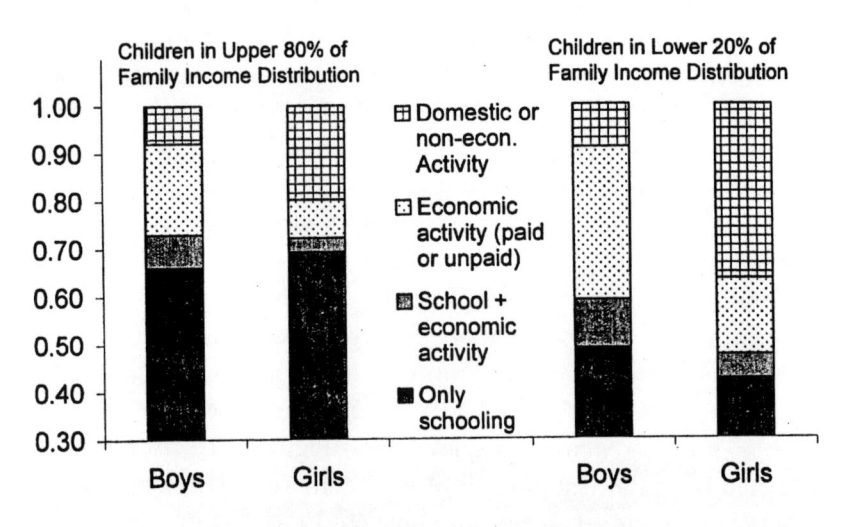

Children in Upper 80% of Family Income Distribution | **Children in Lower 20% of Family Income Distribution**

Y-axis: 0.30 to 1.00

Legend:
- Domestic or non-econ. Activity
- Economic activity (paid or unpaid)
- School + economic activity
- Only schooling

X-axis categories: Boys, Girls (for each group)

Source: Appendix A5.5, multinomial logistic regressions using combined 1992 and 1996 ENIGH. Probabilities control for rural/urban location, sibship size and composition, houshold-head's education, child's age and state proportions of children who are poor.

FIGURE 5.14 Predicted Probability of Weekly Activity by Mexican Children (12-17), by Gender and Poverty Status

these more advantaged girls performed more domestic and non-economic activities than boys, these girls also were far less likely to be employed. The net result was that, among these "non-poor" households, girls and boys were about equally likely to be found in school. The result is quite different among poorer children. For those in the lower 20 percent of the income distribution, girls were less likely than boys to be employed as an alternative to schooling. But, at the same time, compared with boys these poorer girls were *much* more likely to be engaged in domestic or non-economic activities. The net effect of this was to reduce the likelihood that girls would obtain an education, relative to boys.

It is critically important, from a policy perspective, to observe from Figure 5.14 what girls *were* doing, and what they were *not* doing, when they were out of school. Approximately one third of these girls were engaged in some type of economic activity (unpaid as well as paid activities were recorded as "economic" so long as they generated or added value to a product, as in farm work). But about two thirds of these out-of-school girls were performing domestic chores or were in some type of non-economic activity.

THE BASIS OF GENDER INEQUALITY AND ITS IMPLICATIONS FOR WELFARE POLICY

In Mexico, two alternative approaches are thought to have the potential for eliminating the disadvantage of girls in access to schooling. The first approach expands the availability of schooling for all and reduces the opportunity cost. This is the route taken in the wake of the 1993 amendment of the third article of Mexico's constitution (extending compulsory education to the secondary level). In that amendment, education was intended to be "democratic, considering that democracy is not only a juridical structure and political regime but also a system resting on the constant economic, social, and cultural improvement of the people." To achieve these constitutional ideals, the General Law of Education goes further in specifying the objectives of Mexico's system. Article 32 states that "the education authorities will take measures to establish conditions which permit the full exercise of the right to education for every individual, a greater equity of education, as well as the *attainment of effective equality of opportunities of access and continuation in education*" (SEP 1993, pps. 27, 65, emphasis added). Gender equity is not singled out in Mexico's general law, but equalizing the opportunities between daughters and sons would be promoted by truly universalizing secondary education.

A second policy approach to gender equity in school access has been through poverty-alleviation programs. Mexico deserves credit from feminist policy-analysts for having attempted such a wide-ranging and innovative experiment. Regardless of the ultimate outcome, Mexico's attempt should be monitored closely by other nations seeking, through welfare programs, labor laws, and schooling, to move children's activities from a purely domestic to a public policy domain. It is far too early to evaluate the consequences of PROGRESA's extra stipend level provided for girls who continue to secondary. By reducing the family burden of poverty, PROGRESA may have an especially significant impact on girls' access to schooling, since girls in poorer households are more likely than boys not to be in school. However, the evidence presented here suggests that neither compulsory schooling nor income supplements will challenge at least one of the basis for gender as a dimension of educational stratification. Most poor Mexican girls who are out of school are not working for income (nor even working outside of the home in non-remunerated jobs). They are much more likely to be performing non-paid domestic chores. They are most likely to leave school and to perform housework when they have many siblings but few older sisters. It would seem that implicit negotiation and bargaining occur over girls' activities within the household (Sen 1990), leading to predictable situations in which daughters lose out.

What are the possibilities and the limitations on the state, given this domestic basis for gender inequality in the access to schooling? Compulsory school laws reduce the opportunity costs of attending school (by restricting work for pay). They also reduce the direct costs of travel to school, by expanding school availability and proximity. PROGRESA and similar targeted assistance programs provide cash compensation to families whose children attend school, and they transfer additional cash for daughters. But, in a sense, daughters are "priceless" in the Mexican household, and the social expectations that daughters should provide domestic support will need to change before policymakers are able to alter the basis of gender inequality in the access to Mexico's secondary schools.

6

Conclusion: Social Mobilization, NGOs, and Policy Change

At the conclusion of the case studies reported in this book, at century's end, children in Chile, Peru, and Mexico continued to work as well as to attend school. But their likelihood of doing either had changed over the 1990s. Why? What had been most fundamentally altered for children? What had remained constant? During the 1990s, each country's policies and each nation's families encountered a transformed global context for childhood, as the ILO and the CRC changed the norms and expectations about what activities are appropriate for children. Moreover, as discussed in Chapter 3, there were changes both in the national and the family resources available to promote schooling rather than work. These represent important and complementary explanations for the changes reported in this book about children's labor and learning activity. But these explanations are incomplete.

Undeniably, there have been significant modifications in the laws governing education (for example, constitutional reform in two countries). There were also changes in per-pupil public school spending. In Peru, the regulation of educational alternatives changed following a 1992 presidential decree. In Peru, as well as in Mexico, there was increasing poverty for many rural children. These environmental differences, discussed in earlier chapters, surely altered the immediate conditions facing children and families as they allocated their energies to the worlds of work and schooling. But this concluding chapter, in addition to summarizing and interpreting those immediate contextual changes in Chile, Peru, and Mexico, pushes further. Ultimately, we must address a larger question that emerges from our findings: What is it that accounts for the *non-converging* tendencies of each country, given a converging international system of children's rights and given the globalization of the world economy? Why did laws and their implementations continue to differ widely within a region sharing similar cultural and macroeconomic historical experiences? To put the question differently: How did problems like child labor *come to be seen* as "problems" and, finally, once problems became acknowledged as such, why were policies designed to solve them in some countries earlier in others?

Answers to these questions force us to search beyond the stage setting for policy action; we must attend closely to the actors themselves. Advocates for children have followed varied scripts in each country because there has been no single director, no rationale guiding action on each stage according to a consistent, overarching set of principles and priorities. While for simplicity we often refer to actions taken by "Chile," "Peru," or "Mexico," in reality this shorthand notation oversimplifies the interest groups, parties, and organizations that compete with one another to form governments and, concomitantly, to formulate government policies. As in all domains, politics drives the advocacy for children's welfare, and so we must attend to the relationships between actors. These relationships—which ultimately express themselves in national policy environments—link political coalitions and NGOs with the state and with international governing authorities such as the International Labour Organization and the United Nations.

THEORETICAL PERSPECTIVES ON FAMILIES, CHILDREN, NGOS, AND THE STATE

The time periods covered by our case studies were episodes of profound political realignment in Chile, Peru, and Mexico. Chilean families experienced the initiation of a coalition Christian Democrat—Social Democrat government, which followed a period of concerted effort to end military rule through the electoral process and grassroots mobilization. These efforts created a remarkably broad-based alliance by unions, churches, think-tanks, parents' groups, and even some business associations. As a consequence of this alliance, Chilean civil society flourished during the 1987–1996 period, producing viable avenues for participation as the state reconstituted itself with input from a broad array of groups. By contrast with Mexico, social programs in Chile during the early 1990s benefited from partisan competition for issues and reforms to benefit potential voters. As has been argued by the political scientist, Marcus Kurtz (1999, p. 2), "where more than one reformist party competes electorally, politicians cannot take the poor for granted as a constituency, and face the possibility of a policy 'bidding dynamic.'... Without the accountability inherent in a highly competitive political arena, politicians will have a tendency to use antipoverty projects to stave off moments of dissent, not to construct broad and sustained bases of support."

Although Chilean politicians engaged in "bidding" to retain support of poor and working-class voters, there was no such dynamic in either Peru or Mexico. By contrast with Chile, Peru offered far fewer opportunities for incorporating diverse interests or placing stakeholders in positions of responsibility for social policies. Compared with Chile, Peru's political system historically had included an even more diverse array of participants in the years prior 1985. But the hyperinflation, terrorism, and instability in the later years of the Alan Garcia government (1985–90) created such disenchantment with partisan politics that strong leadership by an unknown technocrat appeared attractive to voters in 1990. Fujimori continued to receive popular support even after closing Peru's congress and suspending its constitution in a military-supported "auto-coup" in 1992. For the remainder of the 1990s, there was little engagement by the government with potential stakeholders in civil society.

The number of Peruvian NGOs appears to have increased, but these operated independently of government financial support. They claimed an authority, when advocating for children, that was not dependent on official benediction from the Peruvian legal system. Rather, Peruvian advocates for children claimed a moral authority that was conferred by the ILO, the United Nations, and the CRC (and, less frequently, the Catholic Church). Institutional stakeholders, political parties, and child advocates, in a more pluralist arrangement, might have shared in the responsibility for promulgating Peru's 1992 reforms. Instead, reforms were decreed into law by Fujimori after he closed the congress. The 1992 code of children and adolescents included many legal improvements that could have benefited Peruvian children, but the advocates for children were disengaged from the process of implementation in the view of critics as dissimilar as Isaac Ruiz (who helped lead Peru's "Global March") and Alejandro Cussianovich (who contrarily led the working children's group of MANTHOC).

Frustration with the autonomy of the executive branch boiled over in the presidential campaign of 2000, amid widespread charges of fraud against Fujimori, and this led ultimately to his resignation amid charges of corruption. Even without broad-based support by stakeholders, the Fujimori administrations advanced many programs targeted for poor children. The question now is whether these programs can be institutionalized or sustained under the government of Alejandro Toledo. Peru-watchers have cautioned about the viability the state-centered populism experienced under Fujimori (e.g., Weyland 1999, p. 400).

Mexican children were the heirs to a quite different political dynamic than that of either Chile or Peru. Unlike those South American nations, Mexico was governed by a single organization during the entire period of our Mexican case study. However, opposition parties of the right won control of several state governments, while Cuauhtemoc Cárdenas and his PRD party were

Conclusion: Social Mobilization, NGOs, and Policy Change

elected to lead Mexico City. In the past, potential dissidence over social policy was systematically incorporated—co-opted, critics would say—by Mexico's governing PRI. Leaders and organizations that sought to generate bases for opposition were selected to lead offices within the Secretariat of Public Education or of Social Development or given positions within research institutions heavily dependent on government funding. The PRI thus headed a corporativist state that claimed to represent the interests of the Mexican public generally. Throughout the world, social programs have the potential to become instruments of political expediency under such an arrangement. In her comparative study of the politics of targeted social spending in Mexico, Indonesia, and Ghana, Niles (1999, p. 29) writes that authoritarian leaders often use social spending as a "preemptive strike" to stem the decline of the ruling party in the face of electoral threats from opposition parties or demands for greater democratization. As discussed below, at the conclusion of our Mexican case study, there were hopeful signs that Mexico, like Chile, had begun to engage in pluralist, multiparty debate and advocacy for children, with increased engagement rather than mere co-optation of non-governmental organizations.

Channels of Policy Change: States, NGOs, and the Public

How is grassroots, demographic change effected through the public policy arena? Why should children or their parents, even when they read no daily news reports about constitutional reform or labor bills in their countries, modify their orientations toward work and schooling? Why should the desire for children's labor decline, or the desire for schooling increase, in response to law alone? They should not, at least not from a purely economic perspective. Family behaviors about children's activities may change, but this will occur even when family preferences remain unchanged. In response to changing opportunities to work or to attend school, and in response to greater poverty or wealth, parents in Chile, Peru, and Mexico would alter their decisions about the work and schooling of their children. From this perspective, public policies change the availability or attractiveness of education, and welfare or structural adjustment policies affect family poverty. Together, these provide the simplest explanations for changing children's activities for many economists.

Sociologists and political scientists observe a more complex set of relationships operating on the behavior of children. Aside from the consideration of family resources and constraints, two further questions arise from outside an economic perspective. First, can governments alter the non-material incentives or *symbolic* rewards to children's activities, as these rewards are perceived by families or children? In other words, can the status, prestige, or stigma from school or work be changed by public policy action? Second, in an open society, public policies and governments respond to social mobilization and public demands. Since all governments (except for the most autocratic regimes) are sensitive to public demands, policies that respond to social mobilization are not the fundamental cause of changed patterns of work and schooling. Rather, it would be more accurate to view legal reform, social welfare policies, and public spending as *manifestations* of priorities set by parents. Thus, the second question is: What can explain policy variations? Why does the policy apparatus of some countries treat education and child labor so differently than they are treated in other countries?

The first question has been studied by institutionalist sociologists, who argue that parental values about education and work depend on a host of nonmaterial factors. These include the official evaluation of education and work that are given by both national and international institutions. The state can communicate and—at times—mold, parents' subjective evaluations of the appropriate activities for their children. As Fuller and Rubinson (1992, p. 21) observe, "State action is not limited only to spending. Policies enacted by civic elites signal alleged benefits of school attendance: economic opportunity, individual development, membership in the modern project of nation building." In this view, once the state has enhanced the symbolic and nonmaterial value associated with education, and once governments have

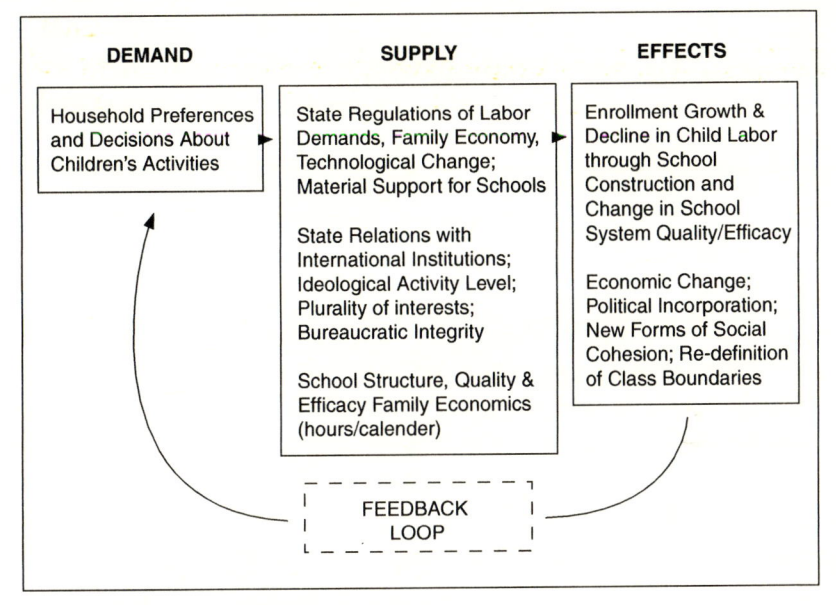

Conclusion: Social Mobilization, NGOs, and Policy Change

Source: adapted from Fuller & Rubinson (1992)

FIGURE 6.1 Material and Symbolic Impact of State Action on Household Decisions and Children's Activities

stigmatized and devalued child labor through official pronouncements, there is a "feedback-loop" (see Figure 6.1). After state policies raise parental evaluations of education, or lower parents' evaluations of child labor, then the public will demand more schooling and will reinforce the restrictions and sanctions on work by children.

The framework proposed by Fuller and Rubinson emphasizes the initial interests and actions of elites controlling the state. Decisionmaking, although responsive to public demands, is channeled through the state itself rather than through intermediary organizations or political parties. In Latin America, even in transient governments such as in Peru and Chile, it certainly appears justified to view governments as the most decisive actors on this stage. As Mickelson (2000, p. 31) argues, from this perspective, "States' adaptations to the new educational demands of global capitalism are not fixed—they will involve choices." But in two of the cases studied in this book—Chile and Peru—governments have proved less durable than some of the intermediary actors, parties, and interest groups acting upon governments. It also is likely that nongovernmental organizations, as well as church orders, unions, business associations, and other units of civil society, have exerted tremendous influence on both the public policy formulation and on family preferences through indirect, international channels. These intermediary organizations have proved capable of joining into alliances with extra-national actors to achieve their own interests. And their symbolic resources include their legitimate authority over an emergent international ideal which they, themselves, have been concerned to promote: the idea of universal human rights.

To understand the ideological material at the disposal of NGOs today, we must be aware of the legacy of human rights campaigns and norms in Latin America and the world, especially as they are molded by the United Nations. Of course, official discourse on human rights did not appear whole cloth in Latin America during the period of our case studies, or arise from nothing. Its historical antecedents date to the end of the American Enlightenment, in 1825–26, when Mexico, Peru, and several other Spanish American countries joined together to declare themselves against slavery at a meeting organized in Panama by Simón Bolivar. In 1928, well before the establishment of the United Nations, Latin American states agreed to protect human rights at the sixth Inter-American Conference. And, several months prior to the adoption of the 1948 U.N. Declaration on Human Rights, the Organization of American States was founded, with its charter members signing the American Declaration on the Rights and Duties of Man (Miró Quesada 1985).

Notwithstanding these antecedents, the impact of human rights ideals on social change has been especially obvious since the signing of the U.N. Charter in June of 1945. In general, the United Nations profoundly altered political dynamics within nations as well as between them, despite Article 2(7), which read that "nothing contained in the present Charter shall authorize the United Nations to intervene in matters which are essentially within the domestic jurisdiction of any state or shall require Members to submit such matters to settlement." For example, within days of the U.N. Charter's adoption, the All-Colonial People's Conference had been organized from an alliance of student groups from West Africa, Ceylon, Burma, India, and elsewhere, making explicit reference to the rights of self-development and nondiscrimination. (Lauren 1998, p. 206). The enforcement of United Nations conventions such as the International Covenant on Economic, Social, and Cultural Rights and the Convention on the Rights of the Child has been delegated to permanent, autonomous committees. International diplomacy and international legal traditions recognized only states as possessing the standing to enjoy rights. But these "horizontal" relations have given way to "vertical" arrangements, whereby individuals, including children, have been transformed into legitimate subjects of international laws, which must be respected (Lauren 1998, p. 260).

Prior to the CRC, another example of the transformative power of the United Nations was seen following the adoption, in 1948, of the Universal Declaration of Human Rights. At that time, UNESCO's director-general was Jaime Torres Bodet, a renowned former secretary of public education from Mexico. Torres Bodet argued that the declaration "is more than a historical summary, it is a program. Every paragraph is a call to action, every line a condemnation of apathy, every sentence a repudiation of some moment of our individual or national history; every word forces us to scrutinize more closely the situation in the world today. The destiny of mankind is an indivisible responsibility which we all must share." By tacit implication, this view authorized and legitimized individuals and groups—not only governments—to advance the human rights doctrine of the declaration. The views of Torres Bodet were prophetic in the subsequent mobilizations in Latin America around human rights, mobilizations that appealed to external sources of moral authority as much as to national constitutions.

What has been the net effect on Mexican, Peruvian, and Chilean public policy from the mobilization around human rights ideals? The effects are diverse because the dynamic has differed in each country. As Stammers (1999, p. 996) argues, human rights mobilizations "both challenge and sustain [state] power, but in different degrees, in different ways, in different places, and at different times." They sustain power insofar as they concede to the state the legitimate means of rectifying abuses. They challenge state power insofar as they invoke legitimated goals and ideals that transcend any particular state. In this regard, there are clear parallels between the emergence of children's welfare, in the context of human rights, and the earlier rise of women's rights as a human right. Nina Berkovitch shows how the initial reluctance of the ILO to embrace the demand for equal pay for women gave way in the face of arguments from feminist international non-governmental organizations, for example the Inter-American Commission on the Status of Women. Close attention to the chronology gives hints of a complex web of causality. Mexican feminists succeeded relatively early, in 1974, in launching a major revision of Mexican legislation to equalize the place of women under Mexican law. Although apparently this was a national movement, in fact this push was anticipatory of the 1975 World Conference of International Women's Year, which was to be held in Mexico City. Following this conference, the United Nation's "Decade for Women" (1976–1985) was catalyzed not by the U.N. itself but by an international non-governmental organization, the Women's International Democratic Federation (WIDF). Together, women's groups succeeded in formulating women's rights as human rights, which legitimately fell within the scope of the United Nation's charter to protect individuals, irrespective of their national citizenship or national rights (Berkovitch 1999, p. 120). In Mexico, one consequence was the establishment by the government of the National Commission for Women at the end of the ten-year period, in 1985 (Poder Ejecutivo Federal 1996, p. 5).

Building on the work by Berkovitch and other collaborators, John Boli (1999) has suggested three distinctive types of authority that can be exercised by international non-governmental organizations (INGOs): autonomous authority, collateral authority, and penetrative INGO authority. For example, scientific organizations exercise authority over their members autonomously from the authority of any national government. The International Committee of the Red Cross, and various population-policy INGOs, have collateral authority along with willing government partners. International population groups such as the Population Council were able to effect change in national population programs and practices, as in Mexico and Chile, but only when governments could be persuaded by the arguments that population control was in their best interests. The third type of authority suggested by Boli, and the one most clearly relevant to the children's rights discourse over child labor and education in the countries of our study, is "penetrative" INGO authority. Some international organizations—Save the Children, Casa Alianza, Amnesty International—achieve their authority through "successful INGO penetration of the boundary-maintenance mechanisms shielding national and local polities from outside influence, as well as on the conscious effort by lower-level units to connect with INGO discourse and programs." Boli argues that "INGOs effect change within countries by inducing states to begin with fundamental elements of our socially constructed world" (pp. 273–74). The form of penetrative authority depends on a rational-voluntaristic structure, in which governments voluntarily participate in and share authority over widely legitimated values, the sanctity of the individual child being one.

The Role of Human Rights NGOs in Latin America

Over the periods of the case studies reported here, non-governmental organizations took on prominent advocacy roles for children with the moral if not legal authority of the United Nations. As the Argentine children rights jurist, Emilio García Méndez (1998, p. 12), has observed:

> During the 1980s a new type of non-governmental organization was born, committed to the cause of children and adolescents, and challenging public policies. These groups created a culture that was to continue long after the demise of the dictators, as they gradually improved their organization, expertise and technical knowledge. In addition, they began to work together and were able to exert influence both at regional and international levels. Because of the seriousness of the crisis and after the experience of

authoritarian governments, these organizations moved away from the State, and lost interest in attempting to influence public policy.

Although NGOs operated independent from state support, they frequently borrowed their legitimacy from the treaty conventions signed by states. The chief international organizations relevant to our study—UNICEF and the ILO—have recognized this and tacitly encouraged social mobilization to implement goals of the CRC and ILO conventions. From the perspective of UNICEF—an organization that is officially composed of governments and not of groups opposing governments—the emergence of opposition NGOs creates special opportunities. One key UNICEF document advises:

> Creating a broad social alliance is a necessary condition for the elimination of child labour. It must reach from the highest levels of global power and influence to the hardest to reach, poorest and most powerless communities and families. This includes all branches and levels of government; civil society organizations, employers and trade unions, consumer groups, the media, families, children, teachers, health professionals, social workers and street educators. The magic of social mobilization and one of its key challenges is ensuring that the impact of the effort is greater than the sum of various separate initiatives, and that all levels of society commit to a common goal. Often, social mobilization includes the need to learn new skills and develop new attitudes among those directly involved. It is about strategic partnerships and agreeing on who plays which role best. It is about inclusion and finding common ground acknowledging each group's contribution to progress made and sustaining the broad commitment to achieving the agreed objectives. (UNICEF 1997, p. 9)

Thomas Risse and Kathryn Sikkink have documented the roles of non-governmental organizations and governments that are "socialized" about international human rights norms. They observe that "socialization processes start when actors adapt their behavior in accordance with the norm for initially instrumental reasons. Governments want to remain in power, while domestic NGOs

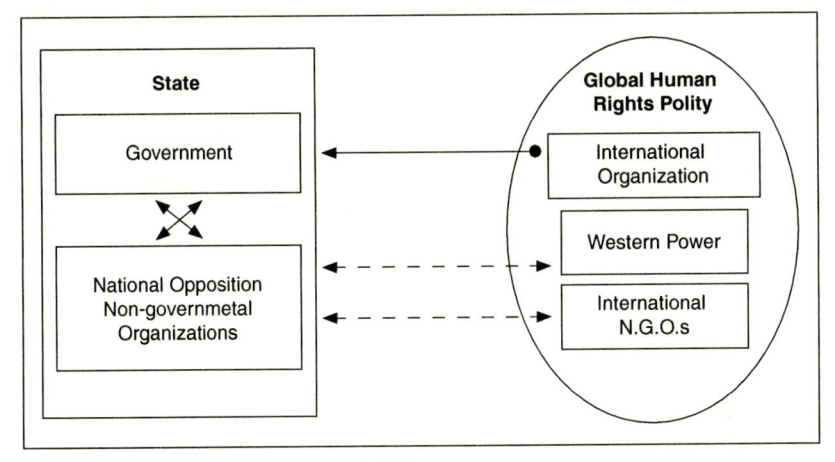

Conclusion: Social Mobilization, NGOs, and Policy Change 227

```
┌─────────────────────────────────────────────────────────────┐
│   ┌─────────────────────┐         ╱‾‾‾‾‾‾‾‾‾‾‾‾‾‾‾‾╲        │
│   │      State          │        ╱  Global Human    ╲       │
│   │                     │       │   Rights Polity    │      │
│   │  ┌───────────────┐  │       │ ┌──────────────┐   │      │
│   │  │  Government   │◄─┼───────┼─│ International│   │      │
│   │  └───────────────┘  │       │ │ Organization │   │      │
│   │        ╲╱           │       │ └──────────────┘   │      │
│   │        ╱╲           │       │ ┌──────────────┐   │      │
│   │  ┌───────────────┐  │       │ │Western Power │   │      │
│   │  │ National      │◄-┼- - - -│ └──────────────┘   │      │
│   │  │ Opposition    │  │       │ ┌──────────────┐   │      │
│   │  │ Non-govern-   │◄-┼- - - -┼►│ International│   │      │
│   │  │ metal         │  │       │ │   N.G.O.s    │   │      │
│   │  │ Organizations │  │        ╲└──────────────┘  ╱       │
│   │  └───────────────┘  │         ╲_____╱        │
│   └─────────────────────┘                                    │
└─────────────────────────────────────────────────────────────┘
```

Source: adapted from Risse & Sikkink (1999)

FIGURE 6.2 Transnational Advocacy and the Socialization of Human Rights Norms

seek the most effective means to rally the opposition. The more they 'talk the talk,' however, the more they entangle themselves in a moral discourse which they cannot escape in the long run" (Risse and Sikkink 1999, p. 16). The diffusion of international norms depends on the establishment and the sustainability of networks among domestic and transnational actors who succeed in linking with international regimes. "International contacts can 'amplify' the demands of domestic groups, pry open space for new issues, and then echo these demands back in the domestic arena" (p. 18). Among the nations Risse and Sikkink studied, Chile is the clearest example of these authors' claims for an expanded agenda opened by NGOs, Church groups, and political opposition. The model suggested by Risse and Sikkink could be schematized as in Figure 6.2. In this model, constituent and opposition national organizations lobby the national government and, in turn, are pressured by governments. But NGO's have powerful alliances outside of the national governance structure: They can leverage government change through these alliances more effectively than through frontal assaults on the state because governments are powerless to retaliate at NGOs through UNESCO, UNICEF, or the ILO. Pressures are thus exerted only in one direction, as represented in Figure 6.2. Organizations, as problem-seeking sets of solutions, try to sell their answers. It is to be expected that they would use international instruments to help legitimize their contributions.

THE INTERNATIONAL LEGAL PROCESS: ILO AND THE CRC

One way to observe changes in the orientation of national child labor policy is through the political negotiations with the International Labour Organization. In 1996, Chile's minister of labor—himself a former ILO official—entered his nation as a participant in the ILO's International Program to Eradicate Child Labour (IPEC). In the same year, during the ILO's session of March 1996, the ILO placed the question of child labor on the agenda of the 1998 session. In preparation for the 1998 session, a survey of official comments about the elimination of intolerable child labor was made of member states. The record of each government's response and counterresponse illuminates the national positions as well as the ability of the ILO to shape those positions through persuasion. By sharp contrast with Chile, Mexico refused to enter the IPEC. The official Mexican response to the survey was that, while eradicating intolerable forms of child labor was a noble objective, the process and time-frame for doing so would depend upon the developmental stage of each member state. In the official view of Mexico, child labor stemmed from the cultural, historical, social, and economic circumstances of ILO members and local communities. Consequently, Mexico argued, it should be up to each ILO member to determine what types of labor were "intolerable." Mexico (together with India) further argued that deciding which forms of labor should be considered "hazardous" must be made independently by member states. Mexico's view was that each government should collaborate with employers and work organizations, with assistance from legal experts in their own national legislation.

Chile, Peru, and the United States replied that the recommendation should take full account of international standards for this decision. The United States was not willing to make to make the consideration of intolerable rights place-specific. Rather, in the U.S. view, standards should be comprehensive and universal. Mexico further argued that the preamble to the new convention should indicate that ILO member states agree to suppress the most intolerable forms of child labor, but that this is best done by progressively enhancing their economic and social circumstances. Mexico also insisted that *any* reference to the total elimination of child labor ought to be avoided in the new convention, as it was only the most intolerable forms of child labor that members had agreed needed to be eradicated. Peru held that the convention should refer only to "children," not to "adolescents." The response to this view was that the convention should focus on types of work that are intolerable at any age. The U.N. Committee on the Rights of the Child also participated in the negotiations. The 1989 conventions (ratified by Peru, Chile, and Mexico but not the United States) had classified all persons under the age of eighteen as legally "children." There was no separate international category for "adolescents" The U.N. committee observed that that the proposed convention had failed to mention education.

There was hope, in Peru, that the ILO could directly influence the government's stance without the need for grassroots mobilization. Strategically, the ILO held its fourteenth assembly in Lima, in August of 1999, creating an expectation of a speech by Peru's chief executive, who had decreed the 1992 Code of Children and Adolescents. Alberto Fujimori did not address the gathering, however. In his place he sent Vice President Ricardo Marquez Flores (the vice presidency is a fluid and transitory position in the Peruvian executive branch and is rotated frequently). While acknowledging that a new international consensus had emerged against child labor, Marquez argued that there were national realities and cultural patterns that validated child and adolescent labor. Marquez focused on the problem of child prostitution, which he agreed must be eliminated under terms of Convention No. 182.

This tardy embrace of ILO standards elicited a cool response from team members of the International Program to Eliminate Child Labor, who worried that Peru's ease in embracing goals of the new convention masked a reluctance to engage the goals of

IPEC. Since the 1996 entry by Peru into this program, the requisite national committee to eliminate child labor was first headed by a renowned advocate for the protection (not elimination) of child labor. Even after her departure, communications were often strained between the ILO and Peru's Ministry of Women (which was delegated with overseeing the eradication of child labor). The position of Peru's IPEC program was thus in sharp contrast to Chile, where the ILO's representative to IPEC enjoyed almost daily communication with his counterpart in the Ministry of Labor and with over twenty grassroots unions, business groups, and advocacy organizations. In Peru the executive branch of government was far more isolated from potential stakeholders. The very active child advocacy Peruvian NGOs were among Latin America's most visible. But their concerted deliberations and manifestos over child labor—much like the actions of Foro Educative—gained no audience with the Fujimori government.

Mexico's official responses to international children's advocacy have been distinct from those of Chile and of Peru. Since the Mexican revolution, the interests of individuals and families have been represented in the state through mass organizations, chiefly the labor and agriculture organizations that constituted the PRI. Rather than openly contest positions taken by the governing party, opposition demands were absorbed into the state apparatus up until the 2000 presidential race. Reciprocal benefits were generated by the co-optation of new interest groups. Legitimacy was added to the PRI's control of the state through the co-optation of potential change-agents within the channels of the ruling party. Identity and constituent politics were minimized as the state responded to collective pressures from its constituent organizations. The organizations that presented themselves as possible threats were rewarded with offices and official places within the ruling bureaucracy.

The weakness of this system, from the perspective of children's well-being in marginalized areas of Mexico, is that vulnerable families and working children are seldom organized, especially in rural Mexico. The interests of working and out-of-school children were neither represented nor integrated within Mexico's corporativist arrangement. This social constitution helps to explain Mexico's resistance, until very recently, to single-interest, broad-based social mobilization outside of the party structure. Historically, the official response to ILO or UNICEF pressures has been to represent a *collective* national interest. That is, governments did not present themselves primarily as guardians, much less as advocates, of individual social freedoms. The third article of Mexico's national constitution has always guaranteed free education for all. However, until 1993, this was presented as the means to national progress rather than as the instrument for individual advancement. This stance changed in the wake of Mexico's ratification of the CRC, which required the government to present periodic reports to the U.N. Committee on the Rights of the Child stating the progress of individual children's welfare and legal protection.

The U.N. report by the Committee on the Rights of the Child responded critically to Mexico's initial submissions regarding national compliance with the convention. The committee called for greater collaboration with non-governmental organizations and further attention to ethnic and regional inequality. Most of all, the committee urged that a single body of law for children under eighteen must be developed in accord with the requirements of the convention. These reactions by the committee were open for public inspection and they were soon invoked by human rights groups, child advocates, and opposition political parties. For example, Rocio Robledo represented the Human Rights Commission of Mexico City at time the capital was governed by the opposition PRD party of Cuauhtemoc Cárdenas. Robledo obliquely criticized the inaction of the PRI to comply with even the letter of the Convention on the Rights of the Child and argued in an opposition newspaper that greater attention was needed to unify and centralize the disperse and disconnected body of legislation related to children. In 1999, she identified fifty-four separate laws, decrees, and codes, each one referring to different ages of children (Monge and Vivas 1999).

Led, in part, by PDR initiatives in Mexico City as well as by UNICEF strategists commemorating the tenth anniversary of Mexico's ratification of the CRC, national legislation was passed to create an integrated legal framework. Three women legislators representing the PAN, PRD, and the PRI co-authored a law to implement new constitutional responsibilities to protect the rights of children and adolescents. First, this law affirmed the precedence the CRC's central tenet, the principle of the best interests of the child. Although the family is considered the "primordial space" for the development of children, the law also affirms the co-responsibility of the Mexican state and society as a whole for protecting children's legal rights and assuring their full development. In terms of labor, the new law reaffirms the prohibitions on contractual relations with children younger than fourteen, as had been established previously in Mexico's Federal Labor Law. But what was most noteworthy about the new legal approach was its recognition of the need for inter-institutional collaboration and a shared responsibility between the federal and state governments. The success of the new law also reflected a desire by each of Mexico's three largest political parties to share credit for the protection of children's rights in the period leading to the presidential campaign.

UNICEF and the CRC appeared conspicuous by their very absence from the law, which refers obliquely only to "compromisos internacionales" (international commitments). Moreover, there was no mention of the NGOs that supported the new law, and this generated some general dissatisfaction from Jorge Valencia, director of COMEXANI and one of the key advocates for children. Mobilization for the protection of children within the CRC framework had broader consequences, in the view of Valencia. "It is also a call to civil society to reassert . . . not only a defense of children's and adolescent's rights, but fundamentally to position them as social subjects with rights." The call to protect children is also a call to illuminate "problems that formerly were invisible to the eyes of the majority of the population, as in this case were children and adolescents (Valencia 2000).

THE MEANING OF TENDENCIES IN CHILDREN'S ACTIVITIES

The finding of increasing rates of school participation in Peru, but not Mexico, at first glance appears counterintuitive. After all, Peru experienced greater overall poverty than did in Mexico (see Figure 1.3). But Peru's demand for education must be viewed in the context of contemporary social history. Prior to the 1968–80 military government, much of Peru's rural population was tied to an oligarchy. Peasants worked as farmers and herders but had no land tenure. Social solidarity was stymied by the clientelistic relationships with the landowners. Lateral relationships and civil institutions were minimal. The structure of rural society, in particular, was characterized as a "baseless triangle": peasants were related to each other primarily through their subservient position in the hierarchy (Cotler 1967). Radical agrarian reforms eliminated the old hierarchy but, in its absence, an educated elite took its place. Similar to the rebirth of inequality in Bolivia, following revolutionary reforms there (Kelley and Klein 1981), parents' expressed demand for children's education—even for those who live in difficult circumstances—is a legacy of radical change and the uncertainty of Peru's political and economic future. Education became the safest bet for all, even for those children who had to work to support themselves. Although schooling may have been unsuccessful in raising productivity or reducing overall income inequality, educational expansion in Peru was seen to have one important benefit for each new government: Education, rather than other, more threatening alternatives, became the preferred route of social progress among the public. When secondary school students were surveyed in 1985 about how Peru could resolve its many social and economic problems, a greater number of young people chose "more education" than any other response (Post 1987). More recently, Ansión and his colleagues (1998) found widespread general agreement that schooling was the "best inheritance." Migdal (1988, p. 27) emphasizes that, "in stitching together strategies of survival, people use myths or symbols to help explain their place and prospects in an otherwise bewildering world. . . . These strategies of survival, sewn from their symbols, rewards, and sanctions, are the roadmaps used to guide one through the maze of daily life, ensuring one's existence and, in rare instances, pointing the way toward upward mobility."

The findings of expanded rates of schooling in the face of Peru's extreme poverty may reflect the absence of alternative paths or social projects, either in the agrarian economy, the labor force, or the political sphere. Education became a type of civic religion to Peruvian families who, migrating to the urban coast, saw few other options for their children's futures. In Mexico, by contrast, the state achieved hegemony over popular demands for education and other indicators of progress. It was the state that promoted national development and initiated social reform projects. In concrete terms, this meant that the supply of schooling was more restricted than in Peru, especially in rural areas. By supporting farm prices in labor-intensive sectors of production, Mexico kept viable many alternatives that, in Peru, disappeared either through neglect or terrorist-inspired urban migration.

CONCLUSIONS: LATIN AMERICAN CHILDREN IN THE GLOBAL MILLENNIUM

The contradictory trends we find in Mexico and Peru, as well as the divergence of those countries from Chile, are indicative of larger tendencies experienced by the world's children. As a recent UNICEF report concludes:

> international trends in the 1980s and 1990s offer a mixed picture of changes in child welfare. While most social indicators improved, on average, in most countries . . . there is evidence that divergence in social achievements is increasing. Roughly one third of the world's children may have been bypassed by improvements in health, education, nutrition and poverty reduction, or may have even witnessed a deterioration since 1980.

In one sense, therefore, the "surprises" seen in Peru and Mexico should come as no surprise at all. Most Latin American children are attending school today. But poverty among children generally—and among students—is not diminishing. For many children in marginalized regions of Mexico, poverty may become intractable. The research indicates that, over the period of the Mexican and Peruvian case studies, poorer children in rural areas became less able to attend school whilst free from the need to work. But this was not the case in Chile, after 1990. In broad terms, the coalition government in that country shifted away from the military's narrow welfare focus on the very poorest of the poor, on families whose children had few opportunities for paid work. There was a relative—not absolute—decline in programs for the poorest Chileans (Kurtz 1999, p. 14) as Chilean subsidies were increased in universalistic policies that broadened away from the narrower focus on the destitute during the military government. Social politics after 1996 also supported urban workers. The minimum wage increases after 1990, for example, cost the government little but affected many more voters than did targeted policies. Child labor made obvious sense as a political issue in the new coalition, including as it did many labor unions.

Mexico's PRI was in a different position from the Coalition government in Chile. Under the PRI, the Mexican state maintained corporatist institutions through labor unions and farming confederations that stretched into civil society. On the one hand, parents who were dissatisfied with the existing alternatives for their children had avenues for redress, and parents could see their positions incorporated into existing organizations. It was less likely they would become threats to those organizations by aligning with opposing parties or with alternative organizations. On the other hand, as compared with rural families in Peru and probably also rural families in Chile, Mexican farm families were presented with better alternatives to the institution of education as a means to achieve stability or social mobility. Children in Mexico's farming economy would naturally see out-of-school-work as a more attractive option than would rural Peruvian children, given the fact that Mexico's state institutions offered legitimacy to involvement in work as opposed to schooling. The conflicting message to families, in the wake of Mexico's 1993 extension of compulsory schooling to nine years, was not only conflicting: It was unlikely to be heard.

The meaning of the tendencies and determinants of children's work and schooling, documented in this book, is that these trends are far from pre-determined. The fact that poverty may become intractable for many Latin American children does not mean that this is inevitable. For, while a global market for goods and services will inevitably reach further into the many societies of Latin America, the political forces unleashed by this transformation lead to no single outcome. Children will not inevitably become more educated; childhood will not "naturally" come to resemble childhood in the countries of the North. Nor will children who are living in poverty inevitably slide backward. The very directionality of development must be seen as problematic, based on the conflicting trends found in populations of children living in three Latin American nations during the 1990s. The fact that there is no single direction, no uniform tendency in children's work patterns suggests a different, clearer role for political leadership than would be suggested had we come to a different conclusion. If poverty were the only cause of child labor in the countries of this study; if there were a consistent trend across the varied policy environments of Chile, Peru, and Mexico; if school attendance were at least becoming equally universal for children in different regions of the same country–these alternative findings would have led to a concluding comment about the nature of contemporary world development and about Latin America's unique position in that development. The absence of these findings, however, leads to a much different conclusion, one stressing the uniqueness of individual policy environments. Both cross-nationally and historically since the 1980s, the varied approaches to school finance, labor code formulation and enforcement, and targeted poverty reduction in Latin America represent a menu of policy alternatives. While governments and political leaders cannot remake childhood exactly as they choose, there is a great deal that they can do to ensure that children's basic needs are met and to guarantee that their rights to a healthy development are protected by the nations that have pledged themselves to their children's futures.

APPENDIX

APPENDIX A1.1 Distribution of Activity by Chilean Children

	Number of children Column Percentage					
	Quintiles of Children's Household Incomes					
A. 1990	Poorest	2	3	4	Richest	TOTAL
Neither Work nor School:	19438	14733	14575	13315	6008	68069
Percent:	7.88	6.01	5.94	5.44	2.45	5.54
Economic activity ONLY:	24701	25094	21123	16756	7236	94910
Percent:	10.01	10.24	8.61	6.84	2.95	7.73
Work AND school:	2964	2321	4015	2389	2555	14244
Percent:	1.20	0.95	1.64	0.98	1.04	1.16
School Attendance ONLY:	199712	202988	205710	212510	229674	1050594
Percent:	80.92	82.81	83.82	86.75	93.56	85.57
Total	246815	245136	245423	244970	245473	1227817
Percent:	100	100	100	100	100	100
	Quintiles of Children's Household Incomes					
B. 1996	Poorest	2	3	4	Richest	TOTAL
Neither Work nor School:	21163	13490	12209	4208	3132	54202
Percent:	7.92	5.19	4.63	1.60	1.19	4.12
Economic activity ONLY:	20605	15075	11821	8387	2575	58463
Percent:	7.71	5.8	4.48	3.20	0.98	4.44
Work AND school:	2877	2415	5213	4047	6837	21389
Percent:	1.08	0.93	1.98	1.54	2.60	1.63
School Attendance ONLY:	222509	229114	234669	245692	250111	1182095
Percent:	83.29	88.09	88.92	93.66	95.22	89.81
Total	267154	260094	263912	262334	262655	1316149
Percent:	100	100	100	100	100	100

Source: weighted tabulations of 1990 and 1996 CASEN. Activities are only for months when school is in session. "Quintiles of children's household incomes" are calculated for all children who are living with at least one parent at the time of the survey, and based on the total income reported for the household head. Quintiles are of children, and not of parents.

APPENDIX A1.2 Distribution of Activity by Peruvian Children

	\multicolumn{6}{c}{Number of children Column Percentage}
	\multicolumn{6}{c}{Quintiles of Children's Household Incomes}
A. 1985	Poorest	2	3	4	Richest	TOTAL
Neither Work nor School:	34477	43425	38363	12299	20251	148815
Percent:	8.09	10.17	9.01	2.88	4.76	6.98
Economic activity ONLY:	95239	75051	67537	45753	29998	313578
Percent:	22.34	17.58	15.85	10.72	7.06	14.71
Work AND school:	126128	123645	104713	120598	103813	578897
Percent:	29.58	28.97	24.58	28.26	24.42	27.16
School Attendance ONLY:	170554	184698	215380	248060	271137	1089829
Percent:	40.00	43.27	50.56	58.13	63.77	51.14
Total	426398	426819	425993	426710	425199	2131119
Percent:	100	100	100	100	100	100
	\multicolumn{6}{c}{Quintiles of Children's Household Incomes}
B. 1997	Poorest	2	3	4	Richest	TOTAL
Neither Work nor School:	31244	29128	24805	27137	27212	139526
Percent:	5.65	5.32	4.5	4.94	4.96	5.07
Economic activity ONLY:	85312	61012	39105	37738	39436	262603
Percent:	15.43	11.15	7.09	6.87	7.19	9.55
Work AND school:	233966	187883	148412	115785	106379	792425
Percent:	42.32	34.32	26.9	21.06	19.4	28.82
School Attendance ONLY:	202277	269360	339464	369039	375238	1555378
Percent:	36.59	49.21	61.52	67.13	68.44	56.56
Total	552799	547383	51786	549699	548265	2749932
Percent:	100	100	100	100	100	100

Source: weighted tabulations of 1985 and 1997 ENNIV. Activities are only for months when school is in session. "Quintiles of children's household incomes" are calculated for all children who are living with at least one parent at the time of the survey, and based on the total income reported for the household head. Quintiles are of children, and not of parents.

Appendix

APPENDIX A1.3 Distribution of Activity by Mexican Children

	Number of children Column Percentage					
	Quintiles of Children's Household Incomes					
A. 1992	Poorest	2	3	4	Richest	TOTAL
Neither Work nor School:	559132	382617	327126	198793	148874	1616542
Percent:	26.30	19.04	15.39	10.45	7.31	15.85
Economic activity ONLY:	528863	301627	314627	231106	188055	1564278
Percent:	24.87	15.01	14.8	12.15	9.23	15.34
Work AND school:	93517	86815	98874	76894	48689	404789
Percent:	4.40	4.32	4.65	4.04	2.39	3.97
School Attendance ONLY:	944812	1238136	1384600	1394821	1651844	6614213
Percent:	44.43	61.62	65.15	73.35	81.07	64.85
Total	2126324	2009195	2125227	1901614	2037462	10199822
Percent:	100	100	100	100	100	100
	Quintiles of Children's Household Incomes					
B. 1996	Poorest	2	3	4	Richest	TOTAL
Neither Work nor School:	467235	521778	384684	241146	124066	1738909
Percent:	19.56	21.53	16.93	10.23	5.42	14.82
Economic activity ONLY:	671910	468393	290886	238245	137003	1806437
Percent:	28.13	19.33	12.8	10.1	5.98	15.4
Work AND school:	259555	163702	150871	127788	121588	823504
Percent:	10.87	6.76	6.64	5.42	5.31	7.02
School Attendance ONLY:	989904	1269210	1446122	1751159	1906773	7363168
Percent:	41.44	52.38	63.63	74.25	83.29	62.76
Total	2388604	2423083	2272563	2358338	2289430	11732018
Percent:	100	100	100	100	100	100

Source: weighted tabulations of 1992 and 1996 ENIGH. Activities are only for months when school is in session. "Quintiles of children's household incomes" are calculated for all children who are living with at least one parent at the time of the survey, and based on the total income reported for the household head. Quintiles are of children, and not of parents.

APPENDIX A4.1 Distribution of Children's Activities by Country, Year, Age, Gender, Residence, and Income Quintile

	Mexico 1992		Mexico 1996		Peru 1985		Peru 1997		Chile 1990		Chile 1996	
Activity	N	Percent	N	Percent	N	Percent	N	Percent	N	Percent	N	Percent
Total												
1. No school or work	683	16.2	640	12.6 *	141	5.1	81	3.2 *	964	8.1	1,071	5.7 *
2. Full-Time Worker	815	19.3	986	19.4	448	16.1	301	11.9 *	859	7.2	1,019	5.4 *
3. Full-Time Student	2,573	60.9	3,126	61.5	1,392	50.2	1,429	56.3 *	9,930	83.3	16,359	87.4 *
4. Works while studies	156	3.7	330	6.5 *	794	28.6	729	28.7	162	1.4	260	1.4
Total	4,227	100.1	5,082	100.0	2,775	100.0	2,540	100.1	11,915	100.0	18,709	99.9
Age 12-14												
1. No work or school	273	12.3	243	9.0 *	56	3.6	24	1.8 *	206	3.6	231	2.4 *
2. Full-Time Worker	156	7.0	230	8.6 *	165	10.7	62	4.6 *	80	1.4	93	1.0 *
3. Full-Time Student	1,727	77.5	2,021	75.6 *	857	55.8	879	64.7 *	5,323	94.2	9,085	95.7 *
4. Works while studies	71	3.2	178	6.7 *	457	29.8	394	29.0	38	0.7	83	0.9
Total	2,227	100.0	2,672	99.9	1,535	99.9	1,359	100.1	5,647	99.9	9,492	100.0
Age 15-17												
1. No school or work	410	20.5	397	16.5 *	85	6.9	57	4.9 *	758	12.1	840	9.1 *
2. Full-Time Worker	659	33.0	756	31.4	283	22.9	239	20.2	779	12.4	926	10.0 *
3. Full-Time Student	846	42.3	1,105	45.9 *	535	43.1	550	46.6	4,607	73.5	7,274	79.0 *
4. Works while studies	85	4.3	152	6.3 *	337	27.2	335	28.4	124	2.0	177	1.9
Total	2,000	100.1	2,410	100.1	1,240	100.1	1,181	100.1	6,268	100.0	9,217	100.0

Appendix

APPENDIX A4.1 (*Continued*)

Boys

Activity	Mexico 1992 N	Percent	Mexico 1996 N	Percent	Peru 1985 N	Percent	Peru 1997 N	Percent	Chile 1990 N	Percent	Chile 1996 N	Percent
1. No school or work	104	4.9	102	3.9 *	52	3.6	23	1.8 *	333	5.5	412	4.3 *
2. Full-Time Worker	611	28.7	692	26.7 *	200	14.0	177	13.6	639	10.5	73	7.7 *
3. Full-Time Student	1,320	61.9	1,573	60.7	703	49.1	682	52.3	4,994	82.1	8,183	86.1 *
4. Works while studies	7	4.5	226	8.7 *	476	33.3	421	32.3	115	1.9	168	1.8
Total	2,132	100.0	2,593	100.0	1,431	100.0	1,303	100.0	6,081	100.0	9,496	99.9

Girls

Activity	1992 N	Percent	1996 N	Percent	1985 N	Percent	1997 N	Percent	1990 N	Percent	1996 N	Percent
1. No school or work	579	27.6	538	21.6 *	89	6.6	58	4.7 *	631	10.8	659	7.2 *
2. Full-Time Worker	204	9.7	94	11.8 *	248	18.5	124	10.0 *	220	3.8	286	3.1 *
3. Full-Time Student	1,253	59.8	1,553	62.4	689	51.3	747	60.4 *	4,936	84.6	8,176	88.7 *
4. Works while studies	59	2.8	104	4.2 *	318	23.7	308	24.9 *	47	0.8	92	1.0 *
Total	2,095	99.9	2,489	100.0	1,344	100.0	1,237	100.0	5,834	100.0	9,213	100.0

Rural

Activity	1992 N	Percent	1996 N	Percent	1985 N	Percent	1997 N	Percent	1990 N	Percent	1996 N	Percent
1. No school or work	438	23.5	351	17.2 *	55	4.6	33	3.2 *	458	14.1	467	9.1 *
2. Full-Time Worker	460	24.7	548	26.8 *	353	29.2	191	18.6 *	455	14.1	525	10.2 *
3. Full-Time Student	901	48.4	979	44.3 *	326	27.0	360	35.0 *	2,284	70.7	4,100	80.0 *
4. Works while studies	63	3.4	168	8.2 *	474	39.2	443	43.1 *	34	1.1	34	0.7
Total	1,862	100.0	2,046	100.0	1,208	100.0	1,027	100.0	3,231	100.0	5,126	100.0

APPENDIX A4.1 (*Continued*)

Urban

Activity	Mexico 1992 N	Percent	1996 N	Percent	Peru 1985 N	Percent	1997 N	Percent	Chile 1990 N	Percent	1996 N	Percent
1. No school or work	1245	10.4	289	9.5 *	86	5.5	48	3.2 *	506	5.8	412	4.3 *
2. Full-Time Worker	355	15.0	438	14.4 *	95	6.1	110	7.3	404	4.7	494	3.6 *
3. Full-Time Student	1,672	70.7	2,146	70.7 *	1,066	68.0	1,069	70.7 *	7,646	88.0	12,259	90.2 *
4. Works while studies	93	3.9	162	5.3 *	320	20.4	286	18.9 *	128	1.5	226	1.7
Total	2,365	100.0	3,035	100.0	1,567	100.0	1,513	100.1	8,684	100.0	13,583	100.0

Household income per capita quintile 1

Activity	N	Percent	N	Percent	N	Percent	N	Percent	N	Percent	N	Percent
1. No school or work	295	25.6	257	21.6 *	35	5.3	18	4.7 *	372	12.0	529	9.3 *
2. Full-Time Worker	246	21.3	364	25.9 *	198	29.9	134	22.5 *	216	6.9	372	5.5
3. Full-Time Student	574	549.7	687	48.8	185	28.0	180	30.3	2,492	80.1	4,762	83.3 *
4. Works while studies	39	3.4	99	7.0 *	243	36.8	262	44.1 *	31	1.0	52	0.9
Total	1,154	100.0	1,407	100.0	661	100.0	594	99.9	3,111	100.0	5,715	100.0

Household income per capita quintile 2

Activity	N	Percent	N	Percent	N	Percent	N	Percent	N	Percent	N	Percent
1. No school or work	180	18.4	189	14.8 *	38	6.4	22	3.7 *	266	8.9	279	6.1 *
2. Full-Time Worker	214	21.9	289	22.6 *	111	18.7	70	11.7 *	245	8.2	297	6.5 *
3. Full-Time Student	560	57.2	716	55.9 *	261	43.9	313	52.3 *	2,448	81.8	3,919	86.2 *
4. Works while studies	25	2.6	87	6.8 *	185	31.1	193	33.6	35	1.2	49	1.1
Total	979	100.0	1,281	100.0	595	100.1	598	100.0	2,994	100.1	4,544	99.9

APPENDIX A4.1 (Continued)

	Mexico				Peru				Chile			
	1992		1996		1985		1997		1990		1996	
Activity	N	Percent	N	Percent	N	Percent	N	Percent	N	Percent	N	Percent
Household income per capita quintile 3												
1. No school or work	123	13.3	119	11.8	24	4.5	14	2.6	185	7.6	170	4.7 *
2. Full-Time Worker	179	19.3	178	17.6 *	69	12.9	48	8.9 *	219	9.0	210	5.8 *
3. Full-Time Student	581	62.7	648	64.2	285	53.4	352	65.4 *	1,979	81.6	3,172	87.8 *
4. Works while studies	43	4.6	64	6.3 *	156	29.2	124	23.0 *	41	1.7	61	1.7
Total	926	100.0	1,009	100.0	534	100.0	538	99.9	82,424	99.9	3,613	100.0
Household income per capita quintile 4												
1. No school or work	66	9.2	52	6.3	19	3.4	12	2.6	95	5.1	65	2.3 *
2. Full-Time Worker	141	19.6	108	13.2 *	47	8.5	35	7.5	121	6.5	103	3.7
3. Full-Time Student	483	67.2	605	73.8 *	343	61.7	320	68.5 *	1,606	86.5	2,603	92.3 *
4. Works while studies	29	4.0	55	6.7	147	26.4	100	21.4 *	35	1.9	50	1.8
Total	719	100.0	820	100.0	556	100.0	467	100.0	1,857	100.0	2,821	100.0
Household income per capita quintile 5												
1. No school or work	10	2.2	23	4.1	25	5.3	15	4.4	46	3.0	28	1.4 *
2. Full-Time Worker	35	7.8	47	8.3	23	5.4	14	4.1	58	3.8	37	1.8 *
3. Full-Time Student	375	83.5	470	83.2	318	74.1	264	77.0	1,405	92.0	1,903	94.4 *
4. Works while studies	20	4.5	25	4.4	63	14.7	50	14.6	20	1.3	48	2.4
Total	449	100.0	565	100.0	429	100.0	343	100.1	1,529	100.1	2,016	100.0

Sources: Mexico: 1992, 1996 *ENIGH*; Peru: 1985/86, 1997 *ENNIV*; Chile: 1990, 1996 *CASEN*.

Notes: 1. Weighted by population weights divided by the mean of the population weight to yield a weighted N approximately equal to the sample size.

2. Percentages may not add to 100 because of rounding.

3. An * indicates that the null hypothesis of no change between survey years is rejected at the 5% significance level.

APPENDIX A4.2 Variables Used in the Multinomial Logit Analysis

Variable	Definition
Dependent Variable:	
Activity	=1 if child does not attend school and does not work (home worker)
	=2 if child does not attend school but does work (full-time worker)
	=3 if child attends school and does not work (full-time student, the Reference category)
	=4 if child attends school and also works (part-time student)
Explanatory Variables:	
Age15-17	=1 for children aged 15-17, =0 for children aged 12-14
Education	Years of education completed by the child
Gender	=1 if child female, =0 if child male
HeadKid	=1 if child is son or daughter of household head, =0 otherwise
Density	Number of siblings within one year of age of child
Num5	Number of siblings aged 5 or younger
Num18M	Number of males in household aged 18 or older (excluding head and spouse)
Num18F	Number of females in household aged 18 or older (excluding head and spouse)
HeadEducation	Years of education completed by the household head
HeadAge	Head's age (in years)
HeadGender	Head's gender (=1 if female, =0 if male)
HeadNotWork	=1 if head is not working, =0 otherwise
HeadSelfEmp	=1 if head is an entrepreneur or self-employed, =0 otherwise
HeadWageEmp	=1 if head is a wage earner, =0 otherwise (Reference category for head's occupational status variables)
NoSpouse	=1 for a single-headed household, =0 otherwise
SpouseWageEmp	=1 if spouse is a wage earner, =0 otherwise or if there is no spouse
SpouseSelfEmp	=1 if spouse is an entrepreneur or self-employed, =0 otherwise or if there is no spouse
SpouseNotWork	=1 if spouse is not working, =0 otherwise or if there is no spouse (Reference category for the spouse variables)
Quintile1	=1 if household is in bottom per capita income quintile, =0 otherwise
Quintile2	=1 if household is in second per capita income quintile, =0 otherwise
Quintile3	=1 if household is in third per capita income quintile, =0 otherwise
Quintile4	=1 if household is in fourth per capita income quintile, =0 otherwise
Quintile5	=1 if household is in top per capita income quintile, =0 otherwise (Reference category for per capita income variables)

APPENDIX A4.2 *(Continued)*

Variable	Definition
Geographic Dummies for Mexico:	
North	=1 if household is in North region, =0 otherwise
NorthPacific	=1 if household is in North Pacific region, =0 otherwise
Gulf	=1 if household is in Gulf region, =0 otherwise
SouthPacific	=1 if household is in South Pacific region, =0 otherwise
Central	=1 if household is in Central region, =0 otherwise (Reference category)
Geographic Dummies for Peru:	
Sierra	=1 if household is in Sierra region, =0 otherwise (Reference category for rural models)
Coast	=1 if household is in Coastal region, =0 otherwise
Selva	=1 if household is in Selva region, =0 otherwise
Lima	=1 if household is in Lima, =0 otherwise (Reference category for urban models)
Geographic Dummies for Chile:	
North	=1 if household is in North region, =0 otherwise
Central	=1 if household is in Central region, =0 otherwise
South	=1 if household is in South region, =0 otherwise
Metro	=1 if household is in Metropolitan region, =0 otherwise (Reference category)

APPENDIX A5.1 Mexican State Indicators of Marginalization, Secondary School Transition Rates, and Female Representation

State	% workers with <2 min. salaries	% homes with dirt floors	% adults without primary	1990 population of state	1984-86 grade 6 primary	1985-86 grade 1 second	1985 transition rate	1994-95 grade 6 primary	1995-96 grade 1 second	% female grade 1 second	1995 transition rate
Aguascalientes	63	34	7	719659	16913	14006	0.83	20040	18287	48.9	0.91
Baja California	40	24	8	1660855	35466	33848	0.95	39484	37928	49.1	0.96
Baja California Sur	54	28	14	317764	6789	6472	0.95	8025	7639	48.7	0.95
Campeche	68	45	24	535185	10491	8800	0.84	13837	12054	47.4	0.87
Coahuila	61	28	8	1972340	49226	43733	0.89	48053	43524	48.6	0.91
Colima	50	36	21	428510	10880	9872	0.91	10697	9975	49.6	0.93
Chiapas	80	62	51	3210496	46237	39082	0.85	68265	52994	45.0	0.78
Chihuahua	53	31	10	2441873	58355	43247	0.74	56810	47126	50.0	0.83
Distrito Federal	60	17	2	8235744	217257	236336	1.09	170749	178352	48.9	1.04
Durango	68	39	20	1349378	36800	27447	0.75	35055	28717	49.6	0.82
Guanajuato	61	47	17	3982593	96768	64405	0.67	103506	77154	47.5	0.75
Guerrero	68	50	50	2620637	58181	46072	0.79	65578	53084	47.5	0.81
Hidalgo	74	46	30	1888366	42733	36473	0.85	54370	46134	47.2	0.85
Jalisco	55	36	13	5302689	134691	98852	0.73	138420	112325	48.7	0.81
Mexico	63	29	13	9815795	226644	180190	0.80	268439	235650	47.9	0.88
Michoacan	60	49	29	3548199	84040	62655	0.75	90560	67442	48.3	0.74
Morelos	60	34	22	1195059	32309	30543	0.95	32377	29297	49.3	0.90
Nayarit	54	42	22	824643	21511	19077	0.89	20676	18711	49.9	0.90
Nuevo Leon	59	23	6	3098736	62889	57125	0.91	73669	69379	48.8	0.94
Oaxaca	79	57	53	3019560	57301	40273	0.70	91961	58729	45.5	0.64
Puebla	72	45	30	4126101	93112	74778	0.80	108898	83748	46.5	0.77
Queretaro	60	40	17	1051235	25521	17465	0.68	29464	24035	46.3	0.82
Quintana Roo	49	39	23	493277	6700	6819	1.02	13838	12770	46.5	0.92
San Luis Potosi	71	45	30	2003187	47420	42499	0.90	51347	41698	47.1	0.81
Sinaloa	56	37	24	2204054	59219	51757	0.87	53131	47741	49.7	0.90
Sonora	53	29	18	1823606	47070	44554	0.95	43371	40861	50.0	0.94
Tabasco	65	44	14	1501744	34361	26720	0.78	41964	37713	46.6	0.90
Tamaulipas	61	32	14	249581	55379	47841	0.86	51768	45878	49.1	0.89
Tlaxcala	72	34	14	761277	19615	17657	0.90	22401	19787	47.4	0.88
Veracruz	72	48	36	6228239	135210	109250	0.81	143996	118061	46.6	0.82
Yucatan	74	48	19	1362940	25821	22540	0.87	31481	27733	45.0	0.88
Zacatecas	73	49	17	1276323	34192	23505	0.69	33636	26351	49.2	0.78

"Marginalization" indicators from 1990 Census. Enrollment information from Secretary of Public Education (SEP)

Appendix

APPENDIX A5.2 Mexican State Proportions of Children's Activities, State Poverty, and State Rural Residence

Survey year:	Numbers of children 12-17 1992	1996	Proportions of them in school 1992	1996	Proportions of students working 1992	1996	Per child income of head (current) 1992	1996	Proportions in lowest quintile 1992	1996	Proportions in highest quintile 1992	1996	Proportions in rural areas 1992	1996
Aguascalientes	152	186	0.59	0.67	0.05	0.13	917	1827	0.23	0.18	0.11	0.19	0.29	0.26
Baja Ca. Nor.	69	131	0.59	0.67	0.09	0.03	2668	3551	0.02	0.01	0.39	0.42	0.18	0.08
Baja Ca. Sur	101	97	0.86	0.81	0.11	0.03	2153	3995	0.06	0.00	0.45	0.39	0.24	0.15
Campeche	107	539	0.68	0.76	0.06	0.10	784	1915	0.21	0.26	0.07	0.13	0.53	0.32
Chiapas	204	233	0.67	0.57	0.08	0.22	502	774	0.43	0.46	0.07	0.03	0.57	0.59
Chihuahua	134	135	0.69	0.64	0.09	0.04	1513	2809	0.05	0.03	0.32	0.23	0.23	0.17
Coahuila	117	546	0.73	0.70	0.04	0.09	1242	2285	0.11	0.10	0.26	0.17	0.10	0.12
Colima	129	134	0.68	0.85	0.13	0.19	1753	2444	0.06	0.08	0.21	0.26	0.21	0.17
Mexico City	472	398	0.87	0.85	0.03	0.02	1810	3558	0.03	0.06	0.35	0.33	0.00	0.00
Durango	178	177	0.64	0.70	0.10	0.05	1303	2329	0.03	0.06	0.14	0.16	0.38	0.43
Guanajuato	235	658	0.50	0.56	0.06	0.12	841	1842	0.21	0.16	0.12	0.15	0.33	0.44
Guerrero	137	211	0.67	0.66	0.10	0.22	780	2163	0.20	0.21	0.08	0.10	0.44	0.47
Hidalgo	132	557	0.56	0.72	0.02	0.13	931	1543	0.32	0.25	0.08	0.12	0.44	0.56
Jalisco	333	562	0.58	0.65	0.07	0.13	1097	2276	0.13	0.23	0.13	0.18	0.18	0.16
Mexico	447	682	0.78	0.78	0.02	0.05	1174	2426	0.08	0.15	0.17	0.18	0.19	0.16
Michoacan	135	228	0.42	0.59	0.08	0.15	676	2128	0.10	0.15	0.16	0.11	0.56	0.44
Morelos	120	167	0.77	0.71	0.04	0.16	888	1939	0.28	0.25	0.09	0.15	0.14	0.13
Nayarit	147	147	0.73	0.80	0.08	0.12	922	2557	0.08	0.11	0.08	0.22	0.40	0.33
Nuevo Leon	297	135	0.73	0.71	0.08	0.04	3266	2337	0.14	0.14	0.19	0.29	0.05	0.10
Oaxaca	164	597	0.67	0.59	0.07	0.19	426	1167	0.07	0.09	0.30	0.09	0.36	0.56
Puebla	170	208	0.65	0.61	0.08	0.25	556	1575	0.38	0.33	0.03	0.15	0.35	0.43
Queretaro	177	202	0.64	0.73	0.10	0.02	827	1779	0.41	0.30	0.05	0.14	0.58	0.42
Quintana Roo	129	149	0.73	0.77	0.11	0.18	1204	2854	0.33	0.21	0.12	0.29	0.19	0.22
San Luis Potosi	135	194	0.64	0.60	0.09	0.09	575	1459	0.03	0.16	0.25	0.07	0.47	0.41
Sinaloa	156	178	0.71	0.82	0.08	0.09	1933	9645	0.28	0.23	0.06	0.07	0.33	0.26
Sonora	99	175	0.90	0.77	0.10	0.03	1273	2983	0.21	0.08	0.29	0.31	0.17	0.23
Tabasco	174	762	0.62	0.74	0.06	0.09	1245	1639	0.07	0.10	0.30	0.23	0.74	0.51
Tamaulipas	118	159	0.66	0.77	0.12	0.04	1421	4449	0.30	0.32	0.20	0.13	0.18	0.17
Tlaxcala	645	168	0.70	0.79	0.05	0.10	806	1589	0.08	0.09	0.17	0.28	0.23	0.20
Veracruz	171	177	0.70	0.75	0.11	0.13	1101	2005	0.28	0.16	0.08	0.08	0.53	0.46
Yucatan	139	153	0.64	0.65	0.15	0.12	1339	2407	0.18	0.15	0.19	0.18	0.17	0.29
Zacatecas	166	210	0.52	0.55	0.08	0.19	856	1209	0.24	0.39	0.25	0.09	0.55	0.53
Total	6089	9255	0.67	0.70	0.07	0.11	1215	2234	0.33	0.31	0.15	0.18	0.31	0.30
									0.19	0.20	0.17			

Note: all figures, except for survey sample numbers in first column, are estimated using sample weights.

APPENDIX A5.3 Determinants of Activities of Mexican Children (12-17), Individual, Family, and State-level Contextual Effects Over Time

(Multinomial Logistic Regression Coefficients)			
	Activity A. rather than full-time schooling	**Activity B.** rather than full-time schooling	**Activity C.** rather than full-time schooling
Time period: survey year is 1996 (not 1992)	-0.873***	-0.918***	-0.319
Household head's years of schooling	-0.225***	-0.275***	-0.072***
Child is FEMALE (not male)	0.946***	-1.028***	-1.092***
Lives in RURAL area of Mexico	0.784***	0.773***	0.328*
Child's age in years	0.552***	0.772***	0.265***
Number of siblings sharing household	0.146***	0.154 ***	0.102***
Income Quintile Dummies (poorest ommited)			
Household head's income is in 2nd Quintile	-0.302*	0.084	-0.676*
Household head's income is in 3rd Quintile	-0.273*	-0.214	-0.092
Household head's income is in 4th Quintile	-0.771***	0.073	-0.541*
Head's income is in 5th Quintile (wealthiest)	-0.789***	-0.261	-1.396***
Period interaction effects, individual level			
Time period * heads years of schooling	0.109***	0.122***	0.022
Time period * living in rural area of Mexico	-0.145	0.271*	0.515**
Time period * 2nd Quintile	0.510***	0.361*	-0.041
Time period * 3rd Quintile	0.285*	-0.313*	-0.197
Time period * 4th Quintile	0.329*	-0.138	-0.163
Time period * 5th Quintile	-0.123	-0.448*	0.276
Time period * being Female	0.080	0.242*	0.351*
Contextual effects and period interactions:			
State's proportion of "poor" children	-1.089**	0.161	-0.801
Time period * proportion poor	1.612***	2.243***	3.025***
Proportion poor * being in 2nd Quintile	0.368	-2.266***	2.117*
Proportion poor * being in 3rd Quintile	-0.182	0.422	-0.142
Proportion poor * being in 4th Quintile	-0.459	-3.138***	1.424
Proportion poor * being in 5th Quintile	-1.090	3.543***	
Constant	-9.243***	-11.937***	-5.818***

Source: 1992 and 1996 ENIGH. The omitted reference category for the income quintiles is the poorest fifth of family income. "Poor" is defined as pertaining to the lowest fifth of the Mexican income distribution. * sig. at .1 level; ** sig. at .01 level; *** sig at .001 level. Activity "A" is domestic or non-economic activity; "B" is economic activity; "C" is economic activity in combination with school attendance.

Appendix

APPENDIX A5.4 Effect of Family Income and State Poverty on Likelihood that Children Attend School

(Predicted Probabilities)

States with fewer than 20% of children (12 – 17) in poverty

	1992			1996		
Income quintile	Only Attends School	Works While Attends	Total prob. In school	Only Attends School	Works While Attends	Total prob. In school
poorest	0.50	0.05	0.55	0.54	0.08	0.62
2nd	0.62	0.04	0.66	0.57	0.04	0.61
3rd	0.66	0.05	0.71	0.67	0.06	0.73
4th	0.73	0.04	0.77	0.76	0.04	0.80
wealthiest	0.82	0.02	0.84	0.86	0.04	0.90
Total, all quintiles	0.68	0.04	0.72	0.70	0.05	0.75

States with 20 – 30% of children (12 – 17) in poverty

	1992			1996		
Income quintile	Only Attends School	Works While Attends	Total prob. In school	Only Attends School	Works While Attends	Total prob. In school
poorest	0.44	0.04	0.48	0.46	0.10	0.56
2nd	0.56	0.05	0.61	0.49	0.08	0.57
3rd	0.61	0.04	0.65	0.59	0.08	0.67
4th	0.75	0.04	0.79	0.69	0.08	0.77
wealthiest	0.80	0.03	0.83	0.78	0.08	0.86
Total, all quintiles	0.61	0.04	0.65	0.58	0.09	0.67

States with more than 30% of children (12 – 17) in poverty

	1992			1996		
Income quintile	Only Attends School	Works While Attends	Total prob. In school	Only Attends School	Works While Attends	Total prob. In school
poorest	0.48	0.04	0.52	0.40	0.13	0.53
2nd	0.65	0.05	0.70	0.44	0.13	0.57
3rd	0.64	0.04	0.68	0.54	0.09	0.63
4th	0.74	0.06	0.80	0.70	0.11	0.81
wealthiest	0.77	0.05	0.82	0.74	0.15	0.89
Total, all quintiles	0.60	0.05	0.65	0.49	0.12	0.61

Source: Estimated from equation in Appendix A.53

APPENDIX A5.5 Determinants of Children's Activities in Mexico, Gender, Poverty, and Gender Differences in Effect of Poverty

	Activity A. rather than full-time schooling	Activity B. rather than full-time schooling	Activity C. rather than full-time schooling
Time period: survey year is 1996 (not 1992)	-0.501***	-0.572***	-0.266
Household head's years of schooling	-0.163***	-0.204***	-0.062***
Child is FEMALE (not male)	0.150	-0.686***	-0.961***
Lives in RURAL area of Mexico	0.833***	0.816***	0.324*
Child's age in years	0.551***	0.766***	0.266***
Number of siblings sharing household	0.149***	0.153***	0.100***
Income Quintile Dummies (poorest ommited)			
Household head's income is in 2nd Quintile	-0.018	-0.329**	-0.098
Household head's income is in 3rd Quintile	-0.137	-0.139	0.012
Household head's income is in 4th Quintile	-0.719***	-0.443***	-0.178
Head's income is in 5th Quintile (wealthiest)	-0.892***	-0.616***	-0.693**
Time period interaction effects, individual level			
Time period * living in rural area of Mexico	-0.264*	0.146	0.483**
Time period * 2nd Quintile	0.598***	0.523***	0.002
Time period * 3rd Quintile	0.423**	-0.105	-0.176
Time period * 4th Quintile	0.568***	0.117	-0.073
Time period * 5th Quintile	0.269	-0.062	0.456*
Time period * being Female	0.152	0.283*	0.364*
Contextual effects and Gender interactions:			
State's proportion of "poor" children	-3.509***	-0.009	0.414
Time period * proportion poor	1.117*	2.219***	3.050***
Being Female * proportion poor living in state	3.419***	-2.533***	-0.829
Being Female * living in a poor family	0.538***	0.631***	0.213
Constant	-9.122***	-12.090***	-6.191***

Source: 1992 and 1996 ENIGH. The omitted reference category for the income quintiles is the poorest fifth of family income. "Poor" is defined as pertaining to the lowest fifth of the Mexican income distribution. * sig. at .1 level; ** sig. at .01 level; *** sig at .001 level. Activity "A" is domestic or non-economic activity; "B" is economic activity; "C" is economic activity in combination with school attendance.

Formal Interviews (with David Post unless otherwise noted)

Alejandro Cussianovich, editor of AutoEducación and a founder of MANTHOC. Lima, November 1986 (with David Post) and July 2000 (with Claudia Galindo).

Ana María Yañez, labor law and woman's rights advocate, ADEC-ATC. Lima, February 1996 (with David Post) and July 2000 (with Claudia Galindo).

Dante Córdova Blanco, former minister of education and head of Fujimori cabinet. Lima, July 1999, with Martín Benavides.

Director of a large urban secondary school. Lima, June 1999 (with Martín Benavides).

Director of Centro Educativo Andrés Bello. Lima, June 1999 (with Martín Benavides).

Director of the primary/secondary school, Maria Reiche. Lima, June 1999 (with Martín Benavides).

Julio Castro Gomez, director of the health-workers union, Federación Medica Peruana. As a congressman under Garcia government, he was member of congressional commission on health, population, and family. Lima, January 1996.

Eliseo Cuadrao, director of IPEC program for ILO in Andean countries. Lima, July 2000 (with Claudia Galindo).

Francisco Rivas, ILO representative to Chile. Santiago, November 1999.

Francisco Verdera, labor economist, Instituto de Estudios Peruanos. Lima, January 1996 and November 1999.

Frederico Alles, child labor specialist, Chilean Ministry of Labor. Santiago, November 1999.

Gloria Helfer, author of United Left education plan for 1985 electoral campaign, public secondary school principal, education minister in first Fujimori government, researcher in NGO Tinkuy. Lima, October 1986 and February 1996.

Grover Pango, union leader and teacher in Catholic school, first APRA minister of education (7/1985–7/1987), activist in civil association Foro Educativo since 1991. Lima, July 1985 and January 1996.

Henry Harmann, vice-minister, Ministry of Education. Lima, February 1996.

Liliana Vega, director of UNICEF's "Street Educators" program in Lima. February 1996 (with David Post) and July 2000 (with Claudia Galindo).

Luis Carlos Gorriti, education adviser to Education Ministry of Alberto Fujimori government. Lima, July 1999 (with Martin Benavides).

Mercedes Cabanillas, APRA congresswoman and later education minister in Alan Garcia government. Lima, June 1999 (with Martin Benavides).

Miek Van Gaalen, child labor specialist with ILO. Lima, November 1999.

Mónica Rodriguez, child labor specialist with ILO. Lima, July 2000 (with Claudia Galindo).

Oscar Collao Montañez, specialist of Peru's Ministry of Education (planning and budget) from 1970 to 1990, and its director from 1985 to 1990. Lima, April 1996.

Pedro Orihuela, director of the Office of Statistics, Ministry of Education. Lima, April 1996

Sonia Peralta, specialist in Office of Statistics, Ministry of Education. Lima, April 1996.

Teresa Tovar, education researcher, DESCO. Lima, January 1996.

Sylvia Smelkes, education researcher, DIE. Aguascalientes, Mexico, October 1999.

Walter Alarcón, child labor consultant for UNICEF. Lima, July 2000 (with Claudia Galindo).

Isaac Ruíz, leader of Peru's "Global March" against child labor and researcher in the Centro de Estudios Sociales y Publicaciones. Lima, July 2000 (with Claudia Galindo).

REFERENCES

Abbott, Edith, and Sophonsiba Breckinridge. 1911. *Truancy and Non-Attendance in the Chicago Schools: A Study of the Social Aspects of the Compulsory Education and Child Labor Legislation of Illinois*. Chicago: University of Chicago Press.

Abbott, Philip. 1981. *The Family on Trial*. University Park, Pa.: Penn State University Press.

Abler, David, Jose Rodriquez, and Hector Robles. 1998. "The Allocation of Children's Times in Mexico and Peru." Working Paper. Population Research Institute, The Pennsylvania State University.

Alarcón, Walter. 1991. *Entry Calles y Plazas: El Trabajo de los Niños en Lima*. Lima: UNICEF/IEP/ADEC-ATC.

Alarcón, Walter, and Liliana Vega. 1995. *Las Calles de los Niños*. Lima: INABIF (Instituto Nacional de Bienestar Infantil y Familiar).

Alston, Philip (ed.). 1994. *The Best Interests of the Child: Reconciling Culture and Human Rights*. New York: Oxford University Press.

Altimar, Oscar. 1984. "Poverty, Income Distribution and Child Welfare in Latin America: A Comparison of Pre- and Post-recession Data." *World Development* 12:261-282.

Anker, Richard, and H. Melkas. 1996. *Economic Incentives for Children and Families to Eliminate or Reduce Child Labor*. Geneva: ILO.

Ansión, Juan, A. Lazarte, S. Matos, J. Rodríguez, and P. Vega-Centeno. 1998. *Educación: La Mejor Herencia*. Lima: Catholic University.

Aries, Philipe. 1960. *Centuries of Childhood*. New York: Alfred Knopf.

Bar Din, Anne. 1998. *Los niños marginados rurales: Estudio de caso en Morelos*. Cuernavaca, Mexico: Centro Regional de Investigaciones Multidisciplinarias.

Barnes, Donna. 1999. "Causes of Dropping Out from the Perspective of Education Theory." Pp. 14–22 in Laura Randall and Joan B. Anderson (eds.), *Schooling for Success: Preventing Repetition and Dropout in Latin American Primary Schools*. New York: M. E. Sharpe.

Barrantes, Emilio. 1989. *Historia de la educación Peruana*. Lima: Mosca Azul Editores.

Basu, Kaushik. 1999. "Child Labor: Cause, Consequence and Cure, with Remarks on International Labor Standards." *Journal of Economic Literature* 37:1083–1119.

Baytelman, Yael, Kevin Cowan, José De Gregorio, and Pablo González. 1999. "Chile." Pp. 237–287 in Enrique Ganuza, Arturo León, and Pablo Sauma (eds.), *Gasto Público En Servicios Sociales Básicos En América Latina Y El Caribe*. Santiago: Economic Commision for Latin America.

Becker, Gary S. 1991. *A Treatise on the Family*. Cambridge, Mass.: Harvard University Press.

———. 1997. "Is There Any Way to Stop Child Labor Abuses?" *Business Week*, May 12, p.22.

Behrman, Jere R. 1996. *Human Resources in Latin America and the Caribbean*. Washington, D.C.: Inter-American Development Bank.

Behrman, Jere R., Nancy Birdsall and Miguel Székely. 1998. "Intergenerational Schooling Mobility and Macro Conditions and Schooling Policies in Latin America." Working paper #386 Inter-American Development Bank.

Behrman, Jere R., Suzanne Duryea, and Miguel Székely. 1999. "Schooling Investments and Aggregate Conditions: A Household Survey-Based Approach for Latin America and the Caribbean." Working paper #407 Inter-American Development Bank.

Bellew, Rosemary, and Elizabeth King. 1993. "Educating Women: Lessons from Experience." In Elizabeth King and M.Anne Hill (eds.), *Women's Education in Developing Countries: Barriers, Benefits and Policies*. Baltimore: Johns Hopkins University Press.

Berhman, Jere R., and Barbara L. Wolfe. 1987. "Investments in Schooling in Two Generations in Pre-Revolutionary Nicaragua: The Roles of Family Background and School Supply." *Journal of Development Economics* 27:395–419.

Berkovitch, Nitza. 1999. "The Emergence and Transformation of the International Women's Movement." Pp. 100–126 in John Boli and George Thomas (eds.), *Constructing World Culture*. Stanford: Stanford University Press.

Berlin, Issiah. 1964. *Four Essays on Liberty*. New York: Oxford University Press.

Berry, Albert. 1997. "The Income Distribution Threat in Latin America." *Latin American Research Review* 32(2):3–40.

Birdsall, Nancy, and Juan Luis Londoño. 1998. "No Tradeoff: Efficient Growth Via More Equal Human Capital Accumulation." Pp. 111–145 in N.Birdsall, C.Graham and R.Sabot (eds.) *Beyond Trade-offs: Market Reform and Equitable Growth in Latin America*. Washington: Brookings Institution Press.

Blair, Sampson Lee. 1992. "Children's Pariticpation in Household Labor: Child Socialization Versus the Need for Household Labor." *Journal of Youth and Adolescence* 21, vol 2, 241–258.

Blake, Judith. 1989. *Family Size and Achievement*. Berkeley: University of California Press.

Boli, John, and George Thomas (eds.). 1999. *Constructing World Culture: International Nongovernmental Organizations Since 1875*. Stanford: Stanford University Press.

Boli, John. 1999. "World Authority Structures and Legitimations." Pp. 267–302 in John Boli and George Thomas (eds.), *Constructing World Culture*. Stanford: Stanford University Press.

References

Borsche, Sven. 1998 "Task Force on National Coalitions of the NGO's Group for the Convention on the Rights of the Child." In proceedings of First European Regional Meeting of National NGO Coalitions for Children's Rights. Berlin.

Boserup, Esther. 1990. "Economic Change and the Roles of Women." In Irene Tinker (ed.), *Persistent Inequalities*. New York: Oxford University Press.

Bowman, Mary Jean, and C. Arnold Anderson. 1980. "The Participation of Women in Education in the Third World." *Comparative Education Review* 24:S13-S32.

Boyden, Jo, and William Myers. 1995. *Exploring Alternative Approaches to Combating Child Labour: Case Studies From Developing Countries*. Innocenti Occasional Papers, Child Rights Series, No. 8. Florence, Italy.

Boyden, Jo, Brigitta Ling, and William Myers. 1998. *What Works For Working Children*. Florence: UNICEF.

Boyden, Jo. 1991. "Working Children in Lima, Peru." Pp. 24–45 in William E. Meyers (ed.), *Protecting Working Children*. London: Zed.

Boylan, Delia. 1996 "Taxation and Transition: The Politics of the 1990 Chilean Tax Reform." *Latin American Research Review* 31(1):7–31.

Bracho, Teresa, and A. Zamudio. 1994. "Los rendimientos económicos de la escolaridad en México." *Economía Mexicana* 3:345–377.

Buchman, Claudia. 1996. "The Debt Crisis, Structural Adjustment and Women's Education: Implications for Status and Social Development." *International Journal of Comparative Sociology* 37:5–29.

Bustillo, Ines. 1993. "Latin America and the Carribean." In Elizabeth King and M.Anne Hill (eds.) *Women's Education in Developing Countries. Barriers, Benefits and Policies*. Baltimore: Johns Hopkins University Press.

Butcher, Kristin, and Anne Case. 1994. "The Effect of Sibling Sex Composition on Women's Education and Earnings." *Quarterly Journal of Economics* 109:531–563.

Capelo, Joaquín. 1902. *Sociologia de Lima*. Lima: La Industria.

Carnoy, Martin. 1982. "Education for Alternative Development." *Comparative Education Review* 26:160–77.

_____. 1998. "National Voucher Plans in Chile and Sweden: Did Privatization Reforms Make for Better Education?" *Comparative Education Review* 42:309-337.

CELADE (Centro Latinoamericano Y Caribeño de Demografia). 1998. *Boletín Demográfico* No. 59.

Chile. 1994. Comisión Nacional Para la Modernización de la Educación.

Chubb, John, and Terry Moe. 1988. "Politics, Markets, and the Organization of Schools." *American Political Science Review* 82:1065-87.

Cisneros, Luis Jaime. 1986. "Commentario." *Debate* [Lima, Peru]. March.

Cohen, Howard. 1980. *Equal Rights of Children*. Totowa, N.J.: Littlefield, Adams.

Colectivo Mexicano de Apoyo a la Niñez (COMEXANI). 1998. "IV informe sobre los Derechos y la Situación de la Infancia en México 1994–1997: Los Hechos se burlan de los Derechos." Mexico, D.F.: Author.

Coleman, J. S., and T.B. Hoffer. 1987. *Public and Private High Schools: The Impact of Communities*. New York: Basic Books.

Consejo Nacional de Población (CONAPO). 1999. "IV Informe de Avances del Programa Nacional de Población." Mexico, D.F.: Author.

Coons, John, and Stephen Sugarman. 1978. *Education by Choice: The Case for Family Control.* Berkeley: University of California Press.

Cooperacción. 1999. *Programa de erradicación del trabajo infantil en el caserío minero artesanal Santa Filomena.* Lima: Author.

Corrales, Javier. 2000. "Political Impediments to Education Reforms, and Some Solutions." Paper presented at CEPAL conference on "Reformas Educativas y Política en América Latina." Santiago, Chile.

Cortés Cáceres, Fernando, and Rosa María Rubalcava Ramos. 1994. *El ingreso de los hogares.* Aguascalientes, Mexico: Instituto Nacional de Estadística, Geografia e Informática.

Cortés, Julio. 1999. "Acerca de la erradicación del trabajo infantil." In Coordinación Sudamericana, *Marcha Global Contra el Trabajo Infantil.* Santiago: Author.

Cotler, Julio. 1967. *La mecánica de la dominación interna y del cambio social en el Perú.* Lima: Instituto de Estudios Peruanos.

Cragg, M. I., and M. Epelbaum. 1996. "Why Has Wage Dispersion Grown in Mexico? Is It the Incidence of Reforms or the Growing Demand for Skills?" *Journal of Development Economics* 51:99–116.

Cussiánovich, Alejandro. 1995. "Los niños y adolescentes trabajadores en el Código." *Autoeducación.* October:19–22.

Dávalos, José. 1996. *Derecho del Trabajo.* México: Editorial Porrua.

De Ibarrola, María. 1996. "Siete políticas fundamentales para la educación secundaria en América Latina. Situación actual y propuestas." Pp. 15–50 in Instituto Estatal de Educación Pública de Oaxaca. *La Educación Secundaria: Cambios y Perspectivas.* Oaxaca, Mexico: Author.

De Janvry, Alain, Gustavo Gordillo, and Elizabeth Sadoulet. 1997. *Mexico's Second Agrarian Reform: Household and Community Responses, 1990–1994.* La Jolla, Calif.: Center for U.S.–Mexican Studies, University of California, San Diego.

De la Madrid, Miguel. 1982–1988. *Informes de Gobierno.* Mexico City: Poder Ejecutivo.

Deaton, Angus. 1997. *The Analysis of Household Surveys: A Micro-Econometric Approach to Development Policy.* Baltimore: Johns Hopkins University Press.

Delgado, Kenneth. 1981. *Reforma Educative: Que Pas?* Lima, Peru: Ediciones SAGSA.

Desai, Sonalde. 1992. "Children at Risk: The Role of Family Structure in Latin America and West Africa." *Population and Development Review* 18:689–717.

Diller, Janelle. 1997. "Child Labor, Trade, and Investment: Toward the Harmonization of International Law." *American Journal of International Law* 91:663–692.

Dore, Ronald. 1976. *The Diploma Disease.* Berkeley: University of California Press.

Dresser, Denisse. 1992. "Pronasol y política: Combate a la pobreza como fórmula de gobernabilidad." In *La pobreza en México. Causas y políticas para combatirla.* Mexico City: Instituto Tecnológico Autónomo de México.

Easton, Peter A., and Simon M. Fass. 1989. "Monetary Consumption Benefits and the Demand for Primary Schooling in Haiti." *Comparative Education Review* 33:176–193.

Economic Commission for Latin America and the Caribbean (ECLAC). 1999. *Social Panorama of Latin America, 1998.* Santiago, Chile: ECLAC.

Edwards, Sebastian. 1995. *Crisis and Reform in Latin America: From Despair to Hope.* New York: Oxford University Press.

Eekelaar, John. 1994. "The Best Interests of the Child and the Child's Wishes: Their Role in Dynamic Self-Determinism." Pp. 42–61 in Philip Alston (ed.), *The Best Interests of the Child: Reconciling Culture and Human Rights.* New York: Oxford University Press.

Elster, Jon. 1983. *Sour Grapes: Studies in the Subversion of Rationality.* New York: Cambridge University Press.

Espínola, Viola. 1992. *Decentralization of the Education System and the Introduction of Market Rules in the Regulation of Schooling.* Documento de Discusion. Santiago: CIDE.

Espinoza, Oscar, and Luis Eduardo González. 1993. *La Experiencia del Proceso de Desconcentración y Descentralización Educacional en Chile, 1974–1989.* Santiago: PIIE.

Esteva, Gustavo, and Madhu Suri Prakash. 1998. *Grassroots Post-modernism: Remaking the Soil of Cultures.* New York: Zed.

Fallon, Peter, and Zafiris Tzannatos. 1998. *Child Labor: Issues and Directions for the World Bank.* Washington, D.C.: The World Bank.

Farrell, Joseph. 1986. *The National Unified School in Chile.* Vancouver: University of British Columbia Press.

Feinberg, Joel. 1980. "The Child's Right to an Open Future." In W.Aiken and H.LaFollette (eds.), *Whose Child? Children's Rights, Parental Authority, and State Power.* Totowa, N.J.: Rowman and Allenheld.

Festinger, Leon. 1962. *A Theory of Cognitive Dissonance.* Stanford: Stanford University Press.

Finn, Jeremy D., Janet Reis, and Loretta Dulberg. 1980. "Sex Defferences in Educational Attainment: The Process." *Comparative Education Review* 24:S33-S52.

Firestone, Shulamith. 1970. *The Dialectic of Sex: The Case for Feminist Revolution.* New York: Morrow.

Fischer, Kathleen B. 1979. *Political Ideology and Educational Reform in Chile, 1964–1976.* Los Angeles: UCLA Latin American Center.

Foro Educativo. 1992. *Descentralización Educativa.* Lima: Author.

Foster, Philip. 1977. "Education and Social Differentiation in Less Developed Countries." *Comparative Education Review* 21:211–229.

Franco, Rolando, and Armando Di Filippo. 1999. "Aspectos Sociales de la Integración Regional." Pp. 19–48 in Franco and Di Filippo (eds.) *Las Dimensiones Sociales De La Integración Regional En América Latina.* Santiago: Economic Commision for Latin America.

Freeman, Michael. 1992. "The Limits of Children's Rights." Pp. 29–46 in Michael Freeman and Philip Veerman (eds.), *The Ideologies of Children's Rights.* Boston: Martinus Nijhoff.

Fuentes Molinar, Olac. 1996. "La Educación Secundaria: Cambios y Perspectivas." Pp. 51–62 in Instituto Estatal de Educación Pública de Oaxaca (ed.),. *La Educación Secundaria: Cambios y Perspectivas*. Oaxaca, Mexico: Author.

Fuller, Bruce, and Richard Rubinson. 1992. *The Political Construction of Education: The State, School Expansion, and Economic Change*. New York: Praeger.

———. 1992. "Does the State Expand Schooling? Review of the Evidence." *The Political Construction of Education*. New York: Praeger.

Fuller, Bruce. 1991. *Growing Up Modern: The Western State Builds Third-World Schools*. New York: Routledge.

Fyfe, Alec. 1989. *Child Labour*. Cambridge: Polity Press.

Gajardo, Marcela, and Ana Maria de Andraca. 1988. *Trabajo Infantil y Escuela*. Santiago: FLACSO

Galeana Cisneros, Rosaura. 1997. *El Trabajo Infantil y Adolescente Como Instancia Socializadora y Formadora En, Para y Por la Vida*. Mexico City: Dirrecion de Investigaciones Educativas.

Gambetta, Diego. 1987. *Were They Pushed or Did They Jump? Individual Decision Mechanisms in Education*. New York: Cambridge University Press.

García Méndez, Emilio. 1998. "Child Rights in Latin America: From 'Irregular Situation' to Full Protection." Innocenti Essays No. 8. Florence: UNICEF.

———. 1999. "Infancia, ley, y democracia: una cuestión de justicia." *Realidad y Utopia* 3:79–94

García-Huidobro, Juan Eduardo, and Cristian Cox. 1999. "La Reforma Educacional Chilena 1990–1998: Vision de Conjunto." Pp. 7–46 in García-Huidobro and Cox (eds.), *La Reforma Educacional Chilena*. Madrid, Spain: Editorial Popular.

Gauri, Varun. 1998. *School Choice in Chile: Two Decades of Educational Reform*. Pittsburgh: University of Pittsburgh Press.

Gershberg, A.I. 1999. "Education 'Decentralization' in Mexico and Nicaragua." *Comparative Education* 35:63–80.

Glewwe, Paul, and Gillette Hall. 1992. *Poverty and Inequality during Unorthodox Adjustment: The Case of Peru, 1985-90*. Washington: The World Bank.

González de la Rocha, Mercedes. 1994. *The Resources of Poverty: Women and Survival in a Mexican City*. Cambridge, Mass.: Blackwell.

González, Pablo. 1999. "Financiamiento, Incentivos, y Reforma Educacional." Pp. 305–31 in García-Huidobro and Cox (eds.) *La Reforma Educacional Chilena*. Madrid, Spain: Editorial Popular.

Graham, Carol. 1991. "The APRA Government and the Urban Poor: The PAIT Program in Lima's Pueblos Jovenes." *Journal of Latin American Studies* 23:91–130.

———. 1994. *Safety Nets, Politics, and the Poor: Transitions to Market Economies*. Washington, D.C.: Brookings.

———. 1998. *Private Markets for Public Goods*. Washington, D.C.: Brookings.

Greenhalgh, Susan. 1985. "Sexual Stratification: The Other Side of 'Growth with Equity' in East Asia." *Population and Development Review* 11:265–314.

Grootaert, Christiaan, and Ravi Kanbur. 1995. "Child Labour: An Economic Perspective." *International Labour Review* 134:187–203.

Grosh, Margaret E., and Paul Glewwe. 1995. *A Guide to Living Standards Measurement Study Surveys and Their Datasets.* Living Standards Measurement Study Working Paper 120. Washington, D.C.: World Bank.

Grosh, Margaret. 1994. *Administering Targeted Social Programs in Latin America. From Platitudes to Practice.* World Bank Regional and Sectoral Studies. The International Bank for Reconstruction and Development/ The World Bank. USA.

Grupo de Iniciativa National (GIN). 1996. "A todo riesgo: trabajo infantil apunte para una discusion." *Realidad y Utopía* 1:103–109.

Guabloche, Maritza. 1993. Administración y Financiamiento Sector Educación. Lima:ESAN

Guerra, María Teresa. 1994. "Seguridad social y condiciones de trabajo de los niños jornaleros agrícolas en Sinaloa." Pp. 111–124 in *Análisis de la situación de los niños jornaleros agrícolas.* Oaxaca, Mexico: Universidad Padagógica.

Guillén-Marroquín, Jesús. 1988. "Child Labour in Peru: Gold Panning in Madre de Dios." Pp. 61–72 in Assefa Bequele and Jo Boyden (eds.), *Combatting Child Labour.* Geneva: International Labour Office.

Hammarberg, Thomas. 1997. *A School for Children with Rights: The Significance of the United Nations Convention on the Rights of the Child for Modern Education policy.* Florence: UNICEF.

Hart, Roger, Jim Himes, and Gerison Lansdown. "Comentario Y Recomendaciones Para Las Iniciativas de Unicef Y Rädda Barnen Relativas al Derecho del Niño a la Participación." Pp. 47–57 in UNICEF 1998. Bogatá: Author.

Hartmann, Heidi I. 1981. "The Family as the Locus of Gender, Class, and Political Struggle: The Example of Housework." *Signs* 6:366–94.

———. 1994. "The Unhappy Marriage of Marxism and Feminism: Towards a More Progressive Union." In David Grusky (ed.), *Social Stratification.* Boulder: Westview.

Harvey, Pharis. 1995. "Where Children Work: Child Servitude in the Global Economy." *Christian Century* 112:362–73.

Herz, Barbara, K. Subbarao, Habib Masooma, and Laura Raney. 1991. *Letting Girls Learn. Promising Approaches in Primary and Secondary Education.* World Bank Discussion Papers 133.

Heward, Christine. 1998. "The New Discourses of Gender, Education, and Development." In Christine Heward and Sheila Bunwaree (eds.), *Gender, Education, and Development.* New York: Zed Books.

Hill, M. Anne, and Elizabeth King. 1993. "Women's Education in Development Countries: An Overview." In Elizabeth King and M. Anne Hill (eds.), *Women's Education in Developing Countries: Barriers, Benefits and Policies..* Baltimore: Johns Hopkins University Press.

Hirschman, Albert O. 1970. *Exit, Voice, and Loyalty: Responses to Decline in Firms, Organizations, and States.* Cambridge, Mass.: Harvard University Press.

Horn, Pamela. 1995. *Children's Work and Welfare, 1780–1890.* New York: Cambridge University Press.

Illich, Ivan. 1970. *Deschooling Society.* New York: Harper & Row.

ILO (International Labour Organization). 1996a. "Child Labour: Targeting the Intolerable." Geneva: Author.
ILO. 1996b. "Child Labour: What is to be Done?" Geneva: Author.
ILO. 1996c. International Labor Conference. 86th Session 1996. Geneva: Author
ILO. 1999. *IPEC Action Against Child Labour*. Geneva: Author.
INEGI (Instituto Nacional de Estadística, Geografia e Informatica). 1998a. *Trabajo doméstico y extradomestico en México*. Aguascalientes, Mexico: Author
INEGI (Instituto Nacional de Estadística, Geografia e Informatica). 1998b. *Infancia y Adolescencia en México*. Aguascalientes, Mexico: Author
Johnson, David. 1992. "Cultural and Regional Pluralism in the Drafting of the UN Convention on the Rights of the Child." Pp. 95–114 in Michael Freeman and Philip Veerman (eds.), *The Ideologies of Children's Rights*. Boston: Martinus Nijhoff.
Kandel, William, and Grace Kao. 2000. "Shifting Orientations: How U.S. Labor Migration Affects Children's Aspirations in Mexican Migrant Communities." *Social Science Quarterly* 81(1):16–32
_____. Forthcoming. "The Impact of Temporary Labor Migration on Mexican Student Outcomes." *International Migration Review.*
Kelley, Jonathan, and Herbert Klein. 1981. *Revolution and the Rebirth of Inequality: A Theory Applied to the National Revolution in Bolivia*. Berkeley: University of California Press.
King, Elizabeth M. 1987. "The Effect of Family Size on Family Welfare: What Do We Know?" In D. Gale Johnson and Ronald Lee (eds.), *Population Growth and Economic Development: Issues and Evidence.* . Madison, Wisc.: University of Wisconsin Press.
_____. 1996. "Education, Work and Earnings of Peruvian Women." *Economics of Education Review* 15:213–230.
King, Elizabeth M., and M. Anne Hill. 1993. *Women's Education in Developing Countries: Barriers, Benefits, and Policies*. Baltimore: Johns Hopkins University Press.
Klaiber, Jeffrey L., S.J. 1986. "The Battle Over Private Education in Peru, 1968–1980." *The Americas* 43:137–158.
Knaul, Felicia. 2000. "Age At Entry Into the Labor Force, Schooling, and Returns to Human Capital in Mexico." Paper presented at the meetings of the Population Association of America, March, Los Angeles.
Knaul, Felicia, and Susan W. Parker. 1998. "Patterns Over Time and Determinants of Early Labor Force Participation and School Drop Out: Evidence from Longitudinal and Retrospective Data of Mexican Children and Youth." Paper Presented at the 1998 Population Association of America Meetings, Chicago.
Knutsson, Karl Eric. 1997. *Children: Noble Causes or Worthy Citizens?* Brookfield, Vt.: Arena.
Kuo, Hsiang-Hui Daphne, and Robert M. Hauser. 1996. "Gender, Family Configuration, and the Effect of Family Background on Educational Attainment." *Social Biology* 43:98–131.
Kurtz, Marcus. 1999. "The Political Economy of Pro-Poor Policies in Chile and Mexico." Memeo, The World Bank. Washington, D.C.: Author.

References

Lächler, Ulrich. 1999. "Education and Earnings Inequality in Mexico." Working Paper 1949, The World Bank.

Langbein, Laura Irwin, and Allan J. Lichtman. 1978. *Ecological Inference*. Sage University Paper series on Quantitative Applications in the Social Sciences. Beverly Hills, Calif.: Sage Publications.

Latapi, Pablo. 1993. "Escolaridad inalterada de 1875 – 1993." *Proceso* 855:37

LaTorre, Carmen Luz. 1997. "Financiamiento de la Educación en Chile: Situación Actual y Posibilidades Futuras." Working Paper No. 6. Programa Interdisciplinario de Investigaciones en Educación (PIIE). Santiago.

Lauren, Paul. 1998. *The Evolution of International Human Rights*. Philadelphia: University of Pennsylvania Press.

Leipziger, Deborah, and Pia Sabharwal. 1993. "Companies That Play Hide and Seek with Child Labor." *Business and Society Review* 95:11.

Levin, Henry M. 1991. "The Economics of Educational Choice." *Economics of Education Review* 10:137–158.

Levinson, Mark. 1999. "Who's in Charge Here?" *Dissent*. Fall: 21–23.

Levison, Deborah, Karine Moe, and Felicia Knaul. 2000. "Youth Education and Work in Mexico." *World Development* 29: 167-188.

Levy, Santiago. 1991. *Poverty Alleviation in Mexico*. World Bank Working Papers, No. 679. Washington, D.C.: The World Bank.

Liao, Tim F. 1994. *Interpreting Probability Models: Logit, Probit, and Other Generalized Linear Models*. Newbury Park, Calif.: Sage Publications.

Lindgren Alves, José. 2000. "The Declaration of Human Rights in Postmodernity." *Human Rights Quarterly* 22:478–500.

Lloyd, Cynthia B., and Ann Blanc. 1996. "Children's Schooling in Sub-Saharan Africa: The Role of Fathers, Mothers, and Others." *Population and Development Review* 22:265–98.

Lloyd, Cynthia B., and Sonalde Desai. 1992. "Children's Living Arrangements in Developing Countries." *Population Research and Policy Review* 11:193–216.

Loker, William. 1999. "Grit in the Prosperity Machine: Globalization and the Rural Poor in Latin America." Pp. 9–40 in William Loker (ed.), *Globalization and the Rural Poor in Latin America*. Boulder: Lynne Rienner.

Lomnitz, Larissa Adler de. 1977. *Networks and Marginality : Life in a Mexican Shantytown*. New York: Academic Press.

Lopatka, Adam. 1992. "The Rights of the Child Are Universal." Pp. 47–52 in Michael Freeman and Philip Veerman (eds.), *The Ideologies of Children's Rights*. Boston: Martinus Nijhoff.

Lopez Acevedo, Gladys. 1999. "Learning Outcomes and School Cost-Effectiveness in Mexico: The PARE Program." Working Paper, The World Bank. Washington, D.C.: Author.

Lustig, Nora. 1990. "Economic Crisis, Adjustment and Living Standards in México 1982–1985." *World Development* 18:1325–1342.

MacPherson, C.B. 1973. *Democratic Theory*. New York: Oxford University Press.

Maddala, G. S. 1983. *Limited-Dependent and Qualitative Variables in Econometrics*. Cambridge: Cambridge University Press.

Marjoribanks, Kevin. 1991. "The Sibling Resource Dilution Theory: An Analysis." *The Journal of Psychology* 125:337-346.

Marx, Karl and Frederick Engels. 1978 [1848]. "Manifesto of the Communist Party." In Robert Tucker (ed.), *The Marx-Engels Reader*. New York: Norton.

Mason, Karen O. 1985. *The Status of Women*. New York: Rockefeller Foundation

Massiah, Jocelin. 1990. "Defining Women's Work in the Commonwealth Carribean." In Irene Tinker (ed.), *Persistent inequalities*. New York: Oxford University Press.

McCorquodale, Robert, and Richard Fairbrother. 1999. "Globalization and Human Rights." *Human Rights Quarterly* 21:735-766.

McEwan, Patrick, Luis Beneviste, and Juan Casassus. 1997. "Resultados preliminares de la Primera Evaluación Internacional del Laboratorio Latinoamericano de Evaluación de la Calidad de la Educación." Stanford University. Memeo.

McGinn, Noel, and Susan Street. 1986. "Education Decentralization: Weak State or Strong State?" *Comparative Education Review* 30:471-490.

McNicoll, Geoffrey. 1997. "Population and Poverty: A Review and a Restatement." Working Paper No. 105. New York: Population Council.

Mecklenburg, Pablo. "Componente juvenes Programa MECE-MEDIA" Pp. 151-160 in J. E. Garcia-Huidobro and C. Cox, eds., *La Reforma Educacional Chilena*. Madrid, Spain: Editorial Popular.

Melchior, Arne. 1996. "Child Labour and Trade Policy." In B. Grimsrud and A. Melchior (eds.), *Child Labour and International Trade Policy*. Oslo: Institute for Applied Social Science and Norwegian Institute of International Affairs.

Mexico, Secretaria de Educación Pública. 1999. *Perfil de la educación en México*. México, D.F.: Author.

Mickelson, Roslyn (ed.). 2000. *Children on the Streets of the Americas: Globalization, Education, and Homelessness in the United States, Brazil and Cuba*. New York: Routledge.

Migdal, Joel. 1988. *Strong Societies and Weak States: State-Society Relations and State Capabilities in the Third World*. Princeton: Princeton University Press.

Miró Quesada, Francisco. 1985. "Human Rights in Latin America." Pp. 304-17 in UNESCO (ed.), *Philosophical Foundations of Human Rights*. Paris: Author.

Modell, John. 1979. "Changing Risks, Changing Adaptations: American Families in the Nineteenth and Twentieth Centuries." In Allan J. Lictman and John R. Challinor, eds. *Kin and Communities*. Washington, D.C.: Smithsonian Institution Press.

Monge, Raúl, and María Luisa Vivas. 1999. "Pobreza, violencia y caos legislativo, verdugos de infancia mexicana." *Proceso* 1204:15-20.

Moreno Mena, José. 1996. "Empleo Infantil en el Sector Agrícola del Valle De Mexicali: Algunas Carateristicas Socioeconomicas." In Araceli Brizzio (ed.), *El Trabajo Infantil en México*. Mexico, D.F.: UNICEF.

MORI (Market Opinion Research International). 1998. *Estudio Caracterización del Trabajo Infantil: 3ra Informe de Resultados*. Santiago de Chile: Author.

Morley, Samuel A. 1995. *Poverty and Inequality in Latin America: The Impact of Adjustment and Recovery in the 1980s*. Baltimore: Johns Hopkins University Press.
Mower, Glenn. 1997. *The Convention on the Rights of the Child: International Law Support for Children*. Westport, Conn.: Greenwood Press.
Muñoz Izquierdo, Carlos. 1994. *La Contribución de la educación al cambio social*. Méxio, D.F.: Universidad Ibero Americana.
Muñoz Salazar, Patricia. 2000. *Poverty, Schooling, and Child Labor: A Portrait of Chile Before and After Democratization*. Ph.D. Dissertation, Rural Sociology and Demography, Penn State University.
Muñoz Vila, Cecilia. 1996. "The Working Child in Colombia Since 1800." Pp. 91–102 in Hugh Cunningham and Pier Paolo Viazzo, eds., *Child Labour in Historical Perspective*. Florence: UNICEF.
Muñoz, Cecilia, and Martha Palacios. 1980. *El Niño Trabajador: Testimonios*. Bogatá: Valencia Editores.
Myers, William E.(ed.). 1991. *Protecting Working Children*. London: Zed Books.
Myers, William E. 1999. "Considering Child Labour." *Childhood* 6:13–26.
_____. 2000. "Educating Children Who Work." New York: Save The Children Alliance.
_____. 2001."The Right Right? Child Labor in a Globalizing World." *Annals of the American Academy of Political and Social Science* 575:38-55.
Nardinelli, Clark. 1990. *Child Labor and the Industrial Revolution*. Bloomington, Ind.: Indiana University Press.
Nelson, Joan(ed.). 1990. *Economic Crisis and Policy Choice: The Politics of Adjustment in the Third World*. Princeton: Princeton University Press.
Nelson, Joan. 1992. "Poverty, Equity, and the Politics of Adjustment." In Stephan Haggard and Robert Kaufman, eds., *The Politics of Economic Adjustment*. Princeton: Princeton University Press.
Nieuwenhuys, Olga. 1995. "The Domestic Economy and the Exploitation of Children's Work: The Case of Kerala." *International Journal of Children's Rights* 3:213–225.
_____. 1996. " The Paradox of Child Labor and Anthropology." *Annual Review of Anthropology* 25: 237–251.
_____. 1998. "Global Childhood and the Politics of Contempt." Pp. 267–289 in *Alternatives, Social Transformation and Human Governance*. Boulder: Lynn Rienner.
Niles, Kimberly. 1999. "Economic Adjustment and Targeted Social Spending:The Role of Political Institutions (Indonesia, Mexico, and Ghana)." Working paper, The World Bank. Washington, D.C.: Author.
Nord, Bruce. 1994. *Mexican Social Policy: Affordability, Conflict and Progress*. New York: University Press of America.
O'Neill, Onora. 1996. *Toward Justice and Virtue*. New York: Cambridge University Press.
Ordóñez, Dwight, and María del Pilar Mejía. 1995. *El Trabajo Infantil Callejero en Lima*. Lima: CEDRO.
Ornelas, Carlos. 1995. *El Sistema Educativo Mexicano: La transición de fin de siglo*. Fondo de Cultura Económica. México.

Osterman, Paul. 1980. *Getting Started: The Youth Labor Market*. Cambridge, Mass.: MIT Press.
Oswald Spring, Úrsula. 1991. *Estrategias de Supervivencia en la Ciudad de México*. Cuernavaca, Mexico: UNAM/CRIM
Pango Vildoso, Grover. 1986. *Educación Para La Vida*. Speech to the Peruvian Congress. Lima: Ministry of Education.
Parish, William, and Robert J. Willis. 1993. "Daughters, Education and Family Budgets: Taiwan Experiences." *Journal of Human Resources* 28:863–898.
Pastor, Manuel Jr., and Carol Wise. 1998. "Mexican-Style Neoliberalism." Pp. 41–81 in Carol Wise (ed.), *The Post-NAFTA Political Economy*. University Park, Pa.: Penn State University Press.
_____. 1992. "Peruvian Economic Policy in the 1980s: From Orthodoxy to Herodoxy and Back." *Latin American Research Review* 27:83-117.
Patrinos, Harry A., and George Psacharopoulos. 1997. "Family Size, Schooling and Child Labor in Peru–An Empirical Analysis." *Journal of Population Economics* 10:387–405.
Paus, Eva. 1991. "Adjustment and Development in Latin America: The Failure of Preuvian Heterodoxy, 1985-1990." *Wrold Development* 19:411-434.
Paxson, Christina, and Norbert Schady. 1999. "Do School Facilities Matter? The Case of the Peruvian Social Fund (FONCODES)." Memo. The World Bank. Washington, D.C.: Author.
Pérez, Jaime Jesús. 1998. "El niño como sujeto social de derechos: Una visión del niño para leer la Convención." Pp. 43–45 in UNICEF (ed.), *La participación de niños y adolescentes en el contexto de la Convención sobre derechos del niño*. Bogatá: Author.
Peru. Presidencia del Consejo de Ministros. 1995. Exposición del señor Presidente del Consejo de Ministros y Ministro de Educación Dr. Dante Cordova Blanco ante el Congreso de la Republica. Lima: Author.
Peru. Ministerio de Educación / Organización de Estados Iberoamericanos (MOE/OEI). 1994. *Sistemas Educativos Nacionales*. Lima: Author.
Peru-MOE. 1986. *Plan Operativo Del Sector Educación*. Lima: Author.
Poder Ejecutivo Federal (Mexico). 1996. Alizanza para la Igualdad: Programa Nacional de la Mujer. Mexico, D.F.:Author.
Portocarrero, Felipe, and Arlette Beltrán, María Elena Romero and Hanny Cueva. 1999. "Economy And Policy Of Government Nutrition Support Programs In Peru: The PRONAA Case." Paper presented at International Development and Research Centre (IDRC) symposium, Washington, D.C.
Post, David. 1985. "Student Expectations of the Returns to Education in Peru." *Comparative Education Review*, 29:189–203.
_____. 1987. "Determinantes de las metas politicas entre los escolares Cusqueños." *Revista Peruana de Ciencias Sociales* 1:173-197.
_____. 1990. "The Social Demand for Education in Peru: Student Choice and State Autonomy." *Sociology of Education* 63: 258–271.
_____. 1991. "Peruvian Higher Education: Expansion Amid Crisis." *Higher Education*, 21(1991), 103–119.
_____. 1994. "Through a Glass Darkly? Indigeneity, Information, and the Image of the Peruvian University." *Higher Education* 27:271–95.

References

———. 1996. "The Massification of Education in Hong Kong: Consequences for Equality of Opportunity." *Sociological Perspectives* 39:155–174.

———. 2000. "Student Movements, User Fees, and Access to Mexican Higher Education: Trends in the Effect of Social Background and Family Income, 1984–1996." *Mexican Studies/Estudios Mexicanos* 16:141–163.

———. 2001. "Region, Poverty, Sibship, and Gender Inequality in Mexican Education: Will Targeted Welfare Policy Make a Difference for Girls?" *Gender and Society* 15:468–488.

Post, David, and Suet-ling Pong. 1998. "The Waning Effect of Sibship Composition on School Attainment in Hong Kong." *Comparative Education Review* 42:99–117.

———. 2000a. "International Policies on Early Adolescent Employment: An Evaluation from the U.S. and TIMSS Participant Nations." *International Journal of Educational Policy, Research, and Practice* 2:153–170.

———. 2000b. "Employment During Middle School: The Effects on Academic Achievement in the U.S. and Abroad." *Educational Evaluation and Policy Analysis* 23:273–98.

Powell, Brian, and Lala C. Steelman. 1990. "Beyond Sibship Size: Sibling Density, Sex Composition, and Educational Outcomes." *Social Forces* 69:181–206.

———. 1993. "The Educational Benefits of Being Spaced Out: Sibship Density and Educational Progress." *American Sociological Review* 58:367–381.

Prawda, Juan. 1987. *Logros, inequidades y retos del sistema futuro del sistema educativo Mexicano.* Mexico City, Mexico: Colección Pedagógica Grijalbo.

Psacharopoulos, George. 1994. "Returns to Investment in Education: A Global Update." *World Development* 22:1325–1343.

———. 1997. "Child Labor versus Educational Attainment: Some Evidence from Latin America." *Journal of Population Economics* 10:377–386.

Purdy, Laura M. 1992. *In Their Best Interest? The Case Against Equal Rights for Children.* Ithaca: Cornell University Press.

Rama, Germán. 1983. "Education in Latin America." *CEPAL Review* 21:1–22.

Ramirez, Francisco O., and John Boli. 1987. "The Political Construction of Mass Schooling: European Origins and Worldwide Institutionalization." *Sociology of Education* 60:2–17.

Reimers, Fernando. 1994. "Education Finance in Latin America: Perils and Opportunities." Pp. 29–66 in Jeffrey M. Puryear and J.J. Brunner (eds.), *Education, Equity and Economic Competitiveness in the Americas.* Washington, D.C.: Organization of American States.

Risse, Thomas, and Kathryn Sikkink. 1999. "The Socialization of International Human Rights Norms into Domestic Practices." Pp. 1–38 in Thomas Risse, Stephen Ropp, and Kathryn Sikkink (eds.), *The Power of Human Rights: International Norms and Domestic Change.* New York: Cambridge University Press.

Robles Vásquez, Héctor. 2000. *A Microeconomic Analysis of Child Labor Force Participation and Education: The Case of Mexico, 1984–1996.* Ph.D. Dissertation, Agricultural Economics and Demography, Penn State University.

Rodríguez, José, and David Abler. 1998. "Asistencia a la Escuela y Participación de los Menores en Fuerza de Trabajo en el Perú, 1985–1994." *Revista de Economía* 21:215–253.

Ropp, Stephen, and Kathryn Sikkink. 1999. "International Norms and Domestic Politics in Chile and Guatemala." Pp. 172–204 in Thomas Risse, Stephen Ropp, and Kathryn Sikkink (eds.) *The Power of Human Rights: International Norms and Domestic Change*. New York: Cambridge University Press.

Rounds Parry, Taryn. 1995. "The Impact of Decentralization and Competition on the Quality of Education." Working Paper. Centro de Investigación y Desarrollo de la Educación.

Saavedra, Jaime, Roberto Melzi, and Arturo Miranda. 1997. "Financiamento de la educación en el Perú." Documento de Trabajo 24. Lima: GRADE.

Salazar, María Cristina. 1990. *Niños y Jovenes Trabajadores: Buscando un futuro mejor*. Bogatá: Universidad Nacional de Colombia

———. 1991. "Young Workers in Latin America: Protection or Self-Determination?" *Child Welfare* 70:269–283.

———. 1996. "Child Work and Education in Latin America." *The International Journal of Children's Rights* 6:155–177.

Salazar, María Cristina, and Walter Alarcón Glasinovich (eds.). 1996. *Child Work and Education: Five Case Studies from Latin America*. Florence: UNICEF.

Salinas de Gortari, Carlos. (1988–1994). Informes de Gobierno : Mexico City: Poder Ejecutivo.

———. 1988. *El reto*. Mexico City: Editorial Diana.

San Miguel B., Javier. 1999. "Programa de educacion basica rural." Pps. 91-110 in J. E. Garcia-Huidobro and C. Cox, eds., *La Reforma Educacional Chilena*. Madrid, Spain: Education Popular.

Sarbaugh-Thompson, Marjorie, and Mayer Zaid. 1995. "Child Labor Laws: A Historical Case of Public Implementation." *Administration and Society* 27:25–52.

Sassler, Sharon. 1995. "Trade-Offs in the Family: Sibling Effects on Daughters' Activities in 1910." *Demography* 32:557–75.

Save the Children. 1996. *Small Hands: Children in the Working World*. London: Author.

Scherer Ibarra, Gabriela. 1995. *Los Hijos de la Calle: Niños sin Infancia*. Mexico City: SNTE (Sindicato Nacional de Trabajadores de la Educación).

Schibotto, Giangi, and Alejandro Cussiánovich. 1994. *Working Children: Building and Identity*. Lima: MANTHOC (Movimiento de adolescentes y niños trabajadores hijos de obreros cristianos).

Schiefelbein, Ernesto. 1991. "Restructuring Education Through Economic Competition: The Case of Chile." *Journal of Educational Administration* 29:17-29.

———. 1997. "Incentivos económicos a la escuela en América Latina." *Realidad y Utopía* 2:33–67.

Schiefelbein, Ernesto, and Joseph Farrell. 1980. "Women, Schooling, and Work in Chile: Evidence from a Longitudinal Study." *Comparative Education Review* 24:S160-S179.

References

Schkolnik, Mariana. 1992. "The Distributive Impact of Fiscal and Laour Market Policies: Chile's 1990-91 Reforms." Innocenti Occasional Papers. Florence, Italy: UNICEF.

Sen, Amartya K. 1990. "Gender and Cooperative Conflicts." In Irene Tinker (ed.), *Persistent Inequalities*. New York: Oxford University Press.

Shavit, Yossi, and Jennifer L. Pierce. 1991. "Sibship Size and Educational Attainment in Nuclear and Extended Families: Arabs and Jews in Israel." *American Sociological Review* 56:321-330.

Sheahan, John. 1997. "Effects of Liberalization Programs on Poverty and Inequality: Chile, Mexico, and Peru." *Latin American Research Review* 32(3):7-37.

———. 1999. *Searching For A Better Society: The Peruvian Economy from 1990*. University Park, Pa.: Penn State University Press.

Shihata, Ibrahim. 1996. "The World Bank's Protection and Promotion of Children's Rights." *International Journal of Children's Rights* 4:383-405.

Smelser, Neil. 1991. *Social Paralysis and Social Change: British Working Class Education in the Nineteenth Century*. Berkeley: University of California Press.

Sorokin, Pitirim. 1954 [1927]. *Social and Cultural Mobility*. New York: Harper.

Sotomayer, Carmen. 1999. "Programa de mejoramiento de la Calidad de Escuelas Basicas de Sectores Pobres (P-900)." Pps. 69-90 in García-Huidobro and Cox (eds.) *La Reforma Educacional Chilena*. Madrid, Spain: Editorial Popular.

Stadum, Beverly. 1995. "The Dilemma in Saving Children from Child Labor: Reform and Casework at Odds with Families' Needs (1900-1938)." *Child Welfare* 74:33-55.

Stammers, Neil. 1999. "Social Movements and the Social Construction of Human Rights." *Human Rights Quarterly* 21:980-1008.

Stepan, Alfred. 1985. "State Power and the Strength of Civil Society in the Southern Cone of Labin America." In Peter B. Evans, et al., eds., *Bringing the State Back In*. Cambridge: Cambridge University Press.

Strauss, John, and Duncan Thomas. 1995. "Human Resources: Empirical Modeling of Household and Family Decisions." In Jere Behrman and T. N. Srinivasan (eds.), *Handbook of Development Economics*, volume III. Amsterdam: Elsevier.

Stromquist, Nelly. 1986. "Decentralizing Education Decision-making in Peru: Intentions and Realities." *International Journal of Educational Development* 6:47-60.

———. 1989. "Recent Developments in Women's Education: Closer to a Better Social Order?" In Rita S. Gallin, M. Aronoff, and A. Ferguson (eds.), *The Women and International Development Annual, Vol. 1*. Boulder: Westview.

———. 1995. "Romancing the State: Gender and Power in Education." *Comparative Education Review* 39:423-54.

———. 1998. "Impact of Structural Adjustment Programs in Africa and Latin America." In Christine Heward and Sheila Bunwaree, eds., *Gender, Education, and Development*. London:: Zed Books.

SUTEP (Sindicato Unico de Trabajadores de Educación Peruana). 1986. "Enfoque Ideologico-Politico de la Educación." Lima: Author.
Taylor, Ronald B. 1973. *Sweatshops in the Sun: Child Labor on the Farm.* Boston: Beacon Press.
Tilley, John J. 2000. "Cultural Relativism." *Human Rights Quarterly* 22:501–547.
Tinker, Irene. 1976. "Women in Developing Societies: Economic Independence Is Not Enough." In Jane Roberts Chapman (ed.), *Economic Independence for Women: The Foundation for Equal Rights.* Beverly Hills, Calif.: Sage.
Turbay, Catalina, and Elvia María Acuña. 1998. "Child labor and Basic Education in Colombia." Pp. 39-65 in Salazar and Alarcón (eds.), *Child Work and Education: Five Case Studies from Latin America.* Florence: UNICEF.
UNICEF. 1993. *The Progress of Nations.* Geneva: Author.
UNICEF. 1996. *Censo II de los Niños y Niñas en Situación de Calle.* Mexico, D.F.: Author.
UNICEF. 1997. "Education and Child Labor." Background paper for October 1997 Oslo Meeting. New York: Author.
UNICEF. 1998. *La Participacion de niños y adolescentes en el contexto de la convencion sobre derechos de nito.* Bogota, Colombia: Author.
UNICEF. 1999. *The State of the World's Children.* New York: Author.
U.S. Department of Labor. 1994. *By the Sweat and Toil of Children, Vol. I: The Use of Child Labor in American Imports.* Washington, D.C.: Author.
U.S. Department of Labor. 1995. *By the Sweat and Toil of Children, Vol. II: The Use of Child Labor in U.S. Agricultural Imports and Forced and Bonded Child Labor.* Washington, D.C.: Author.
U.S. Department of Labor. 1997. *By the Sweat and Toil of Children,* Vol. IV. Washington, D.C.: Author.
Van Bueren, Geraldine. 1999. "Combating Child Poverty—Human Rights Approaches." *Human Rights Quarterly* 21:680–706.
Valencia, Jorge. 2000. *Legislacion Sobre Niñez: Un Paso Obligado.* Mexico City: Colectivo Mexicano de Apoyo a la Niñez (COMEXANI).
Vásquez, Enrique, and Carlos Aramburu, Carlos Parodi and Carlos Figueroa. 1999. "Do Government's Social Programs Reach the People in Extreme Poverty? Methodological Monitoring Proposals Based On The Case Of Peru." Paper presented at International Development Research Centre symposium, Washington, D.C.
Verdera, Francisco. 1995. *El Trabajo Infantil en el Perú: Diagnostico y Propuestas Para una Política Nacional.* Lima: Instituto de Estudios Peruanos.
Verhellen, Eugene (ed.). *Monitoring Children's Rights.* The Hague, Netherlands: Kluwer Law International.
Waiser, Myriam. 1992. "Indicadores de la situación educacional." In MIDEPLAN (Ministerio de Planificacion y Cooperacion), *Poblacion, Educacion, Vivienda, Salud, Empleo y Pobreza.* Santiago, Chile: Author.
Webb, Richard. 1977. *Government Policy and the Distribution of Income in Peru, 1963–1973.* Cambridge, Mass.: Harvard University Press.
Weiner, Myron. 1991. *The Child and the State in India.* Princeton: Princeton University Press.

References

Weissman, Robert. 1997. "Stolen Youth: Brutalized Children, Globalization, and the Campaign to End Child Labor." *Multinational Monitor* 18:10–16.
Weyland, Kurt. 1999. "Neoliberal Populism in Latin Amercian and Eastern Europe." *Comparative Politics* 31(4) 379–402.
White, Ben. 1994. "Children, Work and 'Child Labour': Changing Responses to the Employment of Children." *Development and Change* 25:849–878.
White, Ben. 1996. "Globalization and the Child Labour Problem." *Journal of International Development.* 8:829–839.
White, Ben. 1999. "Defining the Intolerable: Child Work, Global Standards and Cultural Relativism." *Childhood* 6:133–144.
Wise, Carol. 1998. "NAFTA, Mexico and the Western Hemisphere." Pp. 1–40 in Carol Wise (ed.), *The Post-NAFTA Political Economy.* University Park, Pa.: Penn State University Press.
Woodhead, M. 1999. "Combating Child Labour. Listen to What the Children Say." *Childhood* 6:27–49.
World Bank. 1995. *World Development Report: Workers in an Integrating World.* New York: Oxford University Press.
World Health Organization (WHO). 1987. *Children at Work: Special Health Risks.* Geneva.
Zamudio Carrillo, A. 1995. "Rendimientos a la educación superior en México: Ajuste por sesgo utilizando máxima verosimilitud." *Economía Mexicana* 4:69–91.
Zedillo Ponce de León, Ernesto. 1994–1996. *Informes de Gobierno.* Mexico City: Poder Ejecutivo.
Zelizer, Viviana A. 1994. *Pricing the Priceless Child.* Princeton: Princeton University Press.

INDEX

Abbott, Edith, 67
Abler, David, 139–173
Achievement and wealth, 24
Achievement scores, 24, 109–110. *See also* Math achievement
El Acuerdo Nacional, 128
Adolescents. *See* Children
Adult education, 209(fig.)
Age groups, 142–143, 172, 240–243(figs.)
  Chile, 169
  Mexico, 150, 158
  Peru, 157–158, 164
Agriculture, 4, 54–55, 143
All-Colonial People's Conference, 222–223
Allende, Salvador, 86
Alves, José Lindgren, 15
American Declaration on the Rights and Duties of Man, 222
Amnesty International, 225
APAFA. *See* Associations of Parents and Family Members
APRA government, 89, 118–119, 122
Argentina, 99

Artesianal production of bricks, 55
Asia, 14
Association for the Evaluation of Achievement (IEA), xv
Associations of Parents and Family Members (APAFA), 124
Atwood, J. Brian, xii
Aylwin, Patricio, 27, 88, 104, 135, 137

Baja California, 198
Bangkok Declaration of April 1993, 14
Bangladesh, 93
Basica, 111
Becker, Gary, xiii, 59
Belaunde, Fernando, 99, 115, 116, 122
Belgium, 103
Berkovitch, Nina, 224
Bi-census, 33
Birth rates, xii, 6
Bodet, Jaime Torres. *See* Torres Bodet, Jaime
Boli, John, 224–225
Bolivar, Simón, 222

Bolivia, 233
Boys' activities, 37–41, 212(fig.)
Brazil, 18, 70–71, 74
Breckinridge, Sophonisba, 67
Brick production, 55
Britain. *See* England
Burma, 223
By Sweat and Toil of Children, 7

Cabanillas, Mercedes, 118–119, 123
Capelo, Joquín, 114, 127
Cárdenas, Cuauhtemoc, 218–219, 231
Casa Alianza, 225
CASEN. *See* Encuesta de Caracterización Socio-Económica Nacional
Ceylon, 223
Chiapas, 184–186, 195, 197, 198, 208, 209–210
Chihuahua, 209
Childhood. *See* Children
Child labor
  Chile, 164–171
  Colombia, 55–56
  definition, 3–4
  as epiphenomenal, 59, 61
  history, 4–7
  intolerable, xvii, 13, 76
  law enforcement, 81–85. *See also* Laws
  market for, 58
  Mexico, 20, 149–157, 203–204(figs.)
  perspectives on, 44–45, 60–65
  Peru, 157–164
  policies, 1–4
  problem of, 57
  regulations, 73–78. *See also* Laws
  as social disease, 52–56
  as symptom of poverty, 57–60
  tolerable, xvii
  world trade perspective, 67–68
  See also Working children
Children
  activities of, 34–43, 134–138, 140–149, 212(fig.), 219–220, 221(fig.), 232–234. *See also* Child labor; Education
  advocates of, 216–217, 230–232. *See also* Non-governmental agencies
  ages of. *See* Age groups
  conceptual framework, 79(fig.)
  definition, 2–3
  development, 63–64, 68–72
  economic activities, 36–37. *See also* Child labor
  "home workers," 141–142, 155, 158
  Mexico City, 48, 53, 58
  and poverty. *See* Poverty
  rights, 8, 7–12, 68–72. *See also* Human rights
  rights vs. social welfare, 7–12
  school attendance. *See* School attendance
  working. *See* Working children
Chile
  age groups, 169
  boys' activities, 37–40, 171
  child labor, 49–51, 164–171
  child labor laws, 81–85
  children's activities, 37–40, 171, 237(fig.)
  demographics, 25–29

determinants of education, 199(fig.)
economic indicators, 30(fig.)
educational incentives, 86–88, 136–137
education system, 97–98, 102–114, 199(fig.)
families, 87–88, 106–108
girls, 37–40, 171, 205–206, 207(fig.)
household income, 170, 202–204
independent education, 102–104, 105–106
IPEC, 74–75, 228
military repression, 99
per-pupil spending, 113(fig.)
recession, 28–29
rural, 165(fig.), 167(fig.), 186–188
school attendance, 34–36, 164–171
school finance, 114(fig.), 136(fig.)
social change, 217
social mobility, 18
"street" children, 49–50
surveys, 34
teachers, 109
urban, 166(fig.), 168(fig.)
Choice-based reforms, 106–107
Christian Democrat-Socialist Democrat coalition, 28, 86, 102, 217
Clinton, Bill, 7
Code on Children and Adolescents. See Código
Código, 64, 83–84, 126, 229

Colombia
academic performance, 24
child labor in, 55–56
children's rights, 71
IPEC, 75
math achievement, 22, 23
Colombian Instituto for Family Welfare, 71
Colombian March Against Child Labor, 75
Combination of work and school, 20–25
COMEXANI, 232
Compulsory education, 96(fig.)
CONAFE. *See* National Council for Educational Development
CONAPO. *See* National Council on Population
Consequentalism, 9, 11–12, 45, 67, 101
"Conteo," 33
CONUP, 115
Convention 132, 75
Convention 138, xv–xvi, 70, 73–74, 75, 77
Convention 182, xvii, 7, 68, 75, 80, 229
Coordination of the National Plan for Deprived Zones and Marginalized Groups (COPLAMAR), 91
Copelo, Joaquín, 13–14
COPLAMAR. *See* Coordination of the National Plan for Deprived Zones and Marginalized Groups
Córdova, Dante, 123–124
Core labor standards, 67–68
Costa Rica, 28
Covarrubias, José Díaz, 48

CRC. *See* Rights of the Child
Culture specificity vs. universal standards, 13–16
Cussiánovich, Alejandro, 47, 64–65, 218

Decade for Women, 224
Decentralized education, 130–131
Declaration of the Rights of the Child, 68, 69
Declaration on Fundamental Principles and Rights at Work, 8, 76
Declaration on Human Rights, 69
Demand-subsidized education, 105–107
Demographics
  birth rates, xii
  changes in, 4–5, 219–225
  Chile, 25–29
  Mexico, 25–29
  Peru, 25–29
Developmental freedom, 8
Dore, Ronald, 13
Dummy variables, 146–147
Dworkin, Ronald, 9
Dysfunctional families, 58

ECA. *See* Statute on Children and Adolescents
Economics
  and education, 17–18
  indicators, 30(fig.)
  Mexico, 30(fig.), 185(fig.)
  per-capita income, 149
  per-pupil spending, 113(fig.)
  Peru, 30(fig.), 183(fig.)
  small businesses, 4
  survey results, 36–37
  wealth, 24, 143–144
  See also Household income; Poverty
ECOSOC. *See* Temporary Social Commission of the Economic and Social Council
Education
  adult, 209(fig.)
  Chile, 86–88, 97–98, 102–114, 136–137, 199(fig.)
  choice-based reforms, 106–107
  completed by household head. *See* Household heads
  compulsory, 96(fig.)
  decentralized, 130–131
  demand-subsidized, 105–107
  determinants of, 181(fig.)
  and economics, 17–18
  and gender, 177–178, 204–214
  independent, 102–104, 105–106
  international comparisons, 135–138, 234–236
  as investment, 17–18
  Mexico, 88–89, 91–93, 95–97, 127–134, 138, 155, 246–247(fig.)
  and mobility, 175–176
  Peru, 89–91, 97, 114–127, 137–138, 182
  preschool, 111–112, 137
  regional inequality, 176–177
  as social return, 17, 220–221
  values of, 220–221
  worldwide, 95–102
  See also Schools
Educational incentives, 85–93
Education for All movement, xiv, 81, 100
Education Service Units (USEs), 122

Index

ENAHO, 34
Encuesta de Caracterización Socio-Económica Nacional (CASEN), 32, 33, 49, 139, 181–182, 187–188
Encuesta Nacional de Empleo. *See* Mexican National Employment Survey
Encuesta Nacional de Ingresos y Gastos de los Hogares (ENIGH), 33–34, 139–140, 181–182, 184, 189–190, 196
Encuesta Nacional de Niveles de Vida (ENNIV), 34, 139–140, 182
ENE. *See* Mexican National Employment Survey
Engels, Friedrich, 5, 59
England, 4–5
ENIGH. *See Encuesta Nacional de Ingresos y Gastos de los Hogares*
ENNIV. *See Encuesta Nacional de Niveles de Vida*
Equal rights, 8. *See also* Children: rights; Human rights
Estado docente, 108

Families
  and children. *See* Children
  Chile, 87–88, 106–108
  dysfunctional, 58
  household heads. *See* Household heads
  incentives to change, 85–93
  income. *See* Household income
  rural, 143
  spouses. *See* Spouses
  trades, 4
  urban, 143
Feminism, 224
Fertility. *See* Birth rates
Finance. *See* Economics
Flores, Ricardo Marquez. *See* Marquez Flores, Ricardo
FONCODES, 89–90
Fondo de Solidaridad e Inversión Social (FOSIS), 88–89
FOSIS. *See* Fondo de Solidaridad e Inversión Social
Foster, Philip, 176
Freedom for development, 68–72
Frei, Eduardo, 27, 104, 135
Friedman, Milton, 102, 105
Fuentes, Olac, 130
Fujimori, Alberto, 90–91, 119–120, 123–124, 138, 217–218, 229
Fuller, Bruce, 14

Galeana, Rosaura, 48–49, 50
Garcia, Alan, 29, 117–118, 125, 136, 217
GATT. *See* General Agreement on Trade and Tariffs
GDP. *See* Gross Domestic Product
Gender, 172, 177–178, 204–214, 240–243(figs.), 250(fig.). *See also* Boys' activities; Girls
General Agreement on Trade and Tariffs (GATT), 67–68
General Law of Education (Mexico), 128–129
General Law of Education No. 23384 (Peru), 116–117
Germany, 74
Ghana, 219
Gini coefficient of primary income, 28

Girls
  activities, 37–41, 212(fig.)
  Chile, 37–40, 171, 205–206, 207(fig.)
  education of, 178–179. *See also* Gender
  Mexico, 41, 206–214
  Peru, 40–41, 205(fig.)
Global economic integration, 4, 6
Global March Against Child Labor, 56, 75, 77, 218
GNP. *See* Gross National Product
Gold production, 54
Gorriti, Luis Carlos, 122
Gortari, Carlos Salinas de, 128
Great Britain. *See* England
Gross Domestic Produce (GDP), 115, 136
Gross National Product (GNP), 24, 112
Grupo de Iniciativa National, 61
Guadalajara, 58
Guatemala, 93

Hammarberg, Thomas, 12, 101
Heads of households. *See* Household heads
Helfer, Gloria, 121
"Home workers," 141–142, 155, 158
Household heads, 147–148, 196–197
  Chile, 169–170, 188(fig.)
  Mexico, 155–156
  Peru, 163, 206
Household income, 143–144, 172–173, 240–243(figs.), 249(fig.)
  Chile, 170, 202–204
  Mexico, 149, 156, 196–202, 210–211, 247(fig.), 250(fig.)
  per-capita, 149
  Peru, 163
Huachipa, 55
Human rights, 222–224, 225–228. *See also* Children: rights

IACI. *See* Inter-American Children's Institute
Iceland, 22
IDB. *See* Inter-American Development Bank
IEA. *See* Association for the Evaluation of Achievement
Illich, Ivan, 13
ILO. *See* International Labour Organization
Inca Plan, 115
Incentives for change, 85–93
Income. *See* Household income
Independent education, 102–104, 105–106
India, 61, 223
Indonesia, 219
INEGI. *See* National Institute of Statistics, Geography, and Information
Information sources, 29–34
INGOs. *See* International non-governmental organizations
Inter-American Children's Institute (IACI), 71–72
Inter-American Commission on the Status of Women, 224
Inter-American Committee for Culture, 98
Inter-American Conference, 222

Index 277

Inter-American Development Bank (IDB), 80–81, 99
Inter-American Meeting of Ministers of Education, 98–99
International Program to Eliminate Child Labor, 229–230
International Child Labor Elimination Act of 1997, 6–7
International Child Labor Office, 6–7
International Committee of the Red Cross, 224–225
International Covenant on Economic, Social, and Cultural Rights, 223
International Evaluation Association, 20–21
International Labour Organization (ILO), 49, 82, 228–232
   Convention 132, 75
   Convention 138, xv–xvi, 70, 73–74, 75, 77
   Convention 182, xvii, 7, 59, 75, 80, 229
   Declaration on Fundamental Principles and Rights at Work, 8, 76
   history, 73–78
   intervention by, xiii
   minimum work age, xii, xv–xvi
   numbers of working children, xi–xii, 1
International laws, 66–68, 228–232
International non-governmental organizations (INGOs), 224–225. *See also* Non-governmental organizations
International Program for the Elimination of Child Labor (IPEC) 49–50, 56, 74–75, 80, 228
International Save the Children Alliance, 12
International Trade Organization (ITO), 68
Intolerable child labor, xvii, 13, 76
IPEC. *See* International Program for the Elimination of Child Labor
Iran, 23
ITO. *See* International Trade Organization

Jensen, Leif, 139–173
Jotiem, Thailand, 100
Jubilee 2000 movement, 81
JUNAEB. *See* National Council for Scholarships and Student Financial Assistance
Kant, Immune, 7, 9
Kuwait, 22

Lagos, Ricardo, 135
Latin America
   history, 16–19
   mobilization of working children, 51
   political economy, 27–29
   recessions, 28–29
   See also Chile; Mexico; Peru
Law enforcement, 81–85
Law of Mines (England), 5
Laws
   Chile, 81–85
   international, 66–68, 228–232

Mexico, 81–85, 215–216
Peru, 81–85, 215–216
Laws of the Indies, 81
League of Nations, 68
Leveler, Valentine, 106
Lifetree scale, 50–51
Lima, 49, 53–54, 98, 122, 183–184
Living Standards Measurement Survey (LSMS), 139
Lopatka, Adam, 11
LSMS. See Living Standards Measurement Survey (LSMS)
Lunch programs, 111, 136–137

Madrid, Miguel de la, 81, 128
MANTHOC. See Movement of Adolescents and Children Workers of Christian Laborers
Mariátegui, Jose Carlos, 114
Marquez Flores, Ricardo, 229
Marx, Karl, 5, 59
Math achievement, 22(fig.)
Mauráx, Marta, xviii
Méndez, Emilio García, 70, 225–226
Méndez, Juan Carlos, 103
Mexican National Employment Survey (ENE), 42
Mexico
 age groups, 150, 158
 boys' activities, 41
 child labor and education, 20, 149–157, 203–204(figs.)
 child labor laws, 81–85
 children's activities, 41, 239(fig.), 248(fig.)
 children's advocacy, 230–232

constitution, 82
decentralization of education, 130–131
demographics, 25–29
economics, 30(fig.), 185(fig.)
education as investment, 17, 18
education system, 95–97, 127–134, 246–247(fig.)
educational incentives, 88–89, 91–93, 138
girls, 41, 206–214
household income, 149, 156, 196–202, 210–211, 247(fig.), 250(fig.)
IPEC, 75, 228
laws, 81–85, 215–216
population, 127–128
recession, 29
rural, 151(fig.), 153(fig.), 184–186, 189(fig.), 196–199, 246(fig.)
school attendance, 35(fig.), 36, 132–134, 149–157, 184–186, 189–190
school finance, 134(fig.), 136(fig.)
secondary schools, 190–196, 208(fig.), 246(fig.)
social change, 218–219
social mobility, 18
students in, xv, 48–49
surveys, 33–34
trends in activities, 43(fig.)
urban areas, 152(fig.), 154(fig.)
women, 224
Mexico City, 48, 53, 58
Meyer, John, 14
Mill, John Stuart, 7
Minimum work age, xii, xv–xvi
Ministry for the Promotion of

Index

Woman and Human Development (PROMUDEH), 90
Moral Health Act, 4–5
Movement of Adolescents and Children Workers of Christian Laborers (MANTHOC), 46–47, 51, 64–65, 83, 218
Multinomial logistic regression model, 144–149, 171–173, 244–245(fig.)
  Chile, 165–168(figs.)
  Mexico, 151–154(figs.), 201–202
  Peru, 159–162(figs.)
Muñoz, Cecelia, 47
Muñoz, Jose Benavides, 116
Muñoz-Salazar, Patricia, 139–173

NAALC. *See* North American Agreement on Labor Cooperation
NAFTA. *See* North American Free Trade Agreement
National Child Welfare Institute, 53–54
National Council for Educational Development (CONAFE), 92–93
National Council for Scholarships and Student Financial Assistance (JUNAEB), 86
National Council on Population (CONAPO), 58–59, 190, 208
National Indigenous Institute, 127
National Institute of Statistics, Geography, and Information (INEGO), 42
National Population Council, 26
National Program of Solidarity (PRONASOL), 92
National wealth, 24
Negative liberty, 8
"Neoliberalism," 59
Netherlands, 51
NGOs. *See* Non-governmental organizations
Non-governmental organizations (NGOs), 218, 222–228. *See also* International non-governmental organizations; United Nations
North American Agreement on Labor Cooperation (NAALC), 68
North American Free Trade Agreement (NAFTA), 68, 143
Nucleos, 116–117
Nuevo Leon, 195

OAS. *See* Organization for American States
Oaxaca, 184–186, 193, 195, 197, 208, 209–210
OECD. *See* Organization for Economic Cooperation and Development
Organization for American States (OAS), 71, 222
Organization for Economic Cooperation and Development (OECD), 67
OXFAM, 59

P-900 schools, 111
PAIT. *See* Program of Temporary Income Support

Pakistan, 2
Palma, Arturo Alessandri, 86
Pango, Grover, 118
Pardo, José, 97
PARE. *See* Programa para Abatir el Rezago Educativo
Part-time students, 142
PDR party, 218–219
Per-capita income, 149. *See also* Household income
Per-pupil spending, 113(fig.)
Pérez, Jaime Jesús, 52
Peru
 age groups, 157–158, 164
 boys' activities, 40–41
 child labor and education, 20, 157–164
 child labor laws, 81–85
 children's activities, 40–41, 205(fig.), 233–234, 238(fig.)
 constitution, 82–83
 demographics, 25–29
 economic indicators, 30(fig.), 183(fig.)
 education system, 97, 114–127, 182
 educational incentives, 89–91, 137–138
 GDP, 115
 girls' activities, 40–41, 205(fig.)
 household income, 163
 IPEC, 74–75, 229–230
 laws, 81–85, 215–216
 recession, 28–29
 rural, 159(fig.), 161(fig.), 183–184
 school attendance, 35(fig.), 36, 157–164, 183(fig.)
 school finance, 122–125, 136(fig.)
 social change, 217–218
 social mobility, 18
 "street" children, 49, 53–54
 surveys, 34
 teachers, 121–122
 unemployment, 99
 and UNESCO, 115
 urban, 160(fig.), 162(fig.)
 See also Lima
Philippines, 2, 23
PIDER. *See* Program for Integrated Rural Development
Pinochet, Augusto, 28, 36, 103
Positive liberty, 8
Postmodern critiques, 15
Poverty, 41–42, 57–60, 143–144, 172–173, 196–204, 208. *See also* Household income
Preschool education, 111–112, 137
Program for Education, Health, and Nutrition (PROGRESA), 93, 177, 196–197, 207, 214
Program for Integrated Rural Development (PIDER), 91
Program of Temporary Income Support (PAIT), 89
Programa Nacional de Apoyo Alimentario (PRONAA), 90–91
Programa para Abatir el Rezago Educativo (PARE), 93
PROGRESA. *See* Program for Education, Health, and Nutrition
PROMUDEH. *See* Ministry for the Promotion of Woman and Human Development

PRONAA. *See* Programa Nacional de Apoyo Alimentario
PRONASOL. *See* National Program of Solidarity
Protagonismo, 64–65
Public education. *See* Education

Quechua, 115–116, 128

Rädda Barnen, 52, 80
Recessions, 28
Red Cross, 224–225
Regional differentiations, 176–177. *See also* Rural areas; Urban areas
Remunerated work, 3
Rights
  based rationales, 9, 10–12, 45, 80, 101
  children's, 8, 7–12, 68–72
  human, 222–224, 225–228
Rights of the Child (CRC), xvi, 2–3, 10–12, 51–52, 69–70, 77, 78, 81, 223, 228–232
Rights of the Child (League of Nations), 68
Risse, Thomas, 226–227
Robledo, Rocio, 231
Robles-Vásquez, Héctor, 139–173
Rubalcava, Rosa María, 59
Ruiz, Isaac, 218
Rural areas, 143
  Chile, 165(fig.), 167(fig.), 186–188
  Mexico, 151(fig.), 153(fig.), 184–185, 189(fig.), 196–199, 247(fig.)
  Peru, 159(fig.), 161(fig.), 183–184

Santa Filomena, 54, 62, 75
Santiago, 56
Save the Children, 68, 80, 225
Scherer, Gabriela, 53
Schiefelbein, Ernesto, 110
School attendance, 34–36, 100
  Chile, 34–36, 164–171
  Mexico, 134(fig.), 136(fig.), 149–157, 184–186
  Peru, 35(fig.), 36, 157–164, 183(fig.)
School finance
  Chile, 114(fig.), 136(fig.)
  Mexico, 132–134, 136(fig.), 189–190
  per-capita spending, 113(fig.)
  Peru, 122–125, 136(fig.)
Schools
  lunch programs, 111, 136–137
  P-900, 111
  secondary, 190–196, 208(fig.), 246(fig.)
  See also Education
Secondary schools, 190–196, 208(fig.), 246(fig.)
Sendero Luminoso, 30–31, 118
Senegal, 16
Sibship structure, 147, 179
  Chile, 170–171
  Mexico, 156
  Peru, 163
Sikkink, Kathryn, 226–227
Sinaloa, 54–55
Small businesses, 4
Smith, Adam, 105
Social mobility, 18
Social stratification, 174–175

Social welfare vs. children's
    rights, 7–12
Sociologia de Lima (Copelo),
    13–14
Sorokin, Pitirm, 174–175
Sostenedores educacionales,
    104
South Africa, 23
Spouses, 148–149
    Chile, 170
    Mexico, 155–156
    Peru, 163–164
State action on households,
    221(fig.)
The State of the World's Children,
    11, 100–101
Statute on Children and
    Adolescents (ECA), 71
Stratification, 174–175
"Street" children, 31, 47, 49–50,
    53–54
Structural adjustment, 59
Students
    achievement scores, 24,
        109–110. *See also* Math
        achievement
    American, xiv–xv
    Latin American, 35(fig.)
    Mexican, xv, 48–49
    part-time, 142
    per-pupil spending, 113(fig.)
    secondary, 190–196, 208(fig.),
        246(fig.)
    See also Education
Subventions, 104, 105–106,
    137
Surveys, 29–34
Svensson, Ann-Lis, 62
Sweden, 52
Sweeney, John, xiv–xv

Teachers, 109, 121–122
Temporary Social Commission of
    the Economic and Social
    Council (ECOSOC), 68–69
Thailand, 2, 100
Third International Math and
    Science Study (TIMSS), 20–21
TIMSS. *See* Third International
    Math and Science Study
Tobit regressions, 180–181
Tolerable child labor, xvii
Torres Bodet, Jaime, 95, 223
Trends in activities, 34–43,
    85–93, 232–234
Twenty-Twenty movement, 81

UNESCO. *See* United Nations
    Educational, Scientific and
    Cultural Organization
UNICEF. *See* United Nations
    International Children's
    Emergency Fund
United Nations
    International Covenant on
        Economic, Social, and
        Cultural Rights, 223
    intervention by, xiii
    Rights of the Child (CRC), xii,
        xvi, 2–3, 10–12, 51–52,
        69–70, 77, 78, 81, 223,
        228–232
United Nations Declaration on
    Human Rights, 69
United Nations Educational,
    Scientific and Cultural
    Organization (UNESCO),
    xv, 72, 98–99
    and Peru, 115
    surveys, 32
United Nations International

Index

Children's Emergency Fund (UNICEF), 11, 59, 72, 234–235
  and human rights, 226
  needs-based orientation, 80
  rights-based orientation, 80, 101
  school attendance, 100
  and "street" children, 47, 53–54
United States
  birth rates, 6
  elimination of child labor, 68
  ILO Convention 182, 75–76
  IPEC, 229–230
  math achievement, 22
  students, xiv–xv
  working children, 5–6
United States Agency for International Development, 115
United States Bureau of International Labor Affairs, 7
United States Department of Labor, 6–7, 32
United States National Longitudinal Survey, 32–33
Universal Declaration of Human Rights, 15, 222, 334
Universal standards vs. cultural specificity, 13–16
Unremunerated work, 3
Urban areas, 143
  Chile, 166(fig.), 168(fig.)
  Mexico, 152(fig.), 154(fig.)
  Peru, 160(fig.), 162(fig.)
USEs. *See* Education Service Units
Valencia, Jorge, 232
Variables, 146–147, 244–245(fig.)
Verdera, Francisco, 2–3

Vertical stratification. *See* Stratification
Villarán, Manuel Vicente, 114–115
Vouchers, 102–103

Wales, 4
Wealth, 24, 143–144
Weighted maximum likelihood, 146
Welfare programs, 85–93
West Africa, 223
WIDF. *See* Women's International Democratic Federation
Women, 224. *See also* Girls
Women's International Democratic Federation (WIDF), 224
Working children
  as agents of social change, 45–52, 63–64
  definition of, 3–4
  and education, 19–25. *See also* Education
  England, 4–5
  and math achievement, 22(fig.)
  minimum age, xii, xv–xvi
  mobilization of, 51
  motives for working, 50–51
  numbers of, xii, 1
  of "the street," 31, 47, 49–50, 53–54
  as symptoms of poverty, 45, 57–60
  United States, 5–6
  as victims of exploitation, 45, 52–56, 62–63
  Wales, 4
  See also Child labor

World Bank, 80–81, 93, 99
World Conference of International Women's Year, 224
World trade, 67–68
World Trade Organization (WTO), xi, 68
Worldwide education, 95–102

WTO. *See* World Trade Organization

Yañez, Ana María, 83
Year of the Child, 69
Youth. *See* Children
Yucatán, 208, 209–210

Zedillo administration, 129